SECOND EDITION

EASY WAY TO LEARN CHINESE CHARACTERS

柳燕梅 编著
刘林军 翻译

汉字速成课本 | 第 2 版

北京大学出版社
PEKING UNIVERSITY PRESS

图书在版编目(CIP)数据

汉字速成课本/柳燕梅编著.—2版.—北京：北京大学出版社，2014.3
ISBN 978-7-301-23635-2

Ⅰ.①汉…　Ⅱ.①柳…　Ⅲ.①汉字－对外汉语教学－教材　Ⅳ.①H195.4

中国版本图书馆CIP数据核字（2013）第308772号

书　　　名：汉字速成课本（第2版）
著作责任者：柳燕梅　编著
责 任 编 辑：周　鹏
标 准 书 号：ISBN 978-7-301-23635-2 / H·3452
出 版 发 行：北京大学出版社
地　　　址：北京市海淀区成府路205号　100871
网　　　址：http://www.pup.cn　　新浪官方微博：@北京大学出版社
电 子 信 箱：zpup@pup.cn
电　　　话：邮购部 62752015　发行部 62750672
　　　　　　编辑部 62752028　出版部 62754962
印　刷　者：北京大学印刷厂
经　销　者：新华书店
　　　　　　889毫米×1194毫米　16开本　26.75印张　500千字
　　　　　　2001年6月第1版
　　　　　　2014年3月第2版　2019年5月第4次印刷
定　　　价：68.00元（附汉字练习本）

未经许可，不得以任何方式复制或抄袭本书之部分或全部内容。
版权所有，侵权必究
举报电话：010-62752024　电子信箱：fd@pup.pku.edu.cn

序

赵金铭

汉字是汉语的书写符号。它是人与人之间交流信息的约定俗成的视觉信号系统。汉字可以灵活地书写由声音构成的汉语，从而使汉语书面语交际得以达成，并使汉文资料和信息送至远方，传之后代。学习汉语，不能置汉字于不顾，已成不争事实。

汉字又是世界上寿命最长、使用人数最多的一种文字。然而，古往今来，不同的历史时期、不同的人，带着各自不同的政治信仰与文化心态，对汉字的认识也是形形色色，不知凡几。

可喜的是，近年来，人们对古老的汉字又有了新的认识。这首先应归功于汉字信息处理研究与实践所取得的重要成就，它使古老的方块汉字适应了计算机技术的发展与普遍应用，这真是值得载入史册的大事。再者，在汉字与拼音文字的比较研究中，在汉字与人的大脑及思维关系的研究中，都成果迭出，引人注目，这使人们对"东方魔块"汉字的特点与性质有了进一层的认识。

然而在对外汉语教学中，对汉字教学和汉字学习的研究，却历来重视不够。改变汉字教学与汉字学习的滞后现象，国内同行已深有所感，在国外同行中更是呼声甚高。

早在1985年第一届国际汉语教学讨论会在北京香山举行时，德国汉语教学学者柯比德就曾告诉我们："汉字对我们西方人有一定的吸引力，是许多人决定学汉语的先决条件之一。"

到了1993年第四届国际汉语教学讨论会期间，葡萄牙汉语教师孙琳则认为：从汉字所具有的特殊符号表达规律出发，可以采用"认字、写字与听说同步进行"的教学方法，并进一步提出"完全有必要脱离以西方语言学为基础的教学法，创立一套适合汉语语言特征和汉文化社会语言学特征的对外汉语教学理论和教学法"。这些都在提醒我们，在对外汉语教学中，对汉字总是要多加关注的。

汉字比起拼音文字来，确实有"难认、难记、难写"的一面，它曾困扰着一些汉语学习者。但是，汉字具有独特的表意性，蕴含着丰富的文化内涵，有着十分优美的艺术构形，这又吸引了无数海外学子对汉语情有独钟。于是，如何在汉字教学中扬长避短，因势利导，就成了人们探讨的课题。

柳燕梅《汉字速成课本》在如何对非汉字文化圈国家留学生进行汉字教学及指导其汉字学习方面做了有益的尝试。全书选择了858个汉字和135个构字部件作为基本内容。作者认为："要是能全部掌握这些，你就拿到了打开'汉字之门'的'钥匙'，在以后的汉语学习中，汉字将不会成为你学习的障碍。"

在如何使学习者拿到这把开启"汉字之门"的"钥匙"方面，作者做了精心的安排。

一般的汉语教科书，大多是讲解笔画、笔顺，然后就是书写练习。本书与此不同。作为汉字课本，设有四大栏目：汉字知识、奇妙的汉字、学习建议、复习。有关的知识全用英语注释，这就使学习者对汉字的特点和本质有了一个全面、科学的认识，避免了一知半解、道听途说或主观臆测，产生误解。这也有助于学习者树立学好汉字的信心，掌握正确的学习方法，提高学习兴趣。

认汉字、记汉字、写汉字，其中关键在于记忆。记住字形，记住意义，留下声音形象，经过练习，才能会写。因此，如何使学习者记住每一课所出现的新汉字，着实得下一番功夫。唯其如此，才能提高汉字学习效率。本书的做法是将每一课的例字按有效记忆单位（7±2）分成若干小组，并尽量将它们类化，使其具有一定的相似性，为的是便于学习者记忆。书中用了相当篇幅讲"象形字"和"会意字"，而对形声字的"形旁"用力尤多。想方设法使学习者辨别形旁，也是因为形旁与意义有关，便于学习者记忆。比如"冫"跟"冷"有关，例字：冰、冷、凉／次、决。"氵"跟"水"有关，例字：江、河、酒／游、泳、洗、澡／没、法。在讲形声字"声旁"时，特别关照学生不能看到形声字就以声旁判定读音。我们有时揶揄念错了字音的人时，常说真是"秀才认字念半边儿"，这半边儿的读音并不可靠。书中正确地指出，学习声旁的最大意义还在于帮助记忆汉字，而不是确定汉字的读音。

这部教材有几项独特的设计，值得提及。

其一是设计了"同步练习"。所谓"同步练习"，即随着所展示的新教学内容而设计的形式多样、丰富多彩、变幻不拘的各种练习。翻遍全书，读者会发现练习的形式不下几十种。设计如此数量庞大的练习，其目的正在巩固所学、温故知新。为增加所学汉字的实用性，在练习中还将汉字置于词、词组和句子之中。汉字有了上下文，有了富于联想的语境，就更容易记住，且达到提高交际能力的目的。

其二是设计了"奇妙的汉字"。本书借鉴了以往汉字教材和汉字教学中的成功经验，针对学习者普遍存在的学习难点和容易出现偏误的地方，在本栏目中借助汉字的"奇妙"之处，特别予以点明。如：

"不一样的笔画，不一样的汉字"中举出了"土／士，午／牛，己／已，刀／力"等。

"一旁多音"告诉学习者同一声旁可以读音不同，切莫误读。如："江、红、功、空"声旁皆为"工"，读音却不同。

"形似音近字"指出一些汉字构形相似，读音相同或相近，但意义却不同。如："杨／扬，枪／抢，浅／线，剧／据，洁／结，副／幅"。

"形似字"仅仅字形相似，不应混淆。如："历／厉，爪／瓜，折／拆／析，爱／受"。

也许国人对此已习焉不察，然而这正是初学汉字的外国人最容易犯错误的地方。这么一提醒，岂不是让学习者少走了不少弯路？

所憾者，在阐明汉字"奇妙"的同时，对一些字的解释与文字学中的字源说有所不同。如对"人、太、天、大"一系列字的人文阐释，以及对"宿"字为"一百个人住在屋子里"的附会，犹如白玉微瑕。不过作者认为，这都遵循了"利于学习者记忆"的原则，似亦无可厚非。字源学是一门科学，重考据、讲实证，与教学中对某些汉字据字形做有利于记忆的随机解释是两码事。

其三是设计了"学习建议"，针对以往在汉字学习过程中出现的偏差，提出了"先认识汉字再默写"，而不提倡写得越多越好，从而避免了一味地书写，最后竟不知其义、亦不明读音的现象。至于如何记汉字，教材总结了一套"一看，二写，三想，四复习"的记忆汉字的方法，充分运用汉字所具有的形、音、义三位一体的特点，有效地提高了记汉字的能力。在如何写好汉字方面，教材强调在初始阶段一定要按"田"格本，摆好布局，注意间架，规规矩矩地写。这些必要的学习指导看似简单，但对来自非汉字文化圈国家的学生实属必要。

一本汉字速成教材，既要科学，又要实用，兼顾起来，实属不易。学习汉语，必须借助汉字。有声的汉语是第一性的，记录有声汉语的汉字是第二性的。使二者有机地结合起来，相辅相成，互为表里，在教学法中融为一体，不是一件容易的事情。学习汉语，无论是口语还是书面语，首要的是记忆。记不住，头脑中空空如也，一切都谈不上。汉字又不同于拼音文字。如何在记忆方法上动脑筋，指示学习者以门径，也要教者用一番苦心，学习者下一番苦功。以上诸点，这本教材，繁简允当，点到为止，主要精神都体现在所展示的教学内容之中。

许国璋先生在《中国大百科全书·语言文字卷》中讲到语言时认为，语言是"人类特有的一种符号系统。当作用于人与人的关系的时候，它是表达相互反映的中介；当作用于人和客观世界的关系的时候，它是认识事物的工具；当作用于文化的时候，它是文化信息的载体"。旨哉斯言！

语言如此，文字亦然。我们在教语言时，切莫忽视文字在其中的效应。口语固然重要，书面语也不应轻视，汉语尤其如此。而汉字作为汉语书面语的载体，自不可小觑。

2001年1月

第二版前言

《汉字速成课本》从2001年出版至今已经12年了。首先，对所有读者表示衷心的感谢：感谢你们的选用和喜爱，使这本教材有了生命力和再版的必要；也感谢你们的意见和建议，让本教材再版修订时可以进一步提高，为读者提供更多方便。此次再版继续遵循第一版"速成、易记、实用"的编写原则，同时也适当地进行了一些调整、更改和增删。具体如下：

1. 最主要的调整是体例上从第一版的单册变成了由《课本》和《汉字练习本》组成的双册。《课本》中每课体例为三部分："汉字知识""奇妙的汉字"和"学习策略"。而原版中以学生练习为主的两部分"同步练习"和"本课复习"都移到了《汉字练习本》中。尽管体例上进行了如此调整，还是建议在教学中能够根据有效记忆单位（7±2个一组例字）来组织教学，并指导学生及时进行同步练习，以便让学生在短时间内有效掌握一组有共同之处的汉字组块。

2. 经过对第一版课本的仔细审读，再版进行了一些更改和增删。第一，在"汉字知识"中的例字选择上，对少数例字的位置进行了调整，另根据需要删减或增加了个别例字。相应地，《汉字练习本》中的"同步练习"和"本课复习"也进行了微调和更改。第二，对原来的"学习建议"部分进行了补充和调整，并更名为"学习策略"。这部分除了对一些内容进行顺序上的调整外，还补充了一些汉字学习策略，如"笔画分析法"和"利用科技工具和网络资源"。已有的一些汉字学习方法修改后介绍得更加详细具体，如第一版中第4课和第9课的"学习建议"介绍了"回忆默写法"的雏形，经过多年的实践、研究和总结，再版详细介绍了这种策略的具体步骤和活动，并在连续的两课中介绍完。第三，《汉字练习本》中的"写一写"练习分列了一格实写的汉字、四格汉字描红和五格空白，目的是让学生先"观察"第一格中的汉字，然后用描红四格进行汉字"笔画和部件的分析和临摹"，最后用"回忆默写法"在空白的五格中进行"默写"活动。（在进行回忆默写活动的时候，可以用本书附赠的纸卡来遮住前面的汉字。）希望这样的设计对学生汉字学习策略的训练能有更为清晰、有效的指导。

3. 再版修订中仍然坚持原版"利于学习者记忆"的主要服务目的，这一点不曾改变。因为本教材的服务对象依然是汉字初学者，初学者的汉字学习任务主要是识记汉字，特别是记忆字形。这一点决定了对例字的古字形的选取原则：如果古字形与汉字字形差异较大,不利于帮助记忆,本教材就不列出其古字形;列出时,也优先选取与汉字最接近的古字形。也正是坚持这一服务目的,"奇妙的汉字"部分保留了原来与字源说有所不同的一些解释,并在"学习策略"部分增加了对"字形联想"这一记忆策略的介绍。

  总之,希望经过修订的第二版教材能够更好地服务于学生和老师。如果对本教材有任何建议和意见,请与我们联系。在修订再版过程中,得到了北京大学出版社王飙和周鹂两位编辑的大力支持和帮助,特此表示感谢!

编 者

2013 年 11 月

第一版前言

在现有教材中，汉字课本相对较少；而不依附某一综合课本，完全独立、系统地介绍汉字知识的课本就更少。为弥补这一缺憾，我们编写了这本《汉字速成课本》，希望对汉字初学者能有所帮助。

1. 适用对象

本教材适用于希望了解汉字知识、有兴趣学习汉字的初级汉语学习者，尤其是没有汉字背景的非"汉语、汉字文化圈"国家的汉语初学者。

2. 内容与目的

全书共20课。每课分为"汉字知识""奇妙的汉字""学习建议"和"复习"四个部分。

（1）汉字知识

第1～7课介绍笔画、笔顺、部件、汉字结构等基础知识，第8～14课集中介绍形旁，第15～18课介绍声旁，第19、20课介绍多义字和多音多义字。通过对汉字知识的初步系统介绍，使学习者对汉字的构成有一定的理性认识，掌握一些简单的构字规律。每一部分的介绍后都配以相应的例字，以期通过学知识记汉字，达到学以致用的目的。

（2）奇妙的汉字

这一部分以汉字实例介绍了汉字构成中一些奇妙、有趣的现象，目的是增加学汉字的趣味性，让学习者了解到汉字也具有艺术性，并由此记住一些汉字。需要说明的是，有些解释与文字学中的字源说有所不同，但都是遵循"利于学习者记忆"的原则的。

（3）学习建议

我们根据在教学实践中遇到的具体问题以及学生提出的常见问题，在这部分介绍了一些正确、有效的学习方法，希望能切实地帮助汉字初学者。

（4）复习

除了例字后大量的"同步练习"外，每一课还有"复习"部分，针对全课的重点内容，着重认读和书写两方面的训练。

希望学习者通过对本教材的学习，能够尽快掌握一些汉字。同时也希望为授课教师提供必需的教学资料。

另外，我们将每一课的例字按有效记忆单位"7±2"分成若干个小组，并尽量将它们类化，具有一定的相似性，为的是便于学习者记忆，提高学习效率。在练习中还将汉字放到词、短语和句子中，以增加实用性。

3. 使用建议

（1）本教材可用于课堂教学，也可用于自学。课堂教学的设计时间为 2～4 学时一课，平均每学时 15～25 个生字。由于每一课由几个小板块组成，并配以相应的练习，所以可根据教学时间、教学对象的水平任意决定内容量，使用起来比较方便。

（2）将字入词、组句时，不可避免地会遇到语法问题。本教材标明了一些短语的意义，但不安排生成句子的练习，因此教师不必讲解其中的语法。

（3）由于篇幅所限，本教材只选用了部分常用字。如学生水平较高，教师可酌情补充例字。另外，由于某种原因，极个别例字不十分常用（如为说明有些多音字"义同音不同"，我们安排了"薄"的"薄纸"用法，但带出了相应的"薄弱"），教师可不做重点处理。

本教材在编写过程中参考了安子介、陈贤纯、张静贤、张朋朋等先生的教材（恕不一一列举），在此一并表示感谢。由于水平所限，不足之处在所难免，希望大家不吝赐教。

编　者

PREFACE (The First Edition)

Among all the textbooks, those of Chinese characters are relatively few. Even fewer are those independent of a comprehensive textbook and systematic in introducing knowledge about Chinese characters. To enrich such teaching materials, this textbook is compiled with a view to helping the learners in their pursuit of Chinese language study.

I. Intended learners

This book is intended for beginners of Chinese language learning, who are willing to take in some knowledge about Chinese characters and interested in learning the language.

II. Content and aim

There are altogether twenty lessons in this textbook, and each lesson is divided into four sections: Knowledge about Chinese Characters, the Wonder of Chinese Characters, Suggestions and Review.

i. Knowledge about Chinese Characters

Lesson One to Lesson Seven are introductions to the strokes, stroke order, components and structures of Chinese characters; Lesson Eight to Lesson Fourteen cover meaning radicals and the following four lessons cover phonetic radicals; the last two lessons are about multi-meaning and multi-phonetic characters. The elementary but systematic introduction to Chinese characters will enable the learner to gain some rational recognition of the structuring of Chinese characters and master some basic rules governing character construction. Example characters are given immediately after knowledge introduction so that character familiarization can be of help in memorizing characters.

ii. The Wonder of Chinese Characters

Illustrated with characters of particular structures, this section attempts to reveal some peculiarly interesting aspects of Chinese character construction, with a purpose to enhance learners' interest in Chinese character learning. Once the learner has come to realize the art in character construction, his memory will be reinforced. It should be noted here, however, that the interpretation given in this textbook may differ from what is discussed in etymology, while invariably serving the purpose of facilitating memorization of the characters.

iii. Suggestions

Some proper and efficient methods of learning are made available in this section. The suggestions are based on the very practice of language teaching and intended to help learners solve the problems frequently encountered during the course of learning.

iv. Review

This section is to supplement synchronous exercises after the example characters and meanwhile covers the main content of each lesson.

Drills are mainly on recognition and writing of the characters to guarantee a quick mastery over the characters on the part of the learner.

We also group the example characters in memory-effective units of about seven each, and the characters in each unit share some features in common to reduce the task of memorization and improve learning efficiency. To ensure proper usage, we put the characters in different contexts ranging from words and phrases to sentences.

III. How to use this book

i. This book can serve both classroom teaching and independent learning purposes. Each lesson is designed for two to four periods, fifteen to twenty-five characters each period. Since each lesson is divided into several blocks, each accompanied with corresponding exercises, the teacher is able to make his or her own decision on what will be used on the basis of learners' language ability and the time available.

ii. Grammar cannot be excluded when characters are extended to words and sentences. This textbook, however, will not provide grammar exercises on how to construct sentences, with only the meaning indicated. So teachers should use the book accordingly.

iii. Limited by space, this textbook chooses only a number of the characters that are of higher frequency in everyday use. Therefore, the teacher is in a position to add some other characters when the students are of higher language level. Meanwhile, a very small number of less frequently used characters are given for various purposes. For instance, when discussing "薄", the example "薄纸" is what we mean to introduce to the learner, but "薄弱" is also listed, not because of its frequency but because we want to illustrate the point that the meaning of a multi-phonetic character can remain unchanged when pronounced differently. In this case, the teacher does not have to discuss these characters in detail.

During the course of compilation, many textbooks have been used as reference. The authors are An Zijie, Chen Xianchun, Zhang Jingxian, Zhang Pengpeng and some others, to whom we would like to extend our heart-felt gratitude.

The Compiler

目 录 CONTENTS

1 第一课　Lesson One

汉字知识　Knowledge about Chinese Characters ·························· 1
　　　　　1. 象形字　Pictographic characters
　　　　　2. 笔画（1）：基本笔画　Strokes (1): Basic strokes
　　　　　3. 笔顺规则（1）　Rules of stroke order (1)

奇妙的汉字　The Wonder of Chinese Characters ·························· 8
　　　　　一切从"人"开始　Everything starts from"人"

学习策略　Learning Strategy ·························· 10
　　　　　怎样学习汉字（1）——和学习英文有什么不同？
　　　　　How to learn Chinese characters (1) — What's the difference between Chinese character learning and English learning?

2 第二课　Lesson Two

汉字知识　Knowledge about Chinese Characters ·························· 11
　　　　　1. 指事字　Indicative characters
　　　　　2. 笔画（2）：变形笔画和依附笔画
　　　　　 Strokes (2): Transformed and dependent strokes
　　　　　3. 笔顺规则（2）　Rules of stroke order (2)

奇妙的汉字　The Wonder of Chinese Characters ·························· 20
　　　　　不一样的笔画，不一样的汉字（1）
　　　　　Different strokes, different characters (1)

学习策略　Learning Strategy ·························· 22
　　　　　怎样记汉字（1）——"古字形"和"字形联想"
　　　　　How to memorize Chinese characters (1) — "Ancient glyphs" and "Shape association"

3 第三课　Lesson Three

汉字知识　Knowledge about Chinese Characters ·························· 24
　　　　　1. 复合笔画　Complex strokes
　　　　　2. 汉字的结构（1）：独体字
　　　　　 Structures of characters (1): Single-component characters

	奇妙的汉字	The Wonder of Chinese Characters ················· 30
		不一样的笔画，不一样的汉字（2）
		Different strokes, different characters (2)
	学习策略	Learning Strategy ·· 32
		怎样写好汉字　How to write beautiful characters

4　第四课　Lesson Four

	汉字知识	Knowledge about Chinese Characters ··········· 34
		1. 会意字　Associative characters
		2. 汉字的结构（2）：合体字
		Structures of characters (2): Multi-component characters
	奇妙的汉字	The Wonder of Chinese Characters ················· 39
		不一样的笔画，不一样的汉字（3）
		Different strokes, different characters (3)
	学习策略	Learning Strategy ·· 42
		怎样记汉字（2）——"笔画分析法"
		How to memorize Chinese characters (2) — "Stroke analysis"

5　第五课　Lesson Five

	汉字知识	Knowledge about Chinese Characters ··········· 44
		1. 形声字　Pictophonetic characters
		2. 汉字的结构（3）　Structures of characters (3)
	奇妙的汉字	The Wonder of Chinese Characters ················· 48
		既可表意也可表音的偏旁　Radicals both phonetic and meaning
	学习策略	Learning Strategy ·· 51
		怎样记汉字（3）——"回忆默写法"（上）
		How to memorize Chinese characters (3) — "Write by recall" (Part one)

6　第六课　Lesson Six

	汉字知识	Knowledge about Chinese Characters ··········· 54
		部件（1）　Components (1)

目录 CONTENTS

奇妙的汉字   The Wonder of Chinese Characters ·················· 58
不一样的位置，不一样的点儿   Different position, different dot

学习策略   Learning Strategy ································· 61
怎样记汉字（4）——"回忆默写法"（下）
How to memorize Chinese characters (4) — "Write by recall" (Part two)

7   第七课   Lesson Seven

汉字知识   Knowledge about Chinese Characters ············· 63
部件（2） Components (2)

奇妙的汉字   The Wonder of Chinese Characters ·················· 68
部件一样的汉字   Characters with the same components

学习策略   Learning Strategy ································· 71
怎样记汉字（5）——利用部件和偏旁
How to memorize Chinese characters (5) — Using components and radicals

8   第八课   Lesson Eight

汉字知识   Knowledge about Chinese Characters ············· 73
1. 形旁（1） Meaning radicals (1)
    亻、彳、口、讠、女、人
2. 汉字的结构（4） Structures of characters (4)

奇妙的汉字   The Wonder of Chinese Characters ·················· 82
字中字   Characters within characters

学习策略   Learning Strategy ································· 84
学查字典   How to consult a Chinese dictionary

9   第九课   Lesson Nine

汉字知识   Knowledge about Chinese Characters ············· 86
1. 形旁（2） Meaning radicals (2)
    冫、氵、日、月、阝
2. 汉字的结构（5） Structures of characters (5)

	奇妙的汉字	The Wonder of Chinese Characters ·············· 93
		形同但位置不同的形旁
		The same meaning radical taking different positions
	学习策略	Learning Strategy ···································· 96
		汉语中字与词的关系
		Relationship between characters and words in Chinese

10 第十课   Lesson Ten

	汉字知识	Knowledge about Chinese Characters ············ 97
		形旁（3） Meaning radicals (3)
		木、手（扌）、纟（幺）、刀（刂、夕）、心（忄）、火（灬）
	奇妙的汉字	The Wonder of Chinese Characters ·············· 103
		义同形不同的形旁
		Meaning radicals of the same meaning taking different forms
	学习策略	Learning Strategy ·································· 107
		怎样记汉字（6）——利用关键部件
		How to memorize Chinese characters (6) — Using key component

11 第十一课 Lesson Eleven

	汉字知识	Knowledge about Chinese Characters ············ 109
		形旁（4） Meaning radicals (4)
		辶、囗、钅、饣、犭、目、足、艹、竹
	奇妙的汉字	The Wonder of Chinese Characters ·············· 118
		形象字 Graphic characters
	学习策略	Learning Strategy ·································· 119
		怎样记汉字（7）——联想法
		How to memorize Chinese characters (7) — Association strategy

12 第十二课 Lesson Twelve

	汉字知识	Knowledge about Chinese Characters ············ 120
		形旁（5） Meaning radicals (5)
		宀、穴；广、疒；尸、户；礻、衣（衤）；欠、攵

目 录 CONTENTS

奇妙的汉字	The Wonder of Chinese Characters ················ 128
	夹心字　Sandwich characters
学习策略	Learning Strategy ························· 129
	怎样记汉字（8）——自制汉字卡片 How to memorize Chinese characters (8) — Making flashcards

13 第十三课　Lesson Thirteen

汉字知识	Knowledge about Chinese Characters ················ 131
	形旁（6）　Meaning radicals (6) 土、石、山、身、耳、页、马、牛、羊、虫、鱼、鸟
奇妙的汉字	The Wonder of Chinese Characters ················ 139
	合字　Compound characters
学习策略	Learning Strategy ························· 140
	怎样记汉字（9）——利用科技工具和网络资源 How to memorize Chinese characters (9) — Using technology tools and online resources

14 第十四课　Lesson Fourteen

汉字知识	Knowledge about Chinese Characters ················ 142
	形旁（7）　Meaning radicals (7) 王、贝、皿、酉、车、舟、田、米、走、见、力、巾
奇妙的汉字	The Wonder of Chinese Characters ················ 150
	"品"形字　Pyramid-shaped characters
学习策略	Learning Strategy ························· 151
	怎样记汉字（10）——复习 How to memorize Chinese characters (10) — Review

15 第十五课　Lesson Fifteen

汉字知识	Knowledge about Chinese Characters ················ 152
	声旁（1）　Phonetic radicals (1) 巴、马、圣、可、方、青、及、艮、交、己、夬、舌、采、生、其

	奇妙的汉字	The Wonder of Chinese Characters ·············· 155
		一旁多音　One phonetic radical with more than one sound
	学习策略	Learning Strategy ································ 156
		声旁与汉字的关系（1）
		The relationship between the phonetic radical and the character (1)

16　第十六课　Lesson Sixteen

	汉字知识	Knowledge about Chinese Characters ·············· 157
		声旁（2）　Phonetic radicals (2)
		令、氏、监、羊、京、东、扁、乙、果、仑、争、平、包、比
	奇妙的汉字	The Wonder of Chinese Characters ·············· 159
		声旁位于形旁中间的形声字
		Pictophonetic characters with the phonctic radical in the middle of the meaning radical
	学习策略	Learning Strategy ································ 160
		声旁与汉字的关系（2）
		The relationship between the phonetic radical and the character (2)

17　第十七课　Lesson Seventeen

	汉字知识	Knowledge about Chinese Characters ·············· 161
		声旁（3）　Phonetic radicals (3)
		古、良、吉、票、戋、畐、居、正、廷、曼、兑、且、相、冈
	奇妙的汉字	The Wonder of Chinese Characters ·············· 163
		形似音近字　Characters with similar forms and sounds
	学习策略	Learning Strategy ································ 164
		如何辨别形似音近字
		How to distinguish characters from similar forms and sounds

18　第十八课　Lesson Eighteen

	汉字知识	Knowledge about Chinese Characters ·············· 165
		声旁（4）　Phonetic radicals (4)
		隹、白、原、君、曷、竟、专、直、占、成、韦、参、尤、曹

	奇妙的汉字	The Wonder of Chinese Characters ·················· 167
		形似字（1） Characters similar in form (1)
	学习策略	Learning Strategy ······································ 168
		如何辨别形似字
		How to distinguish characters from similar forms

19 第十九课 Lesson Nineteen

	汉字知识	Knowledge about Chinese Characters ·············· 169
		多义字　Multi-meaning characters
	奇妙的汉字	The Wonder of Chinese Characters ·················· 172
		形似字（2） Characters similar in form (2)
	学习策略	Learning Strategy ······································ 173
		上下文的重要性　The importance of the context

20 第二十课 Lesson Twenty

	汉字知识	Knowledge about Chinese Characters ·············· 174
		多音多义字　Multi-phonetic and meaning characters
	奇妙的汉字	The Wonder of Chinese Characters ·················· 178
		多音同义字　Multi-phonetic characters with the same meaning
	学习策略	Learning Strategy ······································ 179
		怎样学习汉字（2） How to learn Chinese characters (2)

生字总表·· 180
形旁总表·· 193
声旁总表·· 194

第一课
Lesson One

汉字知识 Knowledge about Chinese Characters

　　汉字数量很多，但有些汉字并不常用，通用的不过5000～8000个，日常生活中经常使用的只有3000多个。这3000多个字覆盖了一般书报中99.9%的字。如果一个人掌握了其中出现频率最高的950个字，就可以看书读报了，因为它们能覆盖一般书报中90%的字。留学生能学会1000个左右的汉字就可以了。这本书中包括858个汉字和135个构字部件，要是能全部掌握，你就拿到了打开"汉字之门"的"钥匙"，在以后的汉语学习中，汉字将不会成为你的障碍。

　　In Chinese, there are a great number of characters. But as a matter of fact, some characters are seldom used. Those that are widely used total around 5,000 to 8,000, and only 3,000 or so characters are used in everyday life and cover 99.9 percent of characters appearing in books and newspapers. Among these some 3,000 characters, 950 are of the highest frequency of appearance, covering 90 percent of those printed in books and newspapers. If you have mastered these characters, you will be able to read Chinese. So 1,000 characters will be enough for a foreign student. As for this book, 858 characters and 135 components will be discussed, the mastery over which will give you the key to open the door to Chinese characters.

1. 象形字 Pictographic characters

汉字是怎么来的？

　　汉字至少有3000多年的历史，最初的汉字是象形文字，是根据事物的大概样子，用简单的线条勾画出来的。比如那时人们用"𠂉"来表示"人"（rén, person），用"𠀾"来表示天上的"云"（yún, cloud）。

Where do Chinese characters come from?

　　Chinese characters have had a history of more than 3,000 years. Ancient Chinese characters were pictographic, outlining the rough shape of things with simple lines. For example, ancient people used "𠂉" to symbolize "人"(rén, person)and "𠀾" "云"(yún, cloud).

Easy Way to Learn Chinese Characters

❓ **猜一猜**：下面是一些象形字，你能把它们与现代汉字及其意思联系起来吗？试试看！

Have a guess: Can you match the following pictographic characters with their modern version and meaning? Have a try!

1	♡	山	sun
2	∪	口	eye
3	⌒	日	mountain
4	⊖	目	heart
5	ᗰ	心	mouth
6	⁞⁞	月	door
7	☀	门	tree
8	⟩	火	water
9	ᗰ	水	moon
10	門	木	fire

（答案在本课中找）

(The key can be found in this lesson.)

👤 **想一想**：把上面的象形字和现代汉字比较一下，看看它们有什么不一样。

——从事物的形状变成了方块形；

——从柔软的线条变成了硬直的笔画。

Have a think: What's the difference between the pictographic characters above and their modern version?

——The characters are no longer imitations of the things they refer to, but in square forms;

——The soft lines have turned into solid strokes.

2. 笔画（1）：基本笔画 Strokes (1): Basic strokes

现代汉字是方块形的，是由一些笔画组成的。汉字中最基本的笔画是：
Chinese characters, which are in the shape of a square, are made up of strokes. The basic strokes are as follows:

	笔画 Stroke	名称 Name	写法 Way of writing	例字 Example
1	一	Héng 横	从左向右，要平 horizontally from left to right	十
2	丨	Shù 竖	从上到下，要直 vertically from top to bottom	上
3	丿	Piě 撇	从上向左下，稍软 softly from top to lower left	人
4	丶	Nà 捺	从上到右下，稍软 softly from top to lower right	八
5	丶	Diǎnr 点儿	向右下方，顿笔 dot to lower right and pause	六
6	ノ	Tí 提	从左下向右上 dot from bottom-left to top-right	习

📝 **写一写**：请写一写上面的笔画，并记住它们的名称。

Writing exercise: Please write the strokes listed above and remember their names.

➡ 做"同步练习"1～2

横 Héng

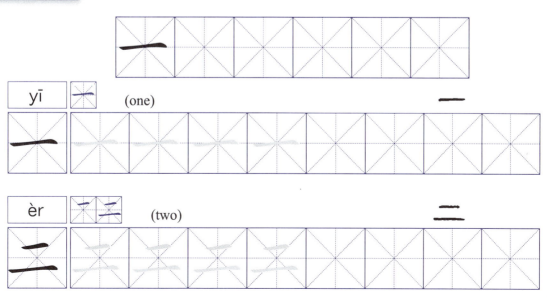

yī (one)

èr (two)

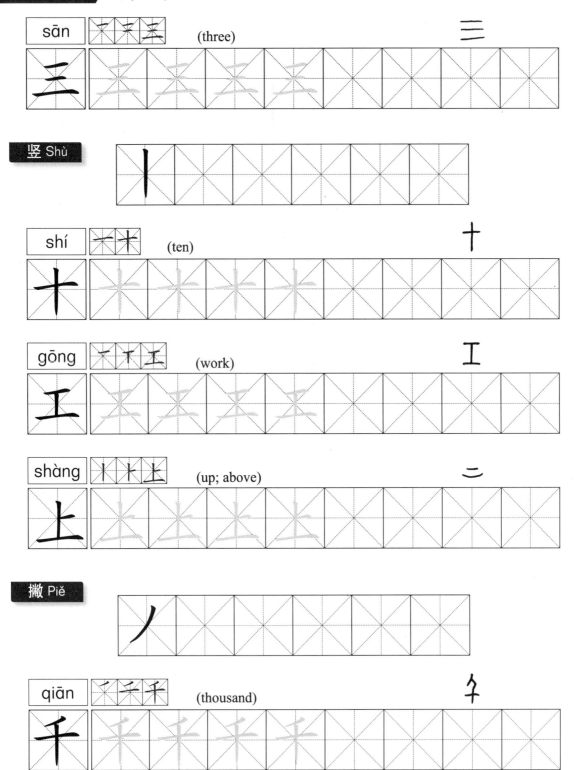

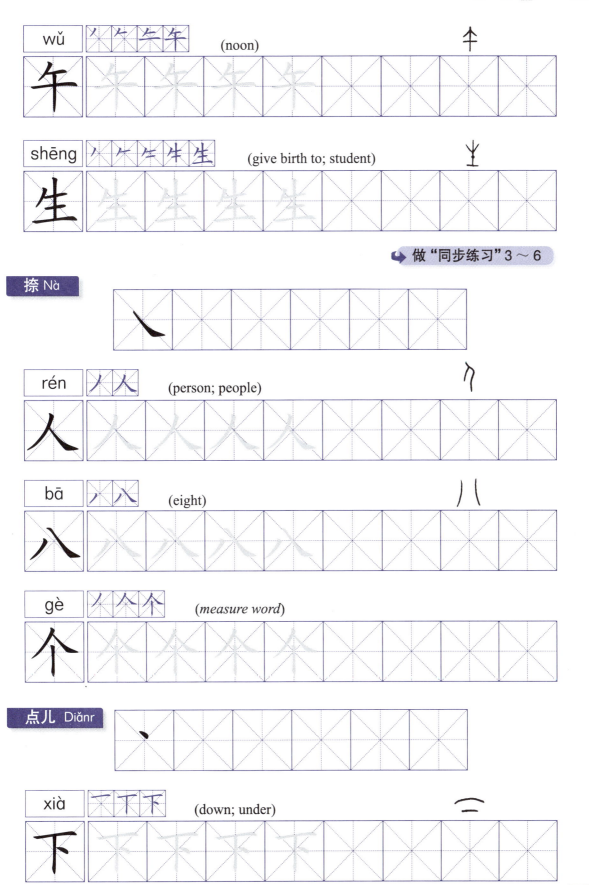

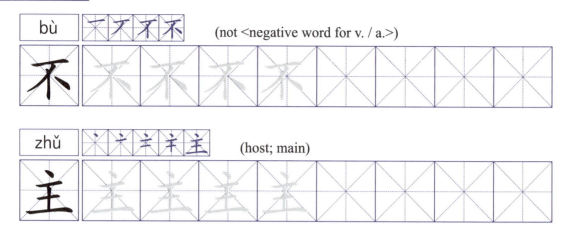

3. 笔顺规则（1） Rules of stroke order (1)

为了写得自然、流畅，写汉字的时候，有一定的书写顺序：

In order to write naturally and fluently, you should observe the rules of stroke order.

（1）**先横后竖**：先写横和由横组成的笔画，再写其他笔画。比如："十"和"丰"。

Heng before *Shu*: fist write *Heng* and the strokes consisting of *Heng*, then other strokes. For example: "十" and "丰".

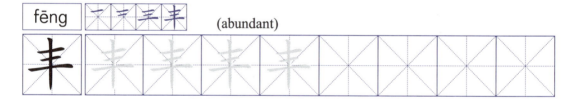

（2）**先撇后捺**：撇和捺相交或相接时，先写撇，后写捺。比如："人"和"文"。

Pie before *Na*: when *Pie* and *Na* join or cross each other, first write *Pie* then *Na*. For example: "人" and "文".

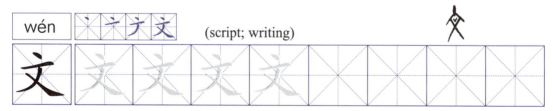

（3）**从上到下**：先写上面的笔画，再写下面的。比如："三"和"土"。

From top to bottom: the upper stroke(s) should be written before lower stroke(s). For example: "三" and "土".

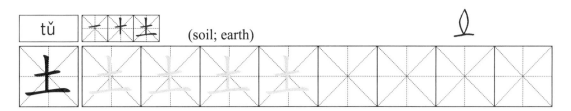

（4）**从左到右**：先写左边的笔画，再写右边的。比如："八"和"木"。

From left to right: write the stroke(s) on the left before stroke(s) on the right. For example: "八" and "木".

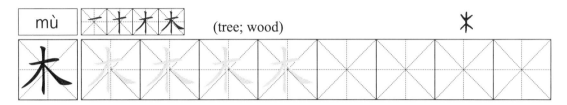

做"同步练习"11～12

奇妙的汉字 The Wonder of Chinese Characters

一切从"人"开始
Everything starts from "人"

人 大 太 天 夫

人： 像"人"站立*。很多汉字都有"人"，也许是因为古老的中国人觉得，"人"是这个世界的中心。

This character resembles a person standing on his feet. In fact, this character is a component of many characters in Chinese, and a possible explanation is that ancient Chinese people regarded human beings as the center of the world.

大： 当人把他的两臂伸展开，就代表着"大"。

When a man stretches both arms, he becomes "大".

太： 尽管人可以伸展开，代表着"大"，但是还有比"人"更大的，于是就在"大"字下面加上一个点儿，变成"太"，表示"很大""很高"。

Although a man can stretch himself to convey the meaning of "big", there are things bigger than a man. So a dot is added below "大" to express the meaning of "very big" and "very high".

---

*为了形象说明，并与下面各字呼应，这里对"人"的解释没有采取文字学中"垂手而立"的说法，而是采用了"像人的两腿站立"。这是因为本教材的基本编写原则是为学习者提供最有利于记忆的汉字解释，不论它是通俗说法还是文字学上的解释。

In order to illustrate the vivid glyphs of the character, and keep all characters in this group consistency, the interpretations here adopt the custom sayings instead of the explanations in academic philology. So "人" is interpreted as "a person standing on his feet" instead of "a bowed standing person" in philology. The primary principle of this textbook composition is to provide the best beneficial descriptions for learners to easily memorize the characters listed, regardless of the description is derived from custom sayings or philology explanation.

第一课 Lesson One

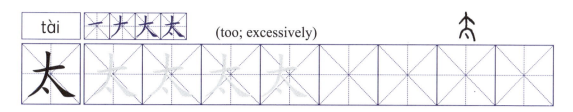

天： 人伸展开就代表着"大"，但是人们也意识到，在"人"的上面还有"天"。
When one stretches himself, he stands for "big". But he also learns that there is the "sky" above him.

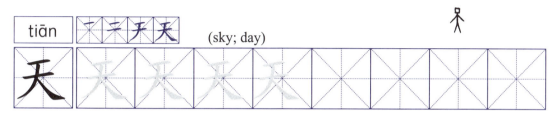

夫： 也许人们早就认识到"人可胖天"，因此用"夫"来表示顶天立地的男人。
Maybe it is just because people came to realize that "man can go beyond the sky" that they uses "夫" to refer to a real man.

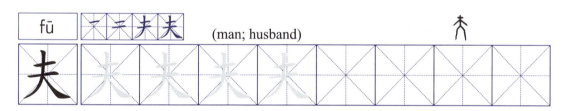

➡ 做"同步练习"13～17

连线练习答案 Key to the matching exercise

1. ♡ — 心 — heart
2. ㅂ — 口 — mouth
3. ⬬ — 目 — eye
4. ⊙ — 日 — sun
5. ⋀⋀ — 山 — mountain
6. ⁝⁝ — 水 — water
7. ⚹ — 木 — tree
8. ☽ — 月 — moon
9. ⋃ — 火 — fire
10. 門 — 门 — door

学习策略　Learning Strategy

怎样学习汉字 (1)
——和学习英文有什么不同？

How to learn Chinese characters (1)
— What's the difference between Chinese character learning and English learning?

　　世界上的文字大致可以分成两种：表音文字和表意文字。汉字是表意文字，也就是说，看到一个汉字，你很难读出它的发音，却可以根据它的字形看出它的大概意义。这与英文是不同的，知道了英文单词的形，也就知道了它的发音，所以记英文单词时，只要记住它的形（或音）与意义的联系就可以了。但是学习汉字，你记住了它的形，还要记它的音，再记住它们与意义之间的联系。看起来，学习汉字要难一点儿，但是汉字是有很多组合规律的，掌握这些规律，学习起来就容易多了，而且越学越容易。中国有句古话："世上无难事，只怕有心人。"你是不是"有心人"呢？

　　Languages in the world can be divided into two groups, phonographic and ideographic, and Chinese is a member of the latter group, which means that you may not know how to read a Chinese character but you can guess the meaning of the character according to how it is written. This is quite different from English, where you can pronounce a word based on its spelling. Thus in English language learning, all you need to do is to relate the spelling or pronunciation to its meaning. In contrast, when you are learning a new Chinese character, you should remember not only its shape and pronunciation but also how the meaning is related to the shape and pronunciation. Therefore, Chinese learning seems somewhat more difficult than English learning. But there are rules governing the makeup of Chinese characters. Once you have mastered the rules, the task will be greatly reduced, and the more you learn, the easier it will become. Just as the old saying goes, "where there is a will，there is a way." Are you a person of strong will?

2 第二课
Lesson Two

汉字知识 Knowledge about Chinese Characters

1. 指事字 Indicative characters

很多东西很难用图画画出来，它们可能是抽象的东西，或者只是图画的一部分，是不能用象形字来表示的，那远古时代的中国人怎么办呢？

他们用抽象的符号来提示字义，一种是纯符号的，如用一个短线条加在另一个长线条上组成"二"，表示方位"上"；还有一种是在象形字上添加一些表示抽象意义的笔画，如在树的根部加一短横（"✳"），表示那里是树根（"本"），后来这个字又有了"事物的根本、基本"的意思。

Many things can hardly be drawn out in pictures, for they may be abstract in meaning or just part of a picture, which cannot be expressed by pictographs. So how could ancient Chinese people do?

They used abstract symbols to indicate the meaning. One class of such symbols is purely symbolic, e.g. one short line over a longer one indicating the meaning of "above" in position. The makeup of the other class is through the addition of some stroke(s) carrying abstract meaning to a pictographic character. For instance, when a short line was added at the lower end of a tree, a character indicating the root came into being. Later on, the character gained some new senses like "the essence of things".

猜一猜：下面是一些指事字，你能把它们与现代汉字及其意思联系起来吗？试试看！

Have a guess: Can you match the indicative characters listed below with their modern version and meaning? Have a try!

1	✳	天	four
2	人	下	up; above
3	三	四	sky
4	一	上	root
5	✳	本	end
6	二	末	down; under

（答案在本课中找）

(The key can be found in this lesson.)

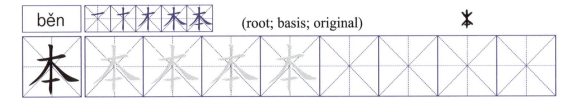

2. 笔画（2）：变形笔画和依附笔画
Strokes (2): Transformed and dependent strokes

（1）变形笔画　Transformed strokes

我们已经学习了汉字的基本笔画"一""丨""丿""乀""、""㇏"等，在有的汉字中，由于所处的位置关系，它们会在方向上、长短上产生变化，形成变形笔画，例如：

We have learned some basic strokes in Chinese, Such as "一", "丨", "丿", "乀", "、" and "㇏". In the Chinese writing system, these strokes may change with their position in direction or in length, which results in transformed strokes. For example：

基本笔画 Basic stroke	变形笔画 Transformed stroke	名称 Name	写法 （与基本笔画比较） Way of writing (in comparison with basic stroke)	例字 Example
、	'	Zuǒdiǎnr 左点儿	向左下方，顿笔 dot to lower left and pause	少
	、	Chángdiǎnr 长点儿	比点儿稍长些 a little longer than a dot	六
丿	一	Píngpiě 平撇	从右向左，接近水平 nearly horizontally from right to left	千
	丨	Shùpiě 竖撇	从上向下，接近垂直 nearly vertically up to down	开
乀	一	Píngnà 平捺	从左向右，接近水平 nearly horizontally from left to right	之

写一写：请写一写上面的笔画，并记住它们的名称。

Writing exercise: Please write the strokes listed above and remember their names.

第二课 2 Lesson Two

左点儿 Zuǒdiǎnr

少 shǎo (few; little; less)

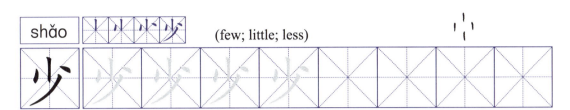

长点儿 Chángdiǎnr

六 liù (six)

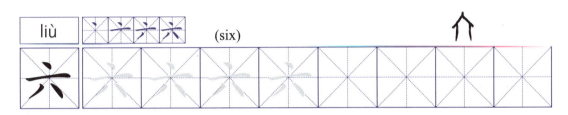

平撇 Píngpiě

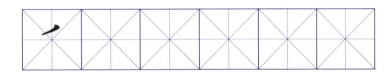

斤 jīn (*measure word*, 1 *jin* = 1/2 kilogram)

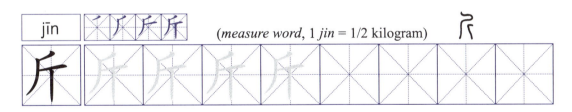

竖撇 Shùpiě

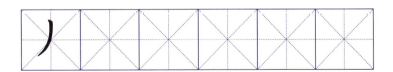

开 kāi (open)

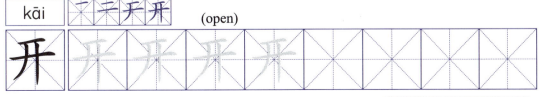

做"同步练习" 1～4

（2）依附笔画　Dependent strokes

有些笔画必须连接在其他笔画后才能形成，这就是依附笔画。依附笔画主要有"折"和"钩"。

The strokes that must be attached to some other strokes are called dependent strokes. *Zhe* and *Gou* are dependent strokes.

①折（Zhé）：自然地连在其他笔画的后面，不是起笔的平笔笔画。主要有：

Zhe is a flat stroke that naturally joined to other strokes, mainly including:

横折	Héngzhé	㇆ ：口　五
竖折	Shùzhé	㇄ ：山　出
撇折	Piězhé	㇜ ：车　云

横折 Héngzhé

(mouth; *measure word*)

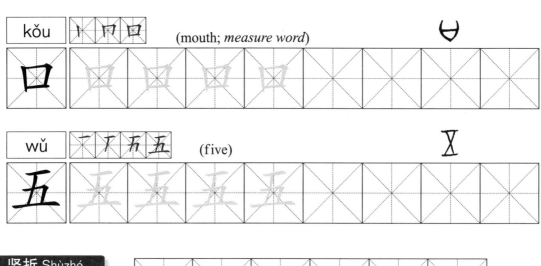

(five)

竖折 Shùzhé

(mountain; hill)

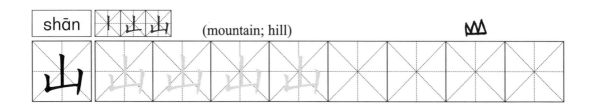

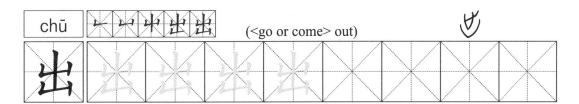

撇折 Piězhé

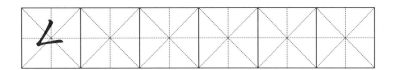

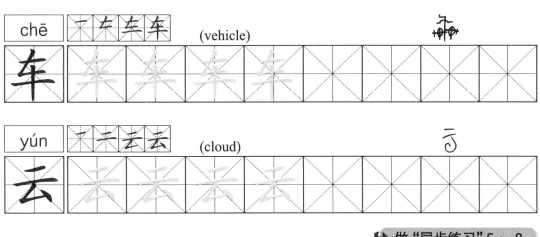

→ 做"同步练习"5~8

② 钩（Gōu）：一画之后，转向另一个方向，然后轻快地提笔，就形成了"钩"。主要有：

Some strokes change in direction and a "hook" is formed by a quick lifting of the pen or a Chinese writing brush, mainly including:

竖钩	Shùgōu	ｊ：小 手 东
横钩	Hénggōu	⁻：了 买
斜钩	Xiégōu	㇂：我
弯钩	Wāngōu	）：（家）*
卧钩	Wògōu	㇃：心

---

* 加括号的字不要求在本课掌握书写，下同。

The character's writing is not required to be achieved within this lesson.

汉字速成课本 *Easy Way to Learn Chinese Characters*

竖钩 Shùgōu

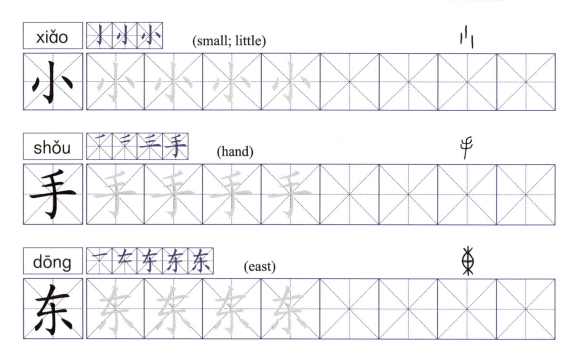

横钩 Hénggōu

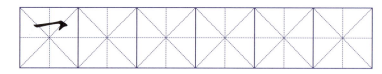

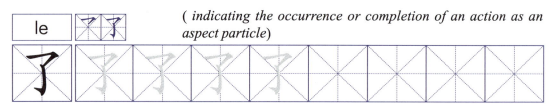

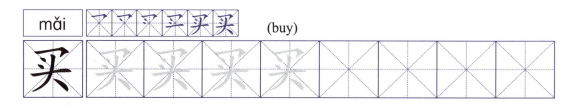

斜钩 Xiégōu

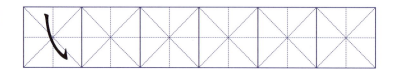

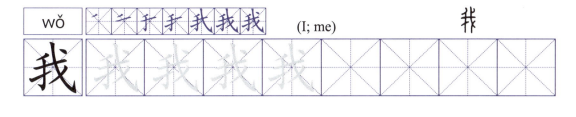

弯钩 Wāngōu

卧钩 Wòyōu

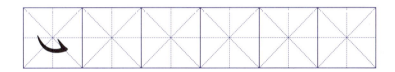

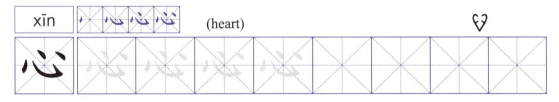

➡ 做"同步练习"9～13

3. 笔顺规则（2） Rules of stroke order (2)

（1）先进后关门　Inside before closing the door

四面包围的结构，要先写左上右三面，然后写里面的字心，最后写下面的横。比如："日"和"田"。

This is a figurative statement which fits the case. When a character is enclosed on all four sides, write the enclosing strokes first and then the enclosed and finally the sealing horizontal stroke at the bottom. It is just like "close the door after one has entered the room". For example: "日" and "田".

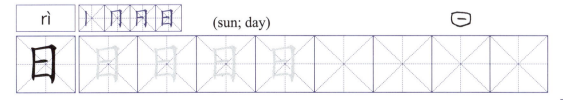

汉字速成课本 Easy Way to Learn Chinese Characters

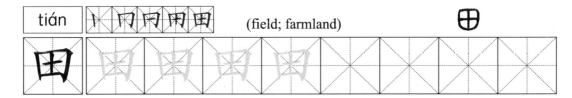

（2）从外到内 From the outer to the inner

从上方包围的结构（左上、右上、左上右），要先写外，后写内。比如："月"。

When a character is enclosed from the upper end (including upper left, upper right and upper left to right), first write the enclosing strokes and then the enclosed. For example: "月".

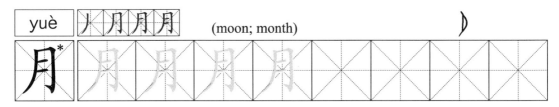

而从下方包围的结构（左下、左下右），要先写内，后写外。比如："画"。

When a character is enclosed form the lower end (including lower left and lower left to right), write the enclosed strokes before the enclosing. For example: "画".

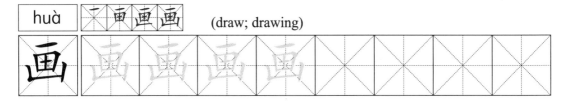

（3）先中间后两边 The middle before two sides

比较突出的竖画在中间，不跟其他笔画相交时，中间的竖画要先写，比如："小"和"业"；如果竖画和别的笔画相交，就后写，比如："中"。

When a vertical stroke is in the middle and prominent position and it does not cross other strokes while it may join others, it should be written first, e.g. "小" and "业"; when it crosses other strokes, however, it should be written last, e.g. "中".

| yè | 丨 丨丨 丨丨 业 业 | (course of study; occupation; industry) |

---

* 不要求在本课掌握书写，下同。

The character's writing is not required to be achieved within this lesson.

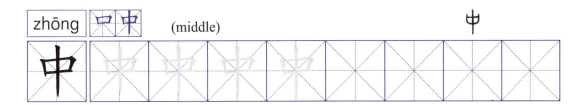

（4）综合规则　　The integrative rule

以上介绍的七种规则可以说是基本的、通常的规则，但不是绝对的。这些规则要综合起来运用，一般先横后竖，但是竖在横的左边时，就先写左边的竖，再写右边的横，比如："上"。有的横在中间，而且比较突出，这个横就最后写，比如："子"。有的先写中间，后写两边，比如："小"。有的先写两边，后写中间，比如："火"。

The seven rules we have learned are the basic rules, which are by no means absolute. They should be applied in an integrative manner. The general rule is to write the horizontal stroke before the vertical stroke. But when the vertical is to the left of the horizontal, the vertical precedes the horizontal, e.g. "上". Another case is when the horizontal stroke is in the middle and takes prominent position, it should be written last, e.g. "子". Some characters are written from the middle to the both sides, e.g. "小"; and some from the both sides to the middle, e.g. "火".

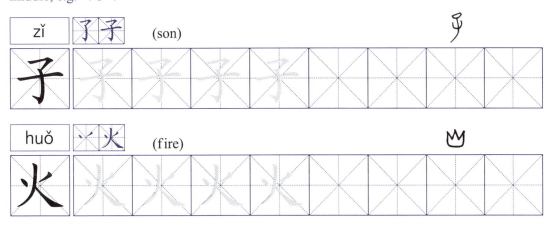

➡ 做"同步练习"14～16

奇妙的汉字 The Wonder of Chinese Characters

不一样的笔画，不一样的汉字（1）
Different strokes, different characters (1)

笔画是汉字最基础的组成部分，笔画的数量不同，所组成的汉字也就完全不同。请看下面几组汉字，看看有什么不同：

Strokes are the basic components of Chinese characters and the difference in stroke number will result in completely different characters. Compare the following pairs of characters and try to see the difference:

{ 日　rì（sun）
{ 目　mù（eye）

{ 白　bái（white）
{ 百　bǎi（hundred）

{ 尸　shī（dead body）
{ 户　hù（door）

{ 白　bái（white）
{ 自　zì（oneself）

{ 厂　chǎng（factory）
{ 广　guǎng（wide）

在学习汉字时，要重视笔画的数量。多一笔或少一笔不是写成了别的字，就是写错了。

You should attach importance to the number of strokes when learning Chinese characters. One more stroke or the omission of a stroke will give you another character or a wrong character.

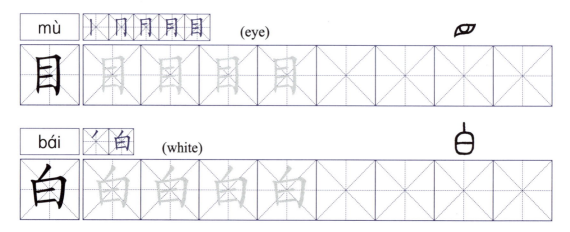

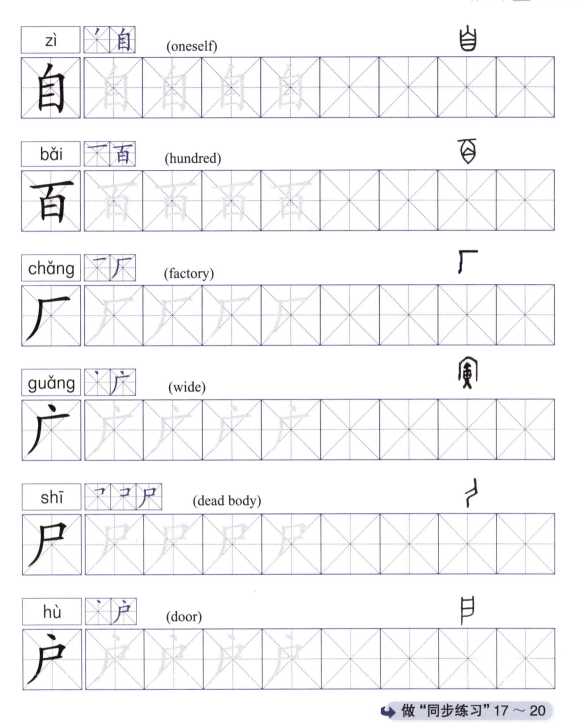

学习策略 Learning Strategy

怎样记汉字（1）
—— "古字形"和"字形联想"

How to memorize Chinese characters (1)
— "Ancient glyphs" and "Shape association"

汉字和拼音文字的字形非常不同，如果你的母语是拼音文字，那么在最初学习汉字的时候，记忆汉字的字形就需要花更多的时间。如果你是一个视觉学习者，可以利用一些汉字的古字形来帮助记忆。当你觉得一个汉字的字形比较难记的时候，可以查找一下这个汉字是否有古字形，这个汉字的字形是怎么来的。如果查找到的古字形和要记忆的汉字非常接近，就可以利用古字形来帮助记忆难记的字形。

可是，并不是所有的汉字都有古字形，而且有古字形的汉字，由于汉字几经演变，现在的字形和原来的古字形已经没有太多相似性了。这个时候，就很难利用古字形来帮助记忆。不过，如果你是一个喜欢想象的人，你可以在自己的头脑里为那些难记的字形想象一幅图画。这种想象可以非常自由随意，你觉得那个汉字看起来像什么，就把它当作什么。有时候，还可以为它编一个小故事。比如这一课的"画"，是不是可以把它想象成你自己画的一幅画儿："四座山的中间是一块田地，东南西三面山都相连，只有北边的山不相连"。这样也许可以帮助你更容易地记住"画"的字形。

虽然你想象的字形和编排的故事不是这个汉字原本的字形和字源，但它们却是你在自己的头脑里记住这些汉字的金钥匙，是你记忆过程中最有效的工具。不过，这种字形联想的方法只适合那些喜欢感性思维的学习者。如果你不喜欢想象，也不知道该怎么去想象或怎么为字形编一个有趣的故事，只想用理性的方式逐步地去记住汉字，那么你可以参考"笔画分析法"（见第四课）和"回忆默写法"（见第五课和第六课）。

Chinese characters are very different from phonographic letters. If your native language is phonographic, you need to make a time investment when starting to learn Chinese characters. If you are a visual learner, you can use ancient glyphs to help memorize some characters. When you think a character is more difficult to memorize, you can find out whether the character has an ancient glyph and how the character was created. If you find the ancient glyph is very close to the character, you can use it to help memorize the difficult character.

However, not all characters have ancient glyphs. Also, since Chinese characters have evolved several times, even for some characters that have ancient glyphs, the original glyphs are quite different from the current characters. In these cases, it is difficult to use ancient glyphs to help memorize characters. But, if you are a person who likes to use your imagination, you can imagine a picture for those characters you find hard to remember. Your imagination can be very casual and free. Whatever you think the characters look like is fine as long as it reminds you of how to write the character. Sometimes, you can also make up a short story for a character. For example, for "画", which you learned in this lesson, you might imagine the character looks just like a picture you drew in which there is a field (田) in the middle of four mountains; the mountains on three sides (East, South and West) are connected, but the mountain of north side is not connected. This may help you more easily remember the character "画"。

Although the picture you imagined and the story you made up are not the same as the character's origin and its own glyph, these may be the most effective tools in your memorization process. However, this method is only suitable for learners who like to attach emotion to their learning process. If you do not like to or do not know how to imagine and make up an interesting story for a character, and instead just want to memorize a character step by step in a rational way, you can refer to the "Stroke analysis" method (in Lesson 4) and "Write by recall" method (in Lesson 5 & 6).

第三课
Lesson Three

汉字知识 Knowledge about Chinese Characters

1. 复合笔画 Complex strokes

在书写时,两个或多个笔画顺势连在一起写成一笔,就构成了复合笔画。上一课学习的"横折""撇折""竖钩"等都是复合笔画,汉字里还有一些:

When two or more strokes are joined together in writing, complex strokes come into being. *Hengzhe*, *Piezhe* and *Shugou* as we have learned in Lesson Two are examples of complex strokes, and there are some more:

(1) 横撇	Héngpiē	フ:	又
(2) 横折提	Héngzhétí	㇊:	(计)
(3) 横折钩	Héngzhégōu	㇆:	月
(4) 横折弯钩	Héngzhéwāngōu	㇌:	几
(5) 横弯钩	Héngwāngōu	㇈:	飞
(6) 横折折撇	Héngzhézhépiě	㇋:	(及)
(7) 横折折折钩	Héngzhézhézhégōu	㇟:	(乃)
(8) 横撇弯钩	Héngpiěwāngōu	㇉:	(队)
(9) 竖弯	Shùwān	㇄:	四
(10) 竖弯钩	Shùwāngōu	㇉:	七
(11) 竖折撇	Shùzhépiě	㇞:	(专)
(12) 竖折折钩	Shùzhézhégōu	㇅:	马
(13) 竖提	Shùtí	㇗:	长
(14) 撇点儿	Piědiǎnr	㇔:	女

写一写:请写一写上面的笔画。

Writing exercise: Please write strokes given above.

➤ 做"同步练习"1～2

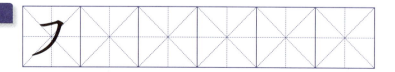

横撇 Héngpiē

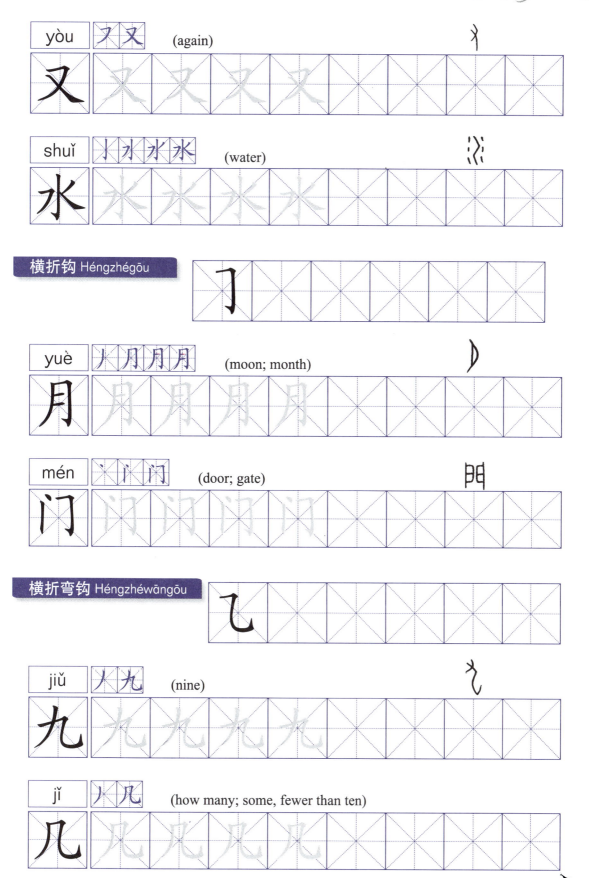

汉字速成课本 Easy Way to Learn Chinese Characters

横弯钩 Héngwāngōu

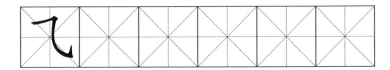

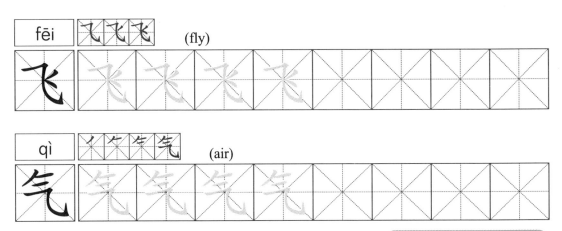

fēi (fly)

qì (air)

➡ 做"同步练习"3～7

竖弯 Shùwān

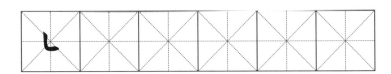

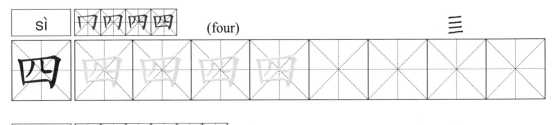

sì (four)

xī (west)

竖弯钩 Shùwāngōu

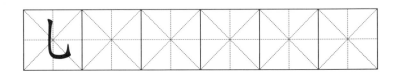

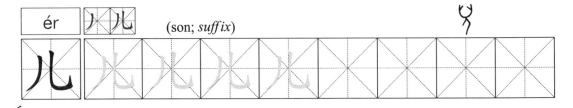

ér (son; suffix)

第三课 3 Lesson Three

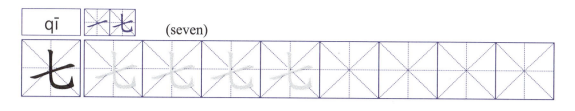

竖折折钩 Shùzhézhégōu

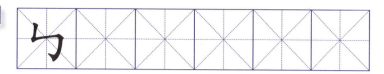

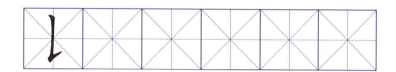

竖提 Shùtí

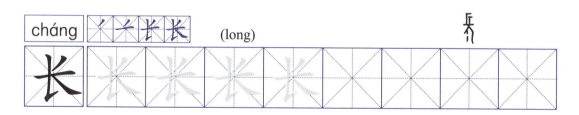

撇点儿 Piědiǎnr

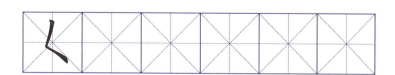

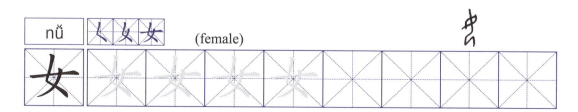

➤ 做"同步练习" 8~12

2. 汉字的结构（1）：独体字
Structures of characters (1) : Single-component characters

汉字是方块形的，汉字的笔画、各个部分需要合理地安排在一个方框中的不同位置上，这要求汉字的结构有一定的规律。汉字的结构大体上分两种：一种是只有一个完整、独立部分的独体字，另一种是由两个或两个以上部分组成的合体字。尽管独体字的比例很小，但它们中的大部分都很常用，或常作为合体字的一部分。本课学习几个常用独体字。

Chinese characters are in the shape of a square. The strokes and components are placed in their proper positions within the square, and the placement is governed by rules. The structures of Chinese characters can be roughly divided into two types: the single component and the compound, where the former includes characters of only one complete and independent component and the latter is made up of characters of more than one component. Despite the small number of single component characters, most of them are widely used or function as a part of the compound characters. In this lesson we will learn several single component characters.

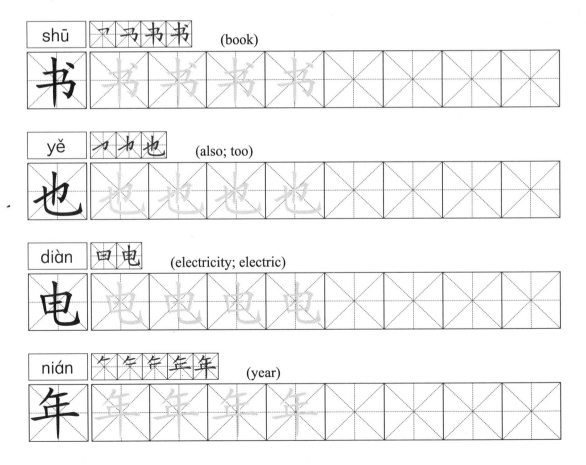

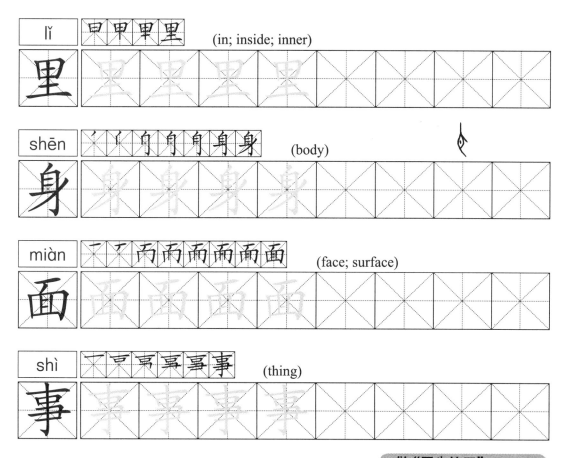

奇妙的汉字 The Wonder of Chinese Characters

不一样的笔画，不一样的汉字（2）
Different strokes, different characters (2)

　　笔画的数量不同可以形成完全不同的汉字。笔画还有长短的不同，这里指在同一个汉字里相对的长短，比如"正"里有三笔"横"、两笔"竖"，它们的长短不一样。相同的笔画，因长短不同也可以形成不同的汉字，看看下面每组的两个字有什么不同：

　　Difference in the number of strokes results in different characters. So does the relative length of a stroke in a character. For instance, there are three *Heng*'s and two *Shu*'s in the character "正", where they are of different length. When the strokes are the same, the difference in length can make different characters. Compare the following two pairs of characters:

$$\begin{cases} 土 & tǔ\ (\text{earth; soil}) \\ 士 & shì\ (\text{solider; scholar}) \end{cases} \qquad \begin{cases} 己 & jǐ\ (\text{oneself}) \\ 已 & yǐ\ (\text{already}) \end{cases}$$

　　汉字中笔画的长短还可以改变笔画的组合方式，比如，使两个相切的笔画变成相交的笔画，从而改变汉字。请看：

　　The varying length of a stroke can also change the combination manner of the strokes. When two conjoined strokes become crossing each other, the character will be different. Compare the following pairs of characters:

$$\begin{cases} 王 & wáng\ (\text{king; }surname) \\ 丰 & fēng\ (\text{abound}) \end{cases} \quad \begin{cases} 午 & wǔ\ (\text{noon}) \\ 牛 & niú\ (\text{cow; ox}) \end{cases} \quad \begin{cases} 刀 & dāo\ (\text{knife}) \\ 力 & lì\ (\text{power; force}) \end{cases}$$

　　汉字中的这些差别虽然很细微，却很重要。希望你在学习汉字的时候能细心观察。

　　Trivial as the differences between the strokes, they are of great significance. So you should be very careful in your observation of Chinese characters.

zhèng 一 丅 下 正 正 (main; just)

正 正 正 正 正

第三课 3 Lesson Three

| shì | 十士 | (scholar; soldier) |

士

| jǐ | 乛㇆己 | (oneself) |

己

| yǐ | 乛㇆已 | (already) |

已

| wáng | 一 二 千 王 | (king; *surname*) |

王

| niú | 𠂉 𠂉 牛 | (ox; cow) |

牛

| dāo | ㇆ 刀 | (knife) |

刀

| lì | ㇆ 力 | (power; force) |

力

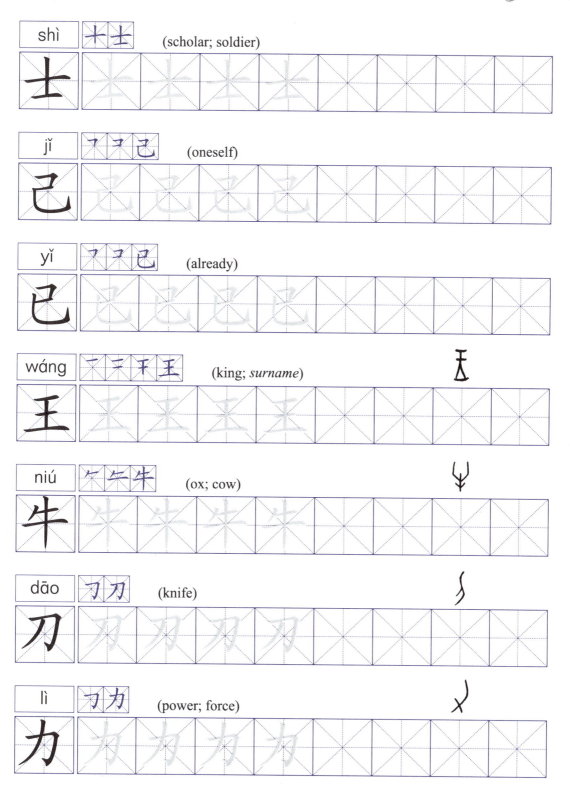

➜ 做"同步练习"17～20

学习策略 Learning Strategy

怎样写好汉字
How to write beautiful characters

学习写汉字要注意两个问题：一是写对，二是写好。

要写好汉字，首先应该写对，在写之前要看清楚汉字的笔画，注意笔画的数量、长短、形状、方向、位置等；其次是要写好每一笔笔画，最基础的有三点：

（1）横平竖直：横要写得平，不能高高低低；竖要写得直，不能弯弯曲曲。

（2）长短适中：注意在一个汉字中，横的相对长短，该长的长，该短的短。

（3）疏密相宜：笔画之间的距离要匀称，笔画多的字要写得紧一些，笔画少的字要写得开一些，不论笔画多还是少，最后写成的字应该是一样大的，比如"我"和"小"，同时写时如写成"我 小"就不好看了。

一个汉字好比是一个建筑，也需要匀称、美观。要想写好一个汉字，就必须注意它的间架结构。各部件要比例恰当，也就是汉字各部分的结构大小要合适，笔画多的部分要写得大一些，笔画少的部分要写得小一些。可以把一个汉字所占的格子根据它部件的多少、大小大致划分为几个部分。比如，左右结构的汉字，如果它是左窄右宽，那么写的时候左边部分可以占格子的三分之一，右边部分占三分之二；如果左右相等，那么各占二分之一，其他同理。所以刚开始学习写汉字时，老师都建议学生使用"田"字格的练习本，这样写出来的汉字又规范又美观。

When learning how to write a Chinese character, you should pay attention to two points: the first is that you should write correctly and the second beautifully.

If you want to write beautiful characters, you should examine the character carefully. How many strokes are there? How long is each stroke? What is it like? Where is it and how does it run? Then you should try to write each stroke properly. The following three criteria are basic to Chinese handwriting:

（1）The horizontal stroke should be level and the vertical stroke upright. The horizontal stroke should not be tipped, while the vertical stroke not zigzagged.

（2）Proper length: You should pay attention to the relative length of the horizontal lines in one character. Longer ones should be written longer and shorter ones shorter.

（3）Balance and symmetry of the character: The distance between strokes should be more or less the same. Therefore, characters with more strokes should be compact and those with fewer strokes should be loose, so that you can write every character in about the same size. For example, when you are writing "我" and "小" side by side like "我 小", they do not look appealing enough.

A character is just like a building where beauty and symmetry should be aimed at. So if you want to write beautifully, you should pay attention to its structure. The components should be well balanced in one character, i.e. the component with more strokes should take larger space than the one with fewer strokes. We can divide the space taken up by a character into several parts according to its components. For instance, if a left-right structured character has a larger right part, we can give it two-thirds of the space; if both parts are of similar size, equal space should be allocated. This explains why the teacher always suggests the students to use workbooks with checks of "田".

第四课
Lesson Four

汉字知识　Knowledge about Chinese Characters

1. 会意字　Associative characters

古人用象形字来表示一些具体的事物，用象形加上一些符号、笔画来表示事物的某个部分或是方位。

那么抽象的概念怎么用汉字表达呢？

聪明的古人把两个或更多的象形字放在一起，表示一些动作、过程或者是抽象的事。比如：用羊大"美"来表示"美"；用一个女子抱着孩子"好"来表示"好"，因为新的生命诞生了是一件好事。汉语里有一些汉字就是古人如此创造出来的。

Ancient Chinese people invented pictographic characters to represent concrete things and the pictographic plus some symbol(s) or stroke(s) to refer to part of a thing or a certain direction and position.

Then how to express an abstract concept?

Ancient Chinese were so clever as to work out the idea of putting two or more pictographic characters side by side to describe an action, a process or something abstract. For instance, they got "美" by putting "羊" and "大" together to express the idea of "beautiful"; they used the imitation of a woman holding her baby in her arms to convey the concept of "good", for it is something desirable for a new life to be born. Some Chinese characters were simply invented by ancient people in this way.

猜一猜：下面是一些会意字，你能把它们与现代汉字及其意思联系起来吗？试试看！

Have a guess: Can you match the associative characters with their modern version and the meaning? Have a try!

Lesson Four 第四课 4

1	从从	休	follow
2	◐	看	bright
3	省	从	forest; woods
4	伏	明	rest
5	分	林	divide
6	林林	分	look

（答案在本课中找）

(The key can be found in this lesson.)

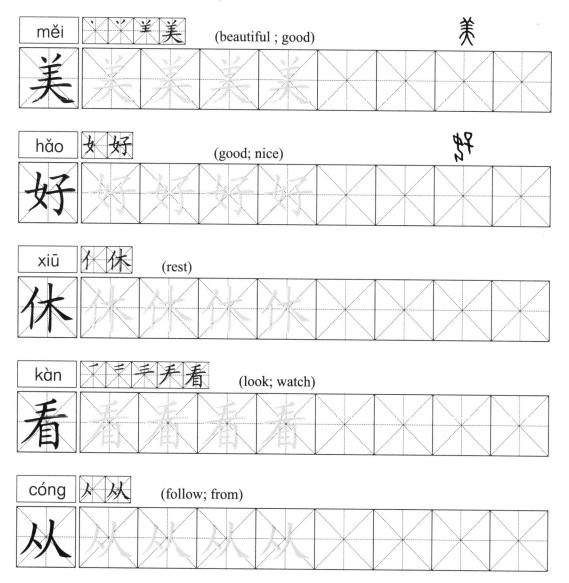

měi (beautiful ; good)

hǎo (good; nice)

xiū (rest)

kàn (look; watch)

cóng (follow; from)

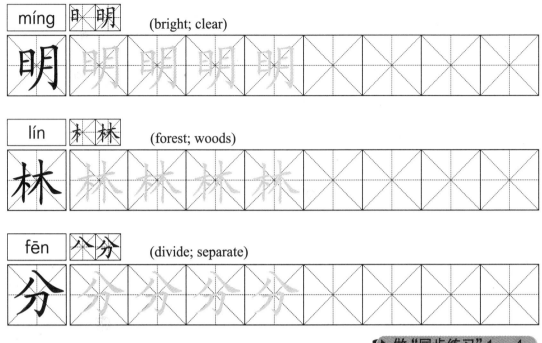

2. 汉字的结构（2）：合体字
Structures of characters (2): Multi-component characters

大部分的汉字都是由两个或两个以上的部分组成的，其中最主要的结构是左右结构和上下结构。现代汉字中，左右结构的字最多，其次是上下结构的，两者约占汉字总数的86%，所以掌握了这两种结构的字就相当于掌握了绝大多数的汉字。

Most Chinese characters are composed of two or more components and the major structures of multi-component characters are left-right structure and top-bottom structure. Of all the characters, those with left-right structure take the first place in number while those with top-bottom structure the second place. Characters of these two structures count for 86 percent of all Chinese characters. So the mastery over characters of these two structures can be regarded as the mastery over most Chinese characters.

（1）左右结构　Left-right Structure

根据左右两个部分的大小，可以分为三种结构：

On basis of the relative size of the left and right parts, it can be subdivided into three sub-structures:

左窄右宽	a smaller left part plus a larger right part	▯：你　汉
左右相等	two parts of equal size	▯：的　以
左宽右窄	a larger left part plus a smaller right part	▯：外　刻

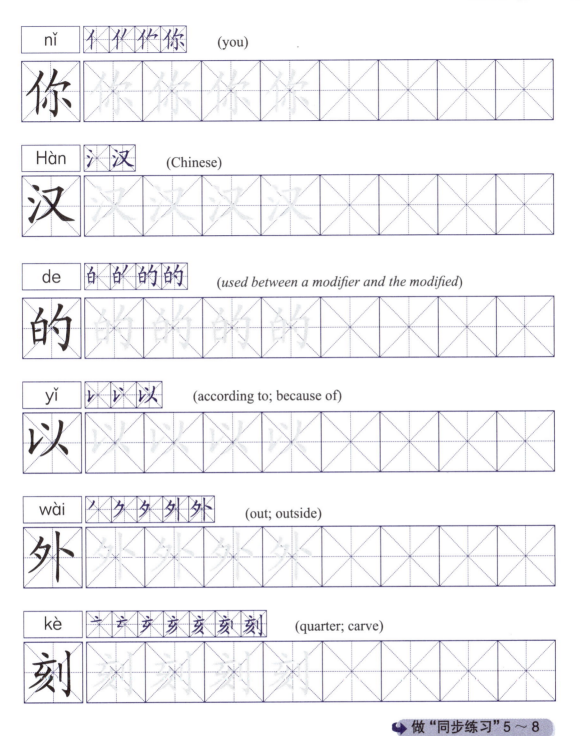

做"同步练习"5～8

（2）上下结构 Top-bottom structure

根据上下两个部分的大小，上下结构也可以分成三种：

For the same reason as in left-right structure, three sub-structures can be observed in top-bottom structure:

汉字速成课本 / Easy Way to Learn Chinese Characters

上短下长　a shorter top part plus a longer bottom part　　囗：字　写
上下相等　two parts of equal length　　　　　　　　　　　囗：是　名
上长下短　a longer top part plus a shorter bottom part　　囗：点　息

| zì | 丶丶宀字 | (character) |

字

| xiě | 冖冖宁写写 | (write) |

写

| shì | 旦旦旦旱是 | (be) |

是

| míng | 夕名 | (name; famous; *measure word*) |

名

| diǎn | 丨卜占占点点点 | (dot; a little; o'clock) |

点

| xī | 自息 | (breath; rest) |

息

➜ 做"同步练习" 9～12

38

奇妙的汉字 The Wonder of Chinese Characters

不一样的笔画，不一样的汉字（3）
Different strokes, different characters (3)

不仅笔画的数量、长短可以区别汉字，笔画的形状、位置等，也可以区别汉字。看看下面几组汉字，每组的两个汉字有什么不同：

Just as the number and length of the stroke can differentiate characters, the shape and position of the stroke can have the same effect. Compare the following pairs of characters:

$$\begin{cases}千\\干\end{cases} \quad \begin{cases}干\\于\end{cases} \quad \begin{cases}贝\\见\end{cases} \quad \begin{cases}才\\寸\end{cases} \quad \begin{cases}名\\各\end{cases} \quad \begin{cases}外\\处\end{cases} \quad \begin{cases}办\\为\end{cases} \quad \begin{cases}旧\\由\end{cases}$$

这里介绍的关于笔画的几个方面，是汉字初学者容易出错的地方。希望你能重视笔画的书写，写时细心观察，也希望你能由此记住一些形似的汉字。

The aspects of the stroke discussed here are beginners' traps in Chinese character learning. So you are advised to be very careful in observing and writing the stroke. Meanwhile, we also hope that you can take advantage of the discussion to remember the characters with similar shapes.

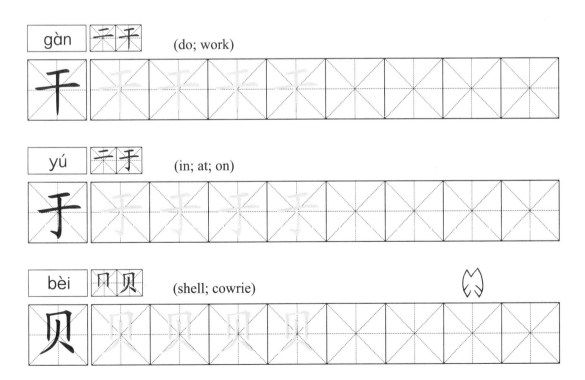

gàn 干　(do; work)

yú 于　(in; at; on)

bèi 贝　(shell; cowrie)

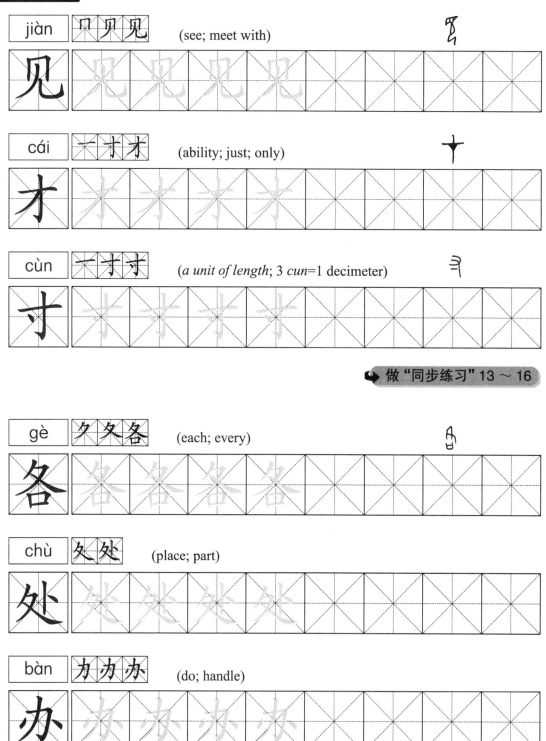

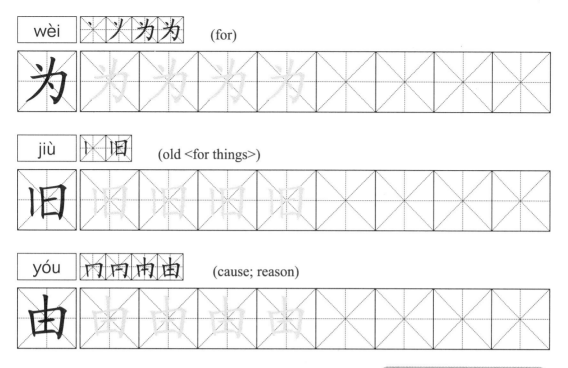

学习策略 Learning Strategy

怎样记汉字（2）
——"笔画分析法"

How to memorize Chinese characters (2)
— "Stroke analysis"

所有的汉字都是由笔画组成的，那么要记住汉字，就得记住这个汉字的所有笔画。第二课和第三课"奇妙的汉字"部分也介绍了"不一样的笔画就会形成不一样的汉字"。笔画有数量、形状、长短、方向、位置和组合方式等多种属性，这些都是汉字的重要区别特征。所以，要想准确地记住一个汉字怎么写，就需要在写以前先仔细地观察汉字，认真地分析这个汉字的每一个笔画。

比如，写之前先数一数这个汉字一共有几个笔画，这样可以帮助区别"日"和"目"这样的汉字；观察笔画的形状，特别是起笔和收笔部分，如"千"和"干"、"贝"和"见"；看看各个笔画是否有长短的不同，如"土"和"士"；如果有"点儿"或"钩"的话，看看它们的方向是怎样的，如"长"和"寸"；注意各个笔画的位置在哪里，如"太"和"犬"中的点儿；也要仔细看笔画与笔画的组合方式是相交还是相切，如"天"和"夫"、"不"和"木"。

在仔细的观察和认真的分析之后，就可以开始书写这个汉字了。实际上，观察和分析都是对汉字字形的记忆加工过程，所以观察和分析后，往往就能基本上记住这个汉字是怎么写的了。这种笔画分析的方法特别适合在开始学习汉字时遇到的笔画数量不多的汉字。如果笔画数量比较多，而且汉字有几个部分了，就可以采用"回忆默写法"（见第五课和第六课）了。

Since every character is formed by strokes, in order to remember characters, you have to memorize all the strokes of the characters. "The Wonder of Chinese Characters" in Lesson 2 and 3 introduce the idea that different strokes will form different characters. Strokes have a variety of attributes, such as number, shape, length, direction, position, and assembling pattern, which are important distinguishing characteristics of Chinese characters. Therefore, in order to remember how to write a character accurately, you need to observe the character carefully and analyze every stroke before writing.

For instance, before writing, it is best to count the number of strokes, which can help differentiate the characters such as "日" and "目"; observe the shape of every stroke, especially for the beginning and ending strokes, for characters such as "千" and "干", "贝" and "见"; check whether the strokes have different lengths, such as in "土" and "士"; check if there is *Dianr* or *Gou* in the character, and if so, take a look their direction, such as in "长" and "寸"; pay attention to the position of each stroke, such as the *Dianr* in "太" and "犬"; carefully note the assembling pattern of strokes and find if strokes are intersecting or tangential, such as "天" and "夫", "不" and "木".

After careful observation and detailed analysis, it is time to begin writing the character. Actually, both observation and analysis are involved the process of memorizing a character's shape, so after performing both functions, most of time you can remember how to write the character. This method of "Stroke analysis" is particularly suitable for beginners trying to memorize characters with few strokes. If a character has more strokes and more than one part, it is better to use the "Write by recall" method (See Lesson 5 & 6) to memorize it.

连线练习答案 Key to the matching exercise

1. 竹 — 从 — follow
2. ☾☉ — 明 — bright
3. 𥄉 — 看 — look
4. 伙 — 休 — rest
5. 八 — 分 — divide
6. 𣏟 — 林 — forest; woods

5 第五课
Lesson Five

✎ 汉字知识 Knowledge about Chinese Characters

1. 形声字 Pictophonetic characters

汉字虽然不是表音的文字，但是在由两个部分组成的一些汉字中，其中一个部分可以表示近似的读音，是声旁；另一个部分可以表示汉字的大概意思或义类，是形旁。比如，"妈"（mā, mom）中"马"表音，"女"表意。这样造出的字就是形声字，声旁和形旁常可以统称为偏旁。

Even though Chinese is not a phonetic language, one component of the characters with two components can give indication to the sound, referred to as the phonetic side/radical, while the other conveys the meaning, termed the meaning side/radical. For example, "马" in "妈" (mā, mom) indicates the sound and "女" carries the meaning. Characters of such make-up are called pictophonetic characters and the two components can be generally referred to as sides or radicals.

📝 **试一试**：下面是一些形声字，请写出它们的形旁（M）和声旁（S），并根据学过的汉字想想它们的意思跟什么有关系。

Have a try: Below are some pictophonetic characters. Please give the meaning side (M) and the phonetic side (S), and guess the possible meaning.

	M	S		M	S
们（men）	___	___	机（jī）	___	___
吗（ma）	___	___	您（nín）	___	___
汽（qì）	___	___	近（jìn）	___	___

| mā | 女 妈 | (mom; mother) |

妈 妈 妈 妈 妈

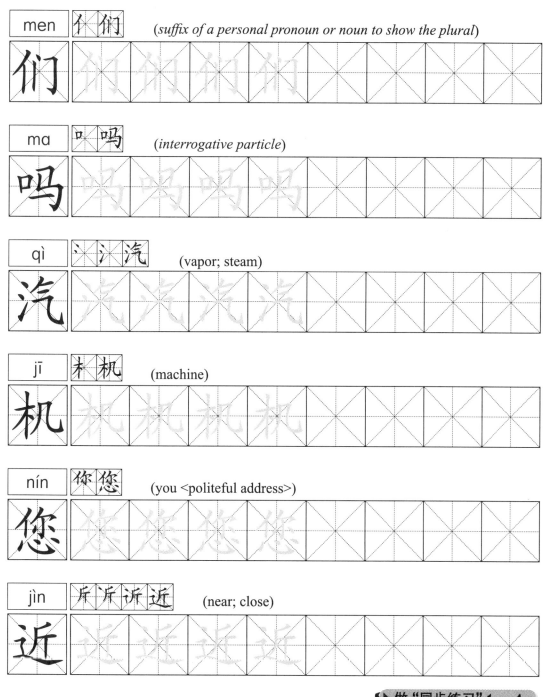

2. 汉字的结构（3） Structures of characters (3)

汉字除了左右和上下两大结构类型以外，还有一种主要的结构类型——包围结构。

In addition to left-right and top-bottom structures, Chinese characters have another important structure—enclosed structure.

(1) 两面包围结构 Enclosed on both sides

　　① 左上包围结构　Enclosed from upper and left　　厂：厅 应
　　② 右上包围结构　Enclosed from upper and right　　习 可
　　③ 左下包围结构　Enclosed from lower and left　　这 起

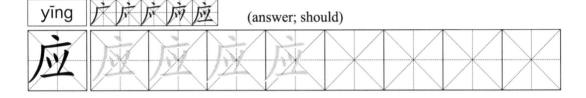

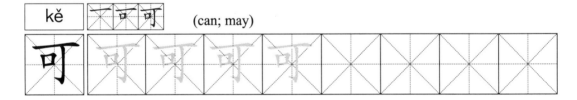

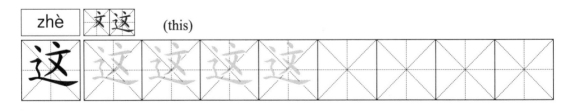

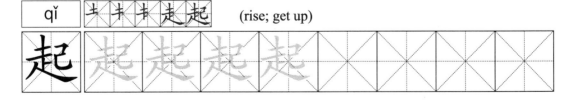

➡ 做"同步练习"5～8

（2）三面包围结构　Enclosed from three sides
　　① 左上右包围结构　Enclosed from left, top and right　　⃞：风　同
　　② 上左下包围结构　Enclosed from top, left and bottom　⃞：医　区
　　③ 左下右包围结构　Enclosed from left, bottom and right　⃞：画

| fēng | 丿 凡 风 风 | (wind) |

风

| tóng | 丨 冂 冂 同 | (same) |

同

| yī | 一 ァ 乑 医 | (medical) |

医

| qū | 一 ㄨ 区 | (area; district) |

区

（3）四面包围结构　Enclosed from four sides　　⃞：国　因

| guó | 冂 囯 国 国 | (country) |

国

| yīn | 冂 冈 因 | (cause; because) |

因

➡ 做"同步练习"9～11

奇妙的汉字　The Wonder of Chinese Characters

既可表意也可表音的偏旁
Radicals both phonetic and meaning

汉语里有些字常用作构字偏旁，比如："人""女"等。其中有的字作为偏旁的构字能力特别强，而且构字时既可以表意，也可以表音，比如："力""门""子""禾"。

Some Chinese characters are often used as radicals, like "人" and "女", and some of them are so active in character construction that they indicate not only the sound but also the meaning, such as "力", "门", "子" and "禾".

	做形旁（as M）	做声旁（as S）
力	男、努	历
门	间	问
子	孩、孙	字
禾	香、秋	和

这些字虽然既可以表意，也可以表音，但是常常以一种为主，比如"禾"多用来表意，表音的只有一个"和"字。

Although these characters can function as both phonetic and meaning radicals, they usually do just one of the two. For instance, "禾" is used as a meaning radical in most cases, the only exception being "和".

nán　甲 男　(male)

男　男　男　男　男

nǔ　女 奴 努　(exert)

努　努　努　努　努

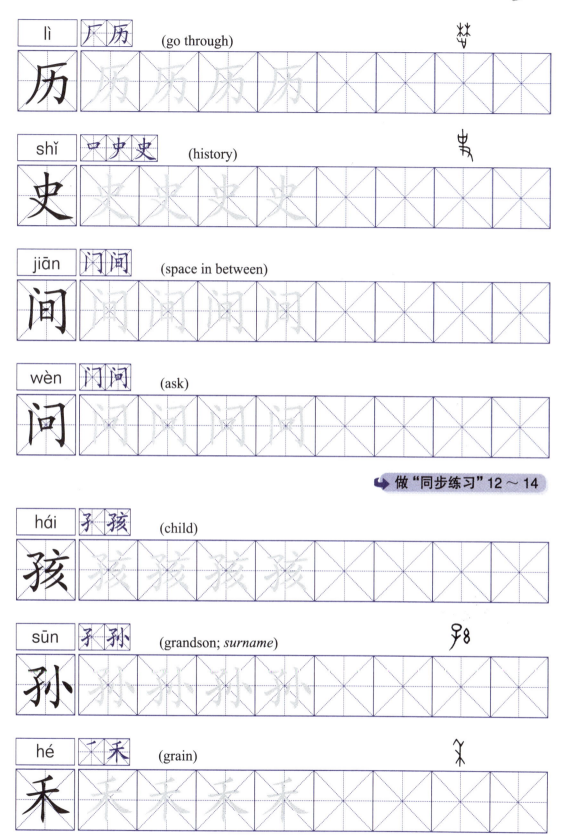

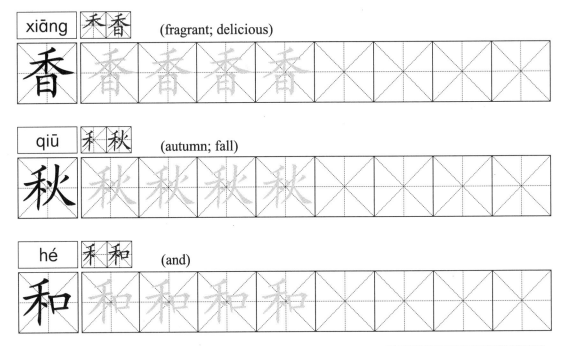

➡ 做"同步练习"15～18

学习策略 Learning Strategy

怎样记汉字（3）
——"回忆默写法"（上）

How to memorize Chinese characters (3)
— "Write by recall"（Part one）

要想记住一个汉字，就要写一写。那么怎样写最有帮助呢？是否写得越多越好呢？不一定，记汉字要采用正确的记写方法。

正确的方法是：写前只看，写时不看，写后再看，直到掌握。具体步骤如下：

第一步：|看 分析| 写汉字之前，应该先看清楚要写的汉字是什么样的，有几个部分，每个部分是什么，哪个部分你已经学过，哪个部分是新的，等等。心里要对这个汉字有一个认识和分析，分析完以后再开始写。

第二步：|写 回想| 写的时候，不看汉字，根据记忆默写。这第一遍写，可能写不对或写不完，没关系。一定不要看一笔写一笔，应该在写不下去的时候再看，或者写完以后再看。

第三步：|再看 修正| 再看的时候，比较自己写的对不对。如果错了，错在哪里；如果写不下去了，是在什么地方。再仔细地观察分析，特别是有问题的部分，以便下次写对。

第四步：|再写 回想| 再写的时候，还是不看汉字，根据记忆来默写。这一遍写，要注意上次没写对的部分，看看现在能否写对。

第五步：|确认 掌握| 如果这次写对了，就可以根据记忆再分别写两遍。如果还是写不对，那就再重复第三步和第四步，直到能够根据自己的记忆写出来为止。

这种"回忆默写"的方法是一种综合性记忆策略，对于独体字和合体字都适用。这样做是经过记忆地写，而不是机械地临摹。用这种方法记汉字，可能不需要写很多遍就能记住了，既节约了时间，又记得牢。你不妨试一试！

Easy Way to Learn Chinese Characters

Writing is essential in your attempt to remember a character. Then what is the most efficient way of writing? Is it true that "the more, the better"? Not necessarily so. It depends more on a proper method than anything else.

The proper method is to 1. look at the character before writing it, 2. write the character without looking at it, 3. check the character after writing it, and then 4. repeat as needed until you have a solid grasp on how to write the character. Below are the detailed steps:

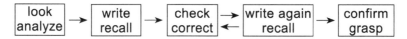

Step 1: [look / analyze] Before you begin to write a character, first examine the character carefully, paying attention to its shape, the components, which part has already been learned, which part is new, etc. When you have gained a general idea about the character, you may begin writing.

Step 2: [write / recall] When you write, do not look at the character, please write it from memory. For the first attempt, you may not be able to write it accurately or successfully, but don't worry — this is normal. However, it must be noted that you should write the character by recall, rather than blindly copying it stroke by stroke. You can check the character if your memory fails you or after writing it.

Step 3: [check / correct] Check by comparing what you just wrote against the original character to see if it is right. If not, find out which part is wrong; if you could not finish writing, identify which part got you stuck. Careful observation and analysis of the character, especially for the part in which you had a problem, will help you write it correctly the next time.

Step 4: [write again / recall] When you write the character again, still write it from memory — do not look at the character. This time, you need to pay attention to the part you did not write correctly last time and check if you can succeed in writing now.

Step 5: [confirm / grasp] If you write the character correctly this time, you can re-write it twice from your memory. If you cannot write it correctly, please repeat Steps 3 and 4 as needed until you can succeed in writing by recall.

This "Write by recall" method is a comprehensive memory strategy. It is suitable for memorizing characters with one or more components. It involves writing from memory rather than mechanically copying what you see in front of you. If you practice writing in this manner, you do not have to write a character many times before you can remember how to write it. In this way, you can save not only time and energy but also create a long-term memory of the characters in your mind. Don't you want to give it a try?

第六课
Lesson Six

 汉字知识　Knowledge about Chinese Characters

部件（1）　Components (1)

　　构成汉字的结构单位有两个：一是笔画，一是部件。笔画是汉字最小的结构单位，部件是由笔画构成的一个自然、独立的部分，并不是汉字的整体。也可以说，笔画是独体字的结构要素，部件是合体字的结构要素。

　　学习部件以后，可以把合体字看成是由几个部件构成的，而不仅仅看到汉字是由笔画构成的。形成这样的习惯有利于认识汉字的结构，有利于记忆汉字。下面介绍一些常见的部件。

There are two units in character construction, the stroke and the component. The stroke is the minimal constructing unit, while the component is a natural and independent part of the character composed of strokes. But the component is not the character yet. It can be said that the stroke structures the single-component character while the component multi-component character.

Knowledge about components will enable you to divide a multi-component character into its components rather than strokes. This will contribute to the recognition and memorization of Chinese characters. Therefore, the following will be devoted to the discussion of components:

（1）厶：么　公　去
（2）十：支　南　卖　直　什
（3）ナ：左　右　在　友　有
（4）儿：元　先　兄　克
（5）厂：反　后

第六课 6 Lesson Six

厶

me	么	(shén) me (what)
gōng	公	(public)
qù	去	(go; leave)

十

zhī	支	(support; *measure word for pens, etc.*)
nán	南	(south)
mài	卖	(sell)

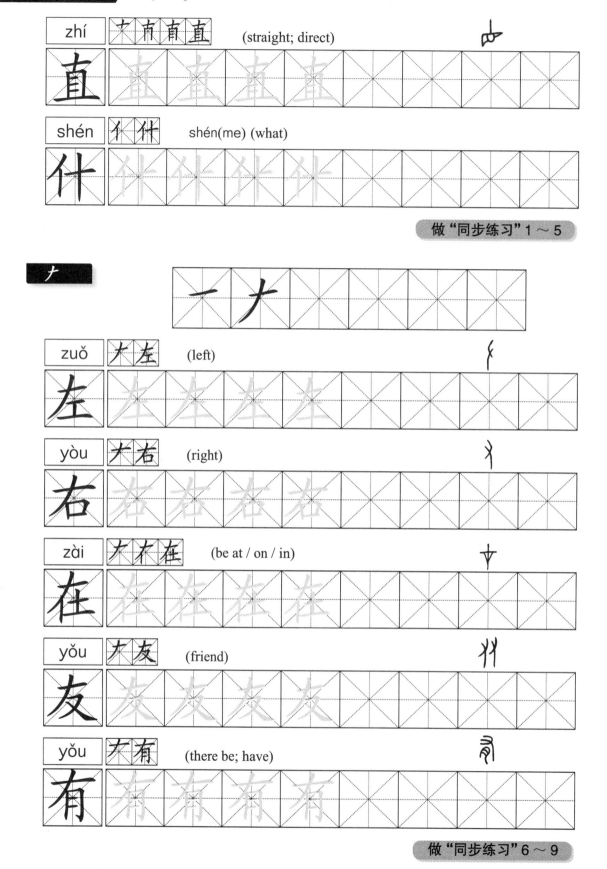

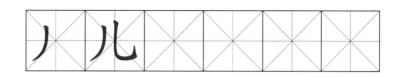

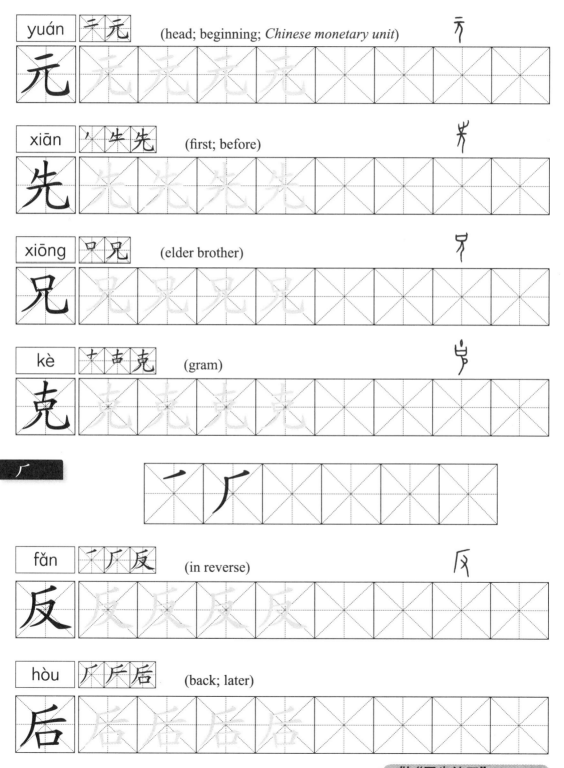

奇妙的汉字 The Wonder of Chinese Characters

不一样的位置，不一样的点儿
Different position, different dot

我们已经学过左点儿"丿"和右点儿"丶"，这两个点儿的方向不同，在不同的汉字中，它们的位置也就不一样。一般只有一个点儿的时候，常常是右点儿"丶"，比如："文""太""我"等。

汉字中常常两个点儿一起用，它们的组合或者是"⸏"，或者是"八"，有时候是"氵"，要看它们在汉字中的位置。请看：

We have learned left dot and right dot, which differ in direction of dotting. In different characters, they take different positions. It is usually the right dot that is used when only one dot is needed, e.g. "文", "太" and "我".

Two dots are often used together. Varying with the position, the component takes the form of "⸏", "八" or "氵". Look at the following table:

形状 Shape	例字 Example	位置 Position
⸏	关、弟、前、半	字头部位、横笔之上 the top position, above a horizontal line
	立、来	两横中间 between two horizontal lines
	只、共	字底部位，横笔之下 the bottom position, below a horizontal line
八	小、办	字的两边 left and right sides
	父、交	撇捺之前 before *Pie* and *Na*
氵	头、雨	字中同一部位 the same position of a character
	母、每	一横上下 above and below one horizontal line

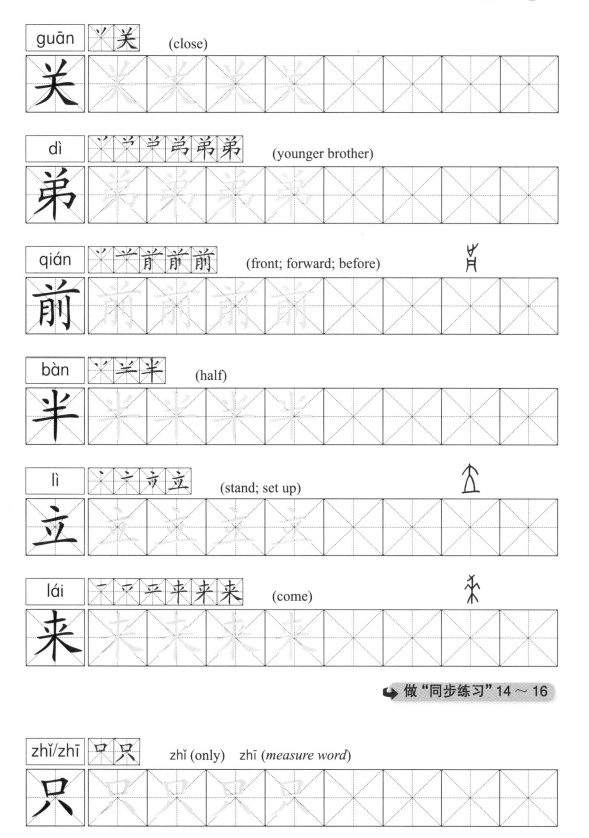

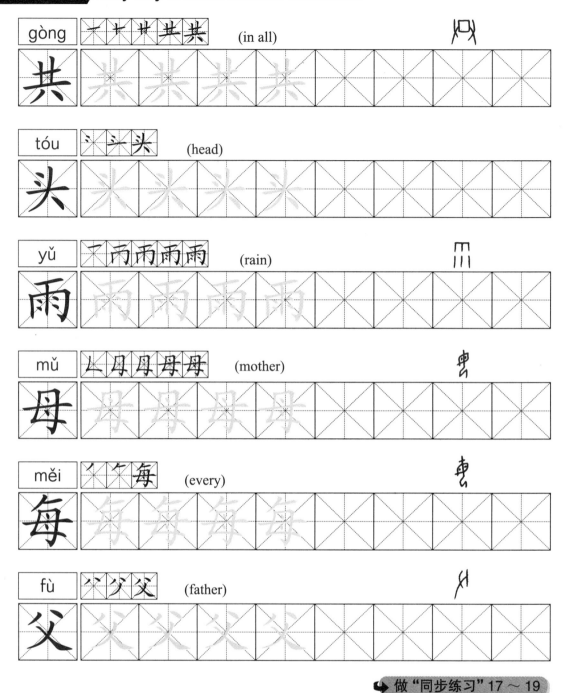

学习策略 Learning Strategy

怎样记汉字（4）
—— "回忆默写法（下）"

How to memorize Chinese characters (4)
— "Write by recall"（Part two）

上一课我们学习了"回忆默写法"的基本步骤。我们已经知道记汉字时，要先看清楚汉字的部件、笔画再动笔写，"写"时要根据自己的回想和记忆来完成。这是记写汉字核心步骤——"看"和"写"的正确方法。为了进一步提高记忆的效率，还需要在上一课学习的基本步骤上附加一些活动。那就是在"看"和"写"的时候，要注意调动多个器官——眼、耳、口、手、脑，采用能够提高效率的多种活动——看、说、听、写、想。具体来说就是，"看"和"再看"的时候，除了分析汉字的字形以外，还要大声读出汉字的发音和英文意思，自己听听读出的发音，脑子里想想汉字的意思。"写"和"再写"的时候，更要一边写，一边说字音，一边想意思。这样并用多个器官的多种活动，可以使汉字记忆的效果更好，保持的时间更长。

"看"的时候，可以利用课本里提供的笔顺描红来帮助观察和分析汉字。这时，不必拿起笔来一笔一笔地描，专注地用脑观察和分析要比用手机械地抄写笔顺更有效，因为将来你要根据脑中的记忆来写。分析完以后，可以盖住例字，利用后面的几个空格来回想默写。一般每个字默写四五遍就可以完成短时记忆了。要想保持记忆的时间更长，就需要以后的复习。

"看"和"写"是记写汉字的两个核心步骤。现在由于电脑的普及，用汉字交流时大多通过打字而不是手写汉字。可能有的人会想：会打字就不用写字了。这其实是不对的，因为这个"写"是为了让你更好地在头脑里记住汉字，而不仅仅只是为了"写"。学习每一个汉字时，你都可以试试用这两课介绍的"回忆默写法"来记汉字，应该比你机械地抄写几十遍更节省时间，效果却更好。

You have learned the basic steps of "Write by recall" method in Lesson 5, which involves first observing and analyzing the components and strokes of Chinese characters, and then writing from memory. This is the proper way to look at and write Chinese characters. In order to further improve the efficiency of memorization, some extra activities can be added to the basic steps. That is, you can add activities to involve more senses in the process of memorization when you observe and write characters. You can involve your eyes, ears, mouth, hands, and brain through looking, saying, listening, writing, and thinking. Specifically, when you "observe" and "check" characters, in addition to analyzing the shape of characters, you also need to read aloud the pronunciation of characters and their English meanings. You can hear your own pronunciations and think of meanings in your mind. When you "write" and "re-write" characters, it is also better to pronounce and think of meaning at the same time. The more senses you incorporate into the memorization activity, the more effective the results of your work will be, and the longer the time that you can retain characters in your memory will be.

When you "observe" characters, you can use the stroke order examples provided in the textbook and workbook to help analyze the characters. At this time, you do not need to use a pen to copy stroke by stroke, it is more effective if you can carefully observe and analyze the characters in your mind, because you will write them out from your memory in the future. After analyzing, it is suggested that you cover the characters and write them by recall to fill in the following four to five boxes provided. Generally, after writing a character several times, it will be placed into short-term memory. If you want to keep characters in your memory for longer, you just need to review them later.

Both "observing" and "writing" are two core steps for memorizing characters. Now due to the popularity of computers, most exchanges with Chinese characters are type-written instead of handwritten. Some may be think that there is no need to write if you can type. In fact, this is not right, because the "writing" enables you to better remember characters in your mind, and not just to "write" them. When you learn each character, you can try to use the "Write by recall" method introduced in this and the previous lesson to memorize the character. It should make your memorization a less laborious task, and may save you a lot of time and energy.

第七课 Lesson Seven

汉字知识 Knowledge about Chinese Characters

部件（2） Components (2)

（1）六字头　Liùzìtóu　　亠：方　交　市　京　高
（2）兴字头　Xīngzìtóu　　⺍：兴　学　觉
（3）冬字头　Dōngzìtóu　　夂：冬　务　条　夏　复
（4）同字框　Tóngzìkuàng　冂：网　两　周
（5）用字框　Yòngzìkuàng　冂：用　周
（6）小字头　Xiǎozìtóu　　⺌：当　堂　常　尝
（7）考字头　Kǎozìtóu　　耂：老　考　者

| fāng | 丶 亠 方 | (square; direction) |

方

| jiāo | 亠 交 | (cross; associate with; hand in) |

交

| shì | 亠 亠 市 市 | (city; market) |

市

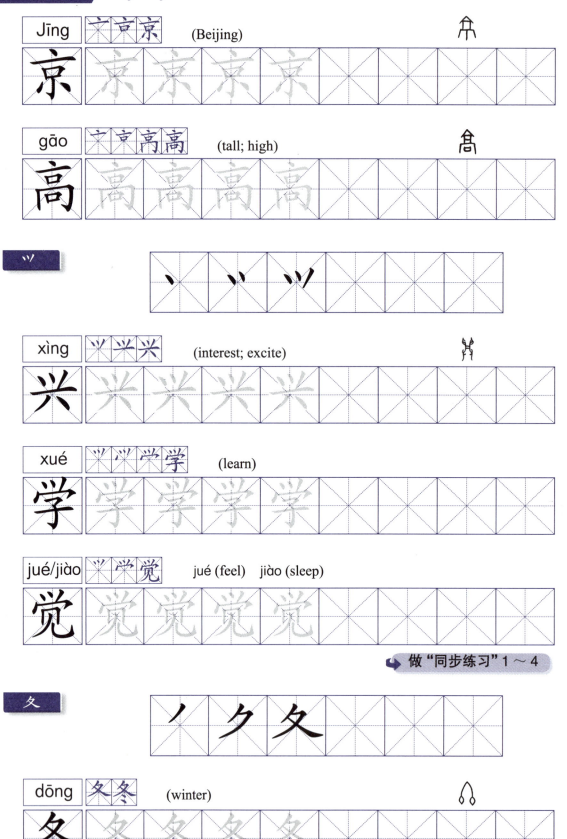

第七课 Lesson Seven

| wù | 夂务 | (serve) |
| 务 | | |

| tiáo | 夂冬条条 | (measure word for long or thin things) |
| 条 | | |

| xià | 一百夏 | (summer) |
| 夏 | | |

| fù | 𠂉自复 | (recover; again) |
| 复 | | |

冂 　丨冂

| wǎng | 冂冈网 | (net) |
| 网 | | |

| liǎng | 一丙丙两 | (two, some, a unit of weight <=50 grams>) |
| 两 | | |

几 　丿几

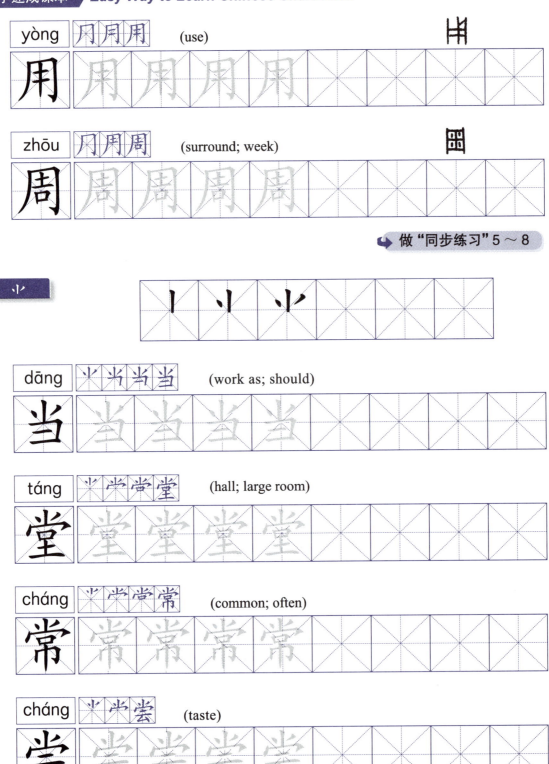

lǎo	老 (old; *prefix*)
kǎo	考 (examine)
zhě	者 (person; *suffix*; -er)

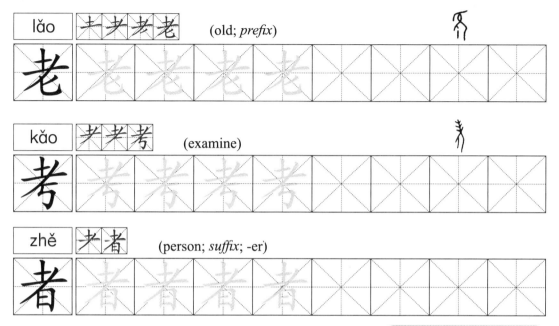

做"同步练习" 9～12

奇妙的汉字　The Wonder of Chinese Characters

部件一样的汉字
Characters with the same components

大部分汉字都由两个或多个不同部件组成，学习的时候需要分别记。有一种汉字非常容易记，因为它们由两个或多个相同部件组成。比如已经学过的"从"，还有"双""朋""林""多""哥""回"等。左右结构的这种汉字，手写体中，第一部件的最后一笔或者第二部件的第一笔会有细小的变化，如"双"的第一个"又"的最后一笔是点儿。这种变化是为了不影响另一个部件的书写，保持整个汉字的美观。

Most characters are made up of two or more components, which have to be remembered separately. But there is a group of characters that are very easy to remember, for their components are exactly the same. "从", which we have learned, is an example. There are still some others, "双", "朋", "林", "多", "哥" and "回", etc. When such a character is of left-right structure, the last stroke of the first component or the first stroke of the second component will be transformed a little in handwriting. For example, the last stoke in the first component "又" of "双" will be written as a dot. The purpose of such transformation is to convenience the writing of the other component and adds beauty to the whole character.

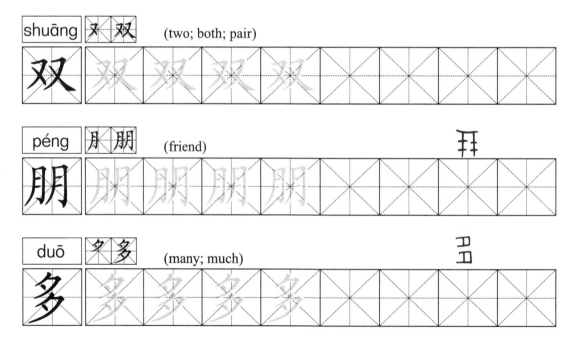

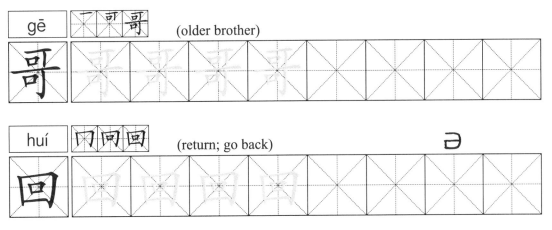

有的汉字两个部件虽然一样，但是形状或方向发生了变化，比如："比""行""竹""北""非"等。

Sometimes transformation can be more serious than discussed above. The shape and direction of the stroke may be changed. "比", "行", "竹", "北" and "非" are examples of this case.

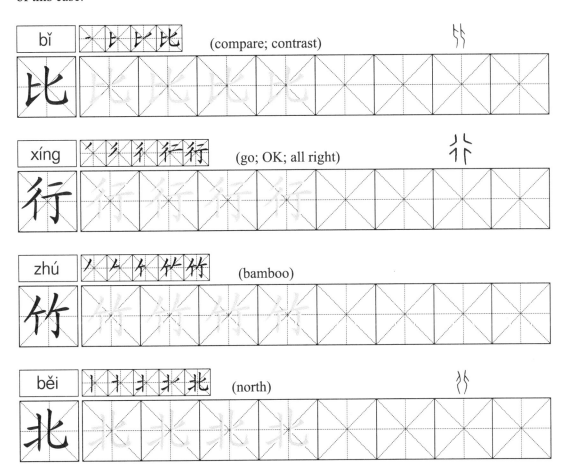

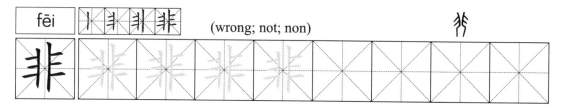

➡ 做"同步练习"13～16

第七课 Lesson Seven

 学习策略 Learning Strategy

怎样记汉字（5）
——利用部件和偏旁

How to memorize Chinese characters (5)
—Using components and radicals

部件是指汉字结构中的一个单位，它相对于笔画、整字。如"哪"字中有三个部件："口""月""阝"；偏旁一般是对形声字进行划分得出来的，表示意义的为形旁，表示读音的为声旁。如"哪"字中，"口"为形旁，"那"是声旁，"哪"有两个偏旁。形声字常被分成两个偏旁，有时候偏旁只有一个部件，如"哪"中的形旁"口"是一个部件；有时候偏旁由两个或多个部件组成，如"哪"中的声旁"那"有两个部件。

这些是关于汉字的术语，这些术语不需要同学们掌握，也可以不必很清楚，但是学习这本书时，会遇到"部件""偏旁"这样的术语，如果觉得不理解的话，可以看看这里提供的说明。同学们学习汉字，怎样方便记忆和掌握，就怎样做。是否了解这些术语，要看你觉得它们对你的汉字学习有没有帮助。

形声字的形旁、声旁具有一定的表意和表音作用，掌握它们对学习汉字和阅读会有很大帮助。在学习过程中，不仅要认识到形旁、声旁的作用，还要正确对待形旁、声旁与汉字的关系，不能绝对地认为每个汉字都一定与它的形旁有关系，也不能认为每个汉字的发音都与它的声旁完全一样，因为我们学习的汉字至少有3000多年的历史，已经有了一些变化。

学习时，遇到表意或表音功能比较强的偏旁，就可以多利用它们记汉字；如果表意和表音功能不强，那么可以不用想它是形旁还是声旁，这个汉字怎么好记就怎么记。

The component is a unit of Chinese characters and is put forward in contrast with the stroke and a complete character. For example, there are three components in the character of "哪", namely "口", "月" and "阝". The radical, however, derives from the discussion over pictophonetic characters, which can be divided into the phonetic radical and the meaning radical. Let's still take "哪" as the example. "口" is the meaning radical and "那" the phonetic radical. Binary division is ususlly adopted in describing pictophonetic characters, where the radical can consist of more than one component. The phonetic radical "那" in the above example is composed of two components.

Don't get confused by these terms. You are not expected to master them. They are provided here just for reference purposes. Whether to remember these terms or not depends entirely on whether it will convenience your learning.

Since the two sides of a pictophonetic character express both meaning and sound, it will help you a lot if you can master them. During the course of learning, you should recognize the significance of the sides, and meanwhile develop a resonable point of view on the relationship between the character and its sides. Not all Chinese characters are related to their meaning sides in meaning, nor are they related to the phonetic sides in sound. You should try to avoid taking things absolutely, for the Chinese language has undergone a history of more than 3,000 years and the characters have experienced some changes.

When the side is powerful in expressing meaning or sound, make full use of this advantage; when it is not so powerful, don't get confused, for your final aim is to remember the character.

第八课
Lesson Eight

汉字知识 Knowledge about Chinese Characters

1. 形旁（1） Meaning radicals (1) ─────────────●

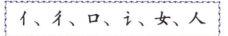

在形声字中，我们把与字的意义有联系的部分叫作形旁，把表示读音的部分叫作声旁。由于汉字中形声字最多，约占现有汉字的80%，所以学会一些常用的形旁和声旁，对记忆汉字会有很大的帮助。

In discussing pictophonetic characters, we use the meaning radical to refer to the part indicating the meaning and the phonetic radical to the part suggesting the sound. Since around 80 percent of Chinese characters are pictophonetic, it will be quite helpful in remembering the characters if you have some knowledge about both kinds of radicals.

亻：跟"人"有关系 related to "person"
　　他　体　位　住　作　信

彳：跟"街"有关系 related to "street"
　　往　很　得

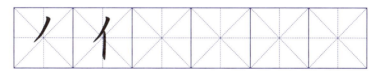

| tā | 亻他 | (he; him) |

| tǐ | 休体 | (body) |

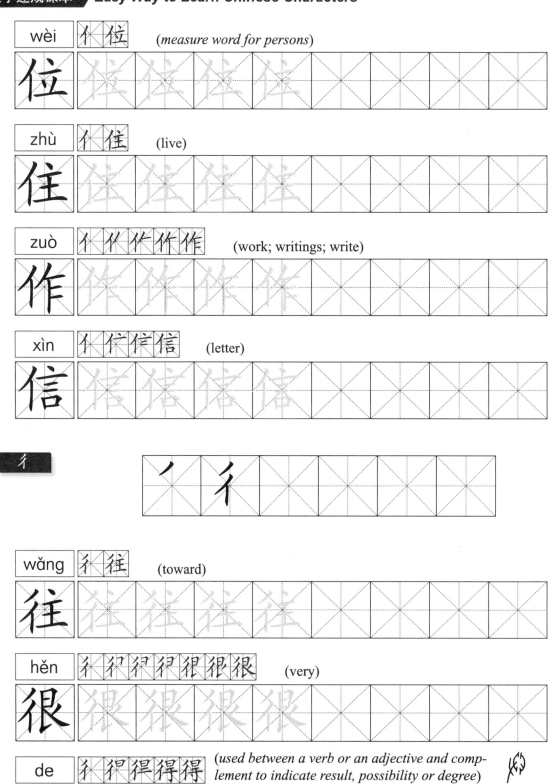

口：跟"嘴"有关系 related to "mouth"
　　叫 吃 唱 吧 呢 听
讠：跟"说、知识"有关系 related to "speaking, knowledge"
　　说 语 话 认 识 请 课 试 让 该

口

丨 口 口

jiào 口 叫 叫 (call)
叫

chī 口 口' 口'' 吃 (eat)
吃

chàng 口 唱 唱 (sing)
唱

ba 口 口' 口'' 叭 吧 (modal particle in suggestion sentences)
吧

ne 口 口' 口'' 呢 呢 呢 (modal particle in question sentences)
呢

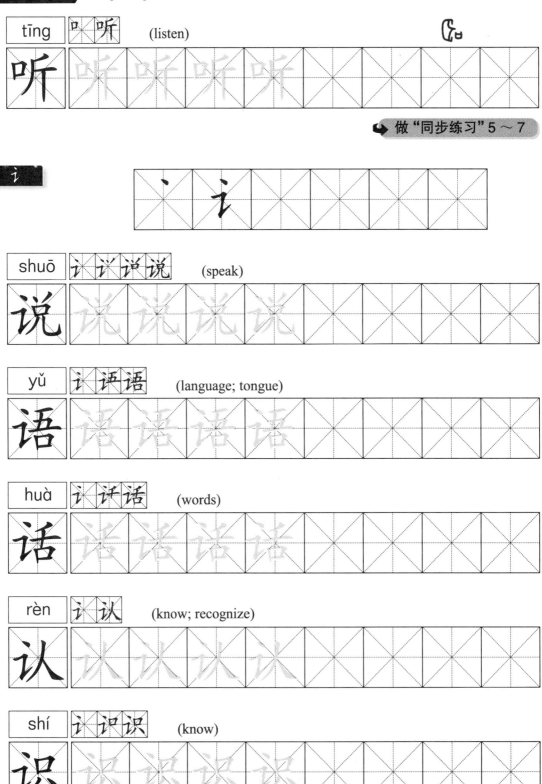

第八课 Lesson Eight

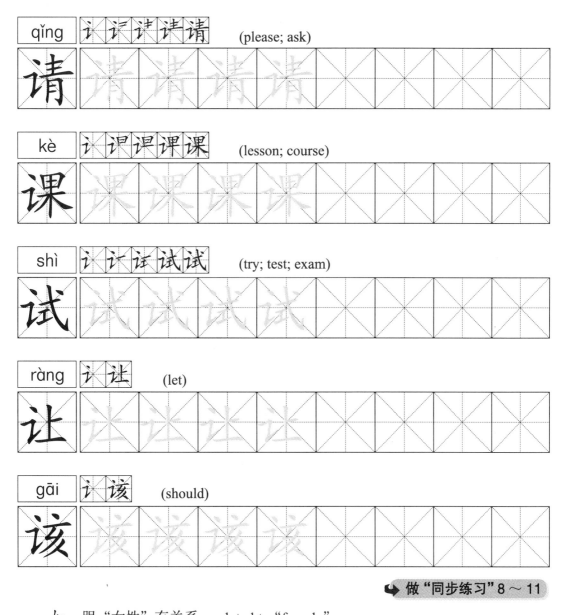

→ 做"同步练习"8～11

女：跟"女性"有关系 related to "female"
她 姐 妹 奶 姓 要 始

人：跟"人"有关系 related to "person"
介 今 会 全 舍 食

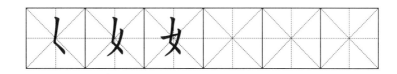

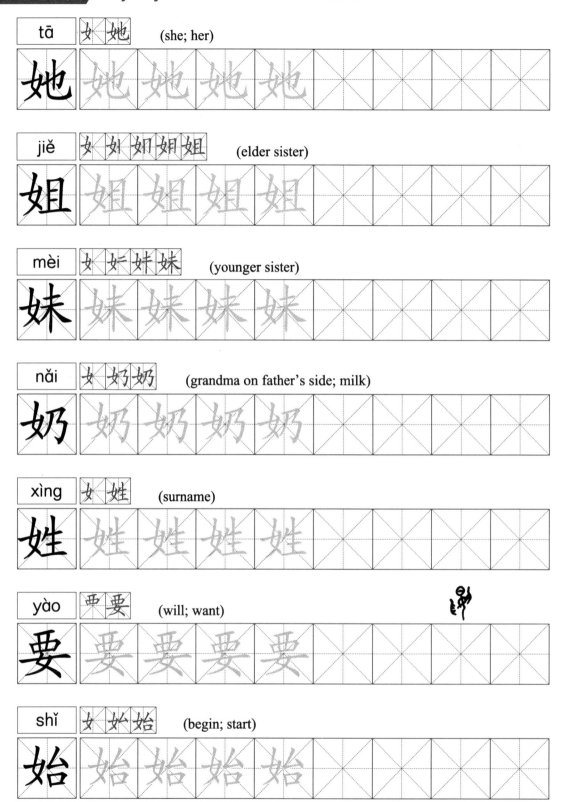

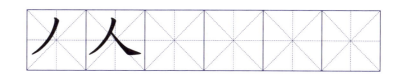
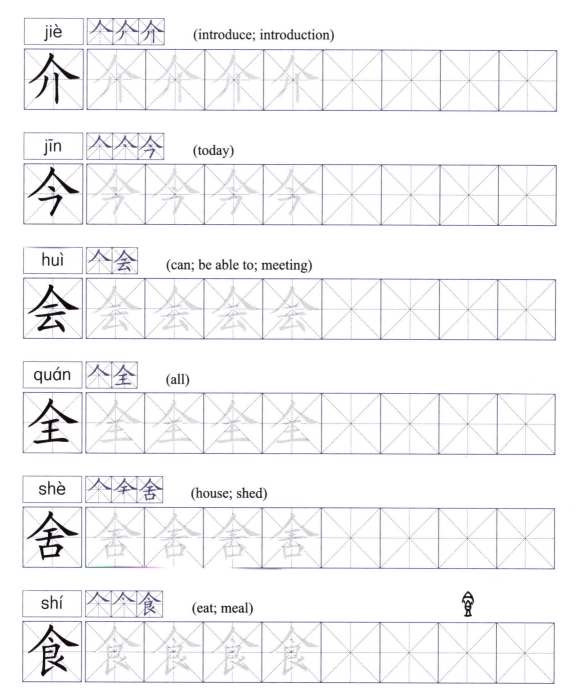

2. 汉字的结构（4）　　Structures of characters (4)

现有汉字中，左右结构和上下结构的汉字最多。还有些汉字不只两个部件，那么就有了左中右和上中下等结构。例如：

Most Chinese characters are either left-right structured or top-bottom structured. But there are some composed of three components, which can be described as left-middle-right structured or top-middle-bottom structured. For example:

左中右　Left-middle-right　　　⊞：谢　做　哪

上中下　Top-middle-bottom　　　☰：意　累　参

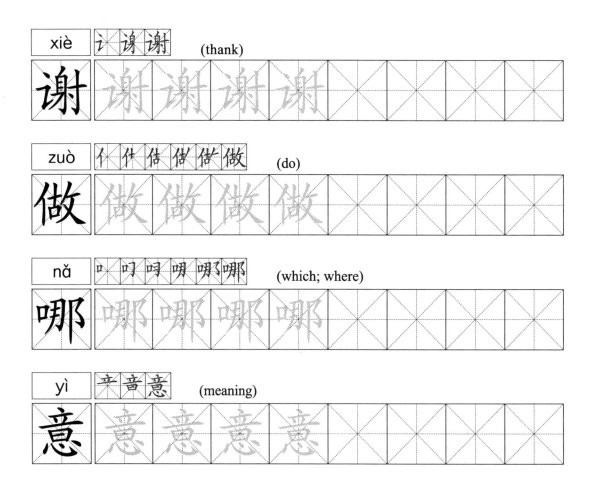

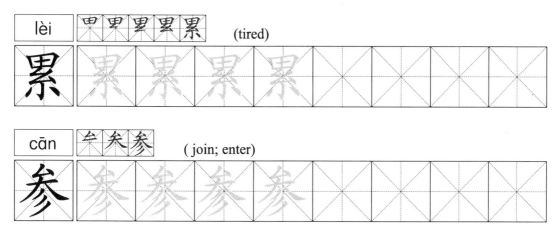

汉字速成课本　Easy Way to Learn Chinese Characters

奇妙的汉字　The Wonder of Chinese Characters

字中字
Characters within characters

大多数汉字由两个或多个部件组成,看起来似乎很难记,但仔细看看,你会发现:在多部件的汉字中,有些部件就是汉字,而且是你学过的汉字,比如"想",三个部件"木""目""心"都是学过的汉字;再如"意",三个部件是"立""日""心"。

其实,"想"字中不仅三个部件是字,"木"和"目"两个部件组成的也是一个字"相",它做"想"的声旁,而"心"是形旁。"意"的上两个部件也是一个汉字"音"。

汉语里有一个很特别的字,不仅它的每个部件是独立的汉字,就是其中的每两个部件组合起来也都是汉字,而且这个汉字还是我们生活中常用到的。它就是"树",其中"木""又""寸"三个部件是独立的汉字,每两个部件可以组合成"村""对""权"三个字,所以"树"一个字里隐藏着其他六个字,学会了一个"树"字,再看其他的字,就会觉得很容易了,是不是?

汉字里有很多有趣的现象,在"奇妙的汉字"部分,我们会继续介绍一些,也希望你能自己发现。随着进一步的学习,你会感到汉字也是一门有意思的艺术。

At first look, characters with two or more components seem difficult to remember. But after closer examination, you will find that some components are characters themselves and that you have already learned them. For example, the three components "木", "目" and "心" of "想" are all among the characters you have learned. So are "立", "日" and "心" of "意".

As a matter of fact, the first two components in "想" form another character "相", which functions as the phonetic radical while "心" is the meaning radical. The upper two components of "意" also make up a character "音".

There is a very special character in Chinese whose three components are three independent characters and the combination of any two of them forms another character. Moreover, this character is very commonly used in daily life. What is it? It is "树", where "木", "又" and "寸" are characters themselves and the combinations of any two of them "村", "对" and "权" are also characters. So there are other six characters in the character "树". When you have learned this character, the characters hidden inside will be quite easy for you.

In fact, there are many interesting phenomena in Chinese characters. We will introduce some more in the section of "The Wonder of Chinese Characters", and at the same time we hope you can find some by yourself. As your learning moves on, we are sure you will find Chinese characters an art of great charm.

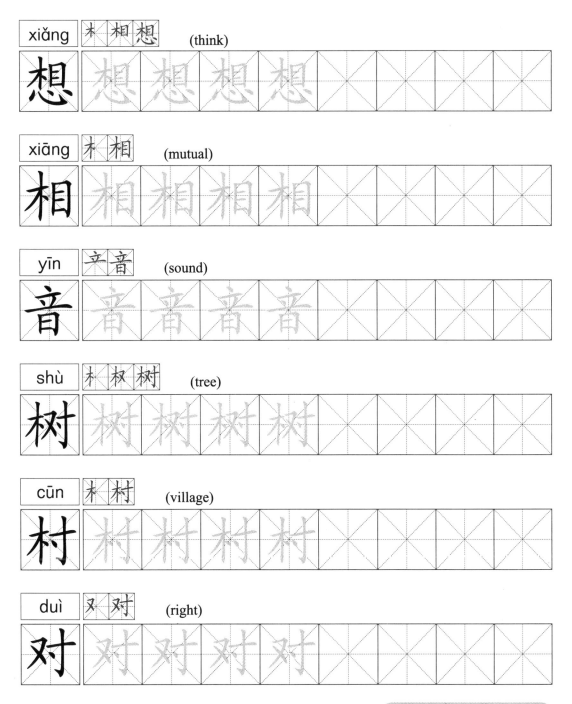

学习策略 **Learning Strategy**

学查字典
How to consult a Chinese dictionary

学习汉语的时候，我们几乎每天都要查字典。查字典最简单的方法是按音序查找，只要知道这个字的读音，再根据拼音排列的顺序，很快就能在字典中找到它。可是我们要查找的汉字并不一定都是认识的，要是不知道汉字的读音，需要在字典中找到它，那怎么办呢？**我们可以用部首检字法。**

什么是部首？

几个汉字有一样的偏旁，那么这个偏旁就是部首，比如"吗""哪"共同的偏旁是"口"，"口"就是部首。"部首"这个词是为查字典用的，平时我们还是常常叫它"偏旁"。

部首检字法需要哪几个步骤？

首先，找到这个汉字的部首，看看它有几画；

其次，在字典的"部首目录"中，根据部首的笔画数找到这个部首的页码（词典中）或号码（字典中），把字典翻到"检字表"，找到这个部首；

再次，看看除了部首以外，这个汉字还有几画；

最后，在这个部首的相应笔画数下，你就可以找到你要查的字了。

这四个步骤简单地说就是：数部首笔画数，找到部首；数剩余偏旁笔画数，找到汉字。比如，你想在字典里找到"深"。"深"的部首是"氵"，3画，在字典的"部首目录"中可以找到"氵"；"深"的另一个偏旁是"罙"，8画，在"检字表""氵"部首下的"8画"中就可以找到这个字。

开始用部首检字法时，你可能不太熟练，多练习几次就容易了。

When we are learning Chinese, we need to consult a dictionary from time to time. The simplest way of consulting a dictionary is the alphabetical method. So long as you know the sound of the character, you can find it very quickly in the dictionary, for the entries are arranged in alphabetical order. The problem is, however, that we may not know how to pronounce the character. Then what should we do? **The *bushou* or radical method will help us out.**

What is *bushou*?

When a radical belongs to a number of characters, we call it *bushou*. For example, "口" appears in both "吗" and "哪", so it becomes a *bushou*. But it should be noted that *bushou* is a term specific to dictionary consultation. In everyday usage, we will still refer to it as the radical.

What is the procedure of the radical method?

First, find out the *bushou* of the character and count its number of strokes.

Second, turn to the *bushou* catalog in the dictionary, and according to the number of strokes find the page number (or code number when it is a pocket dictionary) of the *bushou*; then find the *bushou* in the index pages.

Third, count the strokes of the character, leaving out those of the *bushou*.

Finally, find the character below the corresponding number of strokes.

The procedure can be simplified as: count the strokes in the *bushou* to find the *bushou*, then count the strokes in the rest of the character to find the character. For example, you want to look up "深" in a dictionary. The *bushou* is "氵" with three strokes. Find it in the *bushou* catalog. The rest of the character is composed of eight strokes and you can find the character among those of eight strokes in the index pages below the *bushou* of "氵".

Because the method is new to you, you may feel frustrated at the very beginning. But don't you know the old saying "Practice makes perfect"?

第九课 Lesson Nine

汉字知识 Knowledge about Chinese Characters

1. 形旁（2） Meaning radicals (2)

冫、氵、日、月、阝

冫：跟"冷"有关系 related to "cold"
　　冰　冷　凉　次　决

氵：跟"水"有关系 related to "water"
　　江　深　酒　洗　澡　游　泳　没　法

冫

| bīng | 冫汀汀冰冰 | (ice) |

冰

| lěng | 冫冷冷 | (cold) |

冷

| liáng | 冫凉 | (cool) |

凉

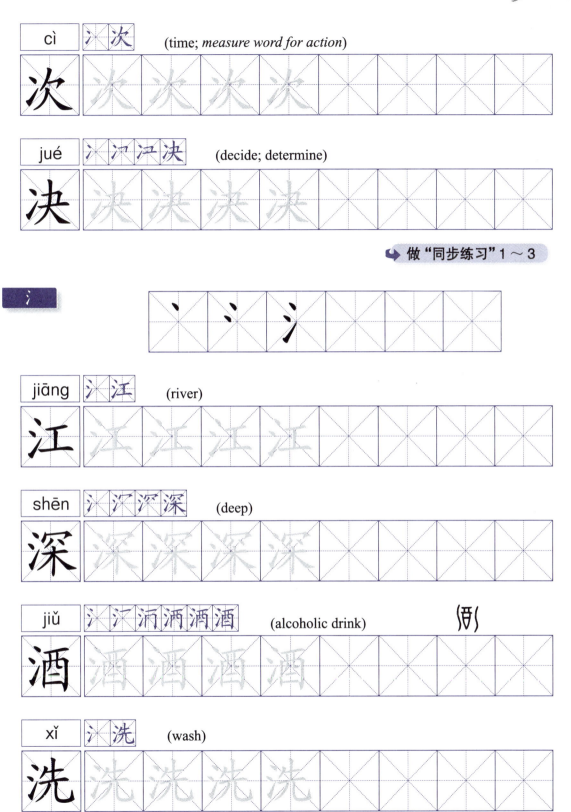

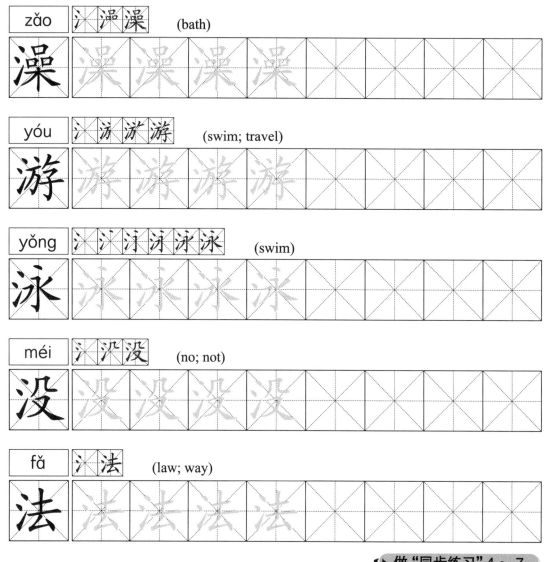

➡ 做"同步练习"4～7

日：跟"太阳""时间"有关系　related to "sun", "time"
　　时　昨　晚

月：居右跟"时间""光线"有关系
　　when positioned on the right, related to "time", "light"
　　期　朝

　　居左跟"身体"有关系
　　when positioned on the left, related to "body"
　　肚　脸　胖　服

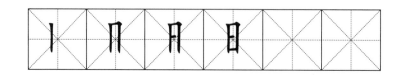

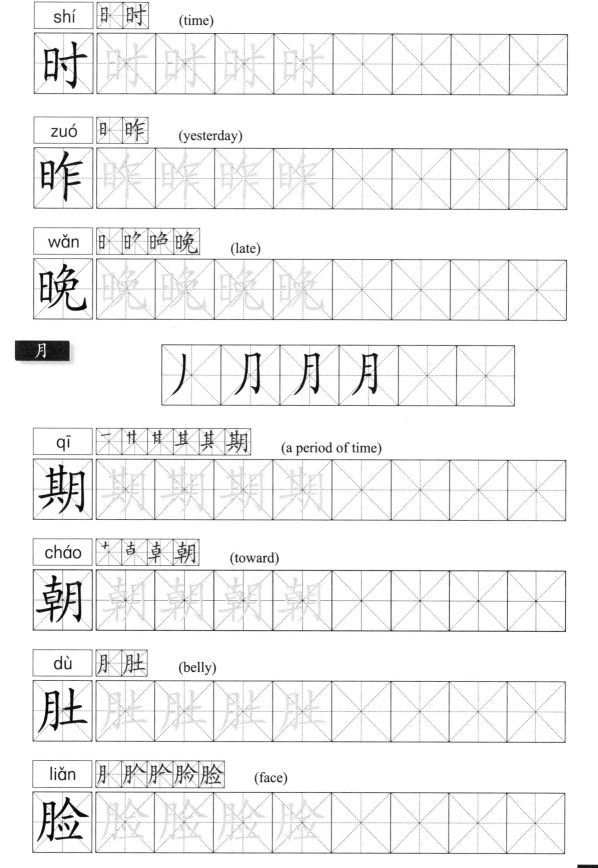

汉字速成课本 Easy Way to Learn Chinese Characters

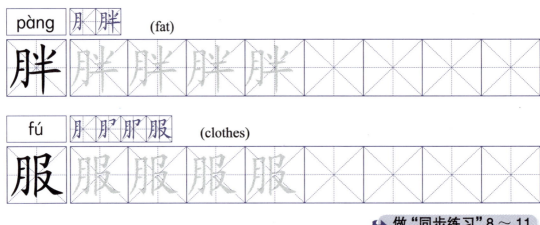

做"同步练习"8～11

阝： 居左跟"土山"有关系　when positioned on the left, related to "fence"
　　队　阳　阴　院　除　附

　　居右跟"城市""地区"有关系　when written on the right, related to "city"
　　那　邮　都

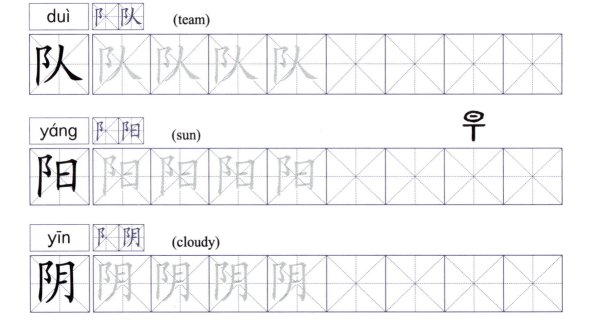

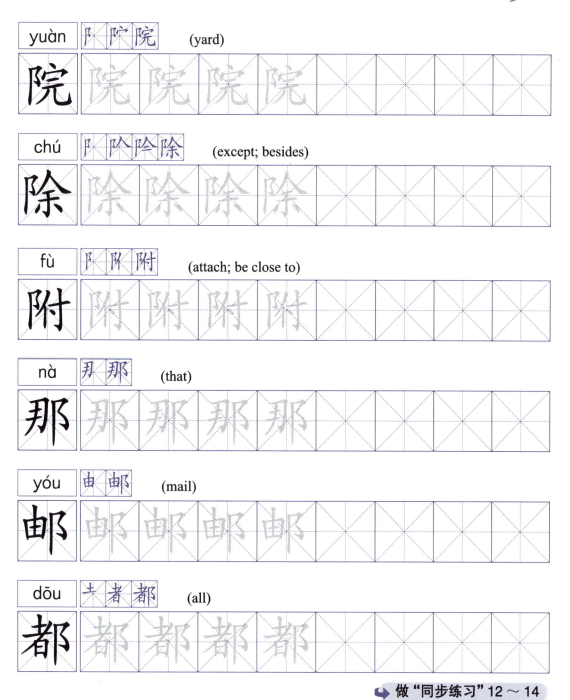

2. 汉字的结构（5） Structures of characters (5)

由于一些汉字不仅仅只有两三个部件，因此它们的结构也不仅是左（中）右、上（中）下、包围等结构。有些多部件的汉字会形成稍微复杂一些的结构，但其实只是以左右、上下、包围三种结构为主，其中又夹杂一种或两种别的结构。比如：

Multi-component characters can be complicated in construction. The structures may be more varied than left-(middle-)right, top-(middle-)bottom and enclosed (also known as outer-inner) structures. Complicated as the structure may be, it has to be based on the three basic structures mentioned above. For example:

⊞ : 够　　⊟ : 都　　⊟ : 些

⊟ : 最　　⊡ : 圆　　⊞ : 能

这些结构的汉字，书写上也遵循一般的顺序：先左后右、先上后下、先外后内。

The writing of these characters will have to observe the general rules as well, that is, from left to right, from top to bottom and from outside to inside.

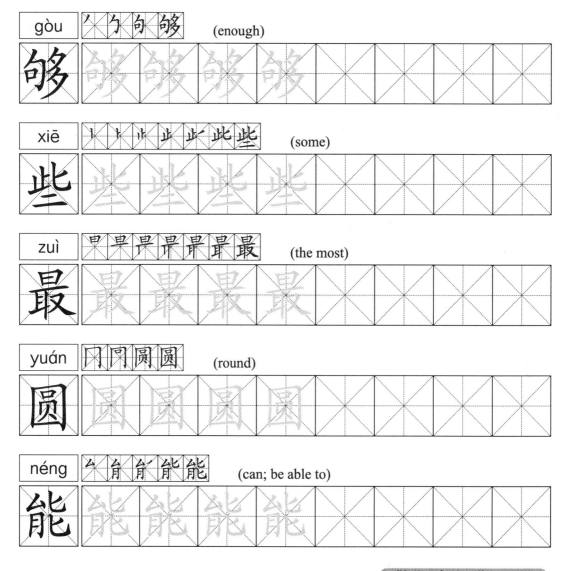

第九课 Lesson Nine

奇妙的汉字 The Wonder of Chinese Characters

形同但位置不同的形旁
The same meaning radical taking different positions

形旁可以在汉字中的任何一个位置,但某个形旁的位置总是相对固定的,比如"亻"总是在左。汉字中也有些形旁可以有两个或两个以上的位置,有时在左边,有时在右边,比如上一课学习的"口""女"和本课的"日""月"等,都不只有一个位置。请看下表(不包括居左的位置):

Meaning radicals can take different positions in different characters although some of them have a fixed position. For example, "亻" is always positioned on the left. Others are of more freedom: sometimes on the left, sometimes on the right. "口" and "女" in Lesson Eight and "日" and "月" to be learned in this lesson belong to this group of meaning radicals. Have a look at the table below (not include the position on the left):

形旁 Meaning radical	位置 Position	例字 Example
口	右边 right	知、和
口	上边 top	号
口	下边 bottom	合
口	里边 inside	问
日	上边 top	早、景、易
日	下边 bottom	春
月	右边 right	期、朝
月	下边 bottom	育

最有趣的是"阝"和"咅"两个部件,因组合时位置不同,从而形成了两个完全不同的汉字:"陪"和"部"。

It may interest you that the difference in position of "阝" and "咅" can result in two different characters, "陪" and "部".

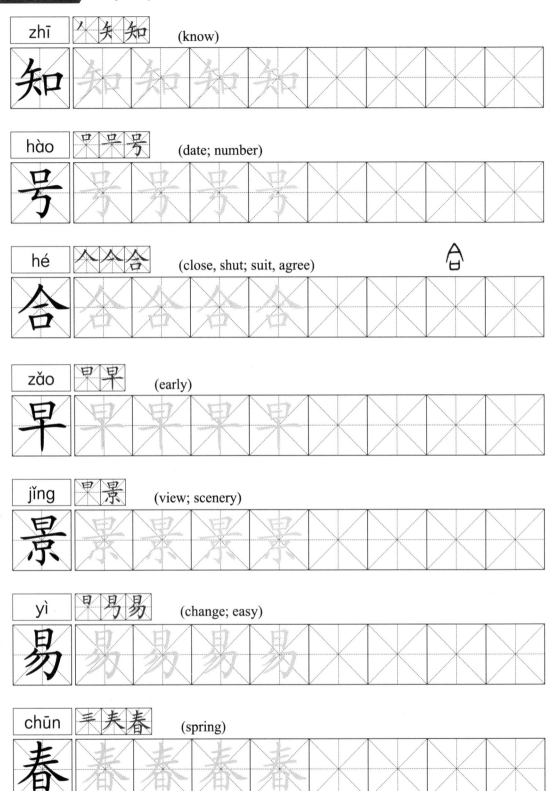

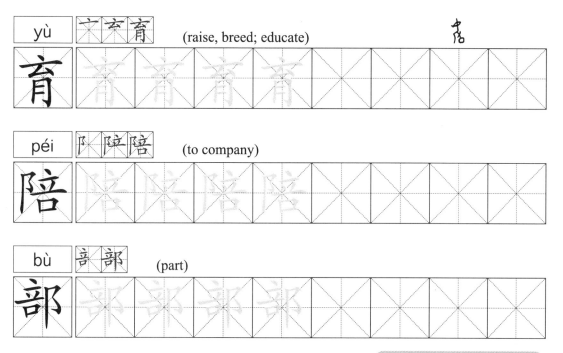

学习策略 **Learning Strategy**

汉语中字与词的关系
Relationship between characters and words in Chinese

汉字是书写的单位，可以说记录了汉语的形。词是意义单位，是运用中最小的音和义的结合体。汉语中字和词的关系有点儿像英语中语素和词的关系一样。

汉语中单个汉字大部分都有意义。其中有的汉字可以单用，比如"买""小"等，它们就是词；有的汉字不可以单用，要和别的汉字组合后才可以使用，比如"子"也有意思，但是要和"日""本"等组合成"日子""本子"等再用在句子中，所以"子"就不是一个词。

英语中的词有一些是由一个语素构成的，但大多数是由两个、三个或更多的语素组合成的；汉语里由一个字组成的词有很多，也有两个或两个以上的字组成的词，其中最多的是两个汉字组成的词。

汉字基本上是和音节相对应的，一般情况下，一个汉字记录一个音节。两个字组成的词，叫作"双音节词"，汉语里双音节词最多。

The Chinese character is a writing unit, recording the shape of things, while the word is a meaning unit, the smallest combination of sound and meaning. The relationship between characters and words in Chinese is somewhat similar to that between morphemes and words in English.

In Chinese most Chinese characters can convey meaning independently. Some Chinese characters can be used by itself, e.g."买"and"小", and they are words themselves. Other characters, however, cannot be used independently. They have to be used together with other characters. For instance, the character"子"has its own meaning, but when it is to be used in a sentence, it has to be used together with"日"and"本"to form such words as"日子"and"本子". In this case,"子"is not a word.

Some words in English consist of only one morpheme; most words are made up of two, three or even more morphemes. In Chinese, there are many words having only one character. Words of two or more characters are also frequently observed, and as a matter of fact, words of two characters are the most in number in Chinese.

Chinese characters correspond with syllables in general. One character usually records a syllable and two-character words are referred to as two-syllable words, which are the most in number.

第十课
Lesson Ten

汉字知识　Knowledge about Chinese Characters

形旁（3） Meaning radicals (3)

木、手（扌）、纟（幺）、刀（刂、夕）、心（忄）、火（灬）

木：跟"树木"有关系　related to "trees"
　　桌 架；* 校 板 椅 楼

扌：跟"手"有关系　related to "hand"
　　打 找 报 扫 把 挂 挤

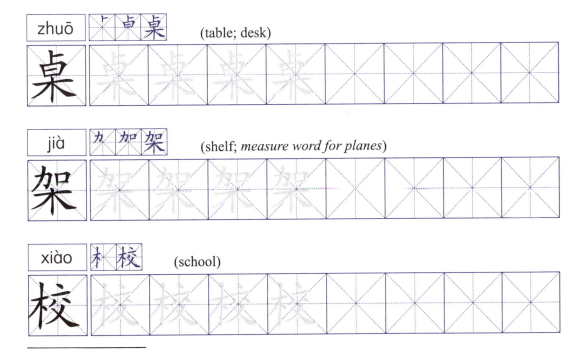

* 分号表示形旁的位置不同。
The semi-colon is to show the different positions of the meaning radical.

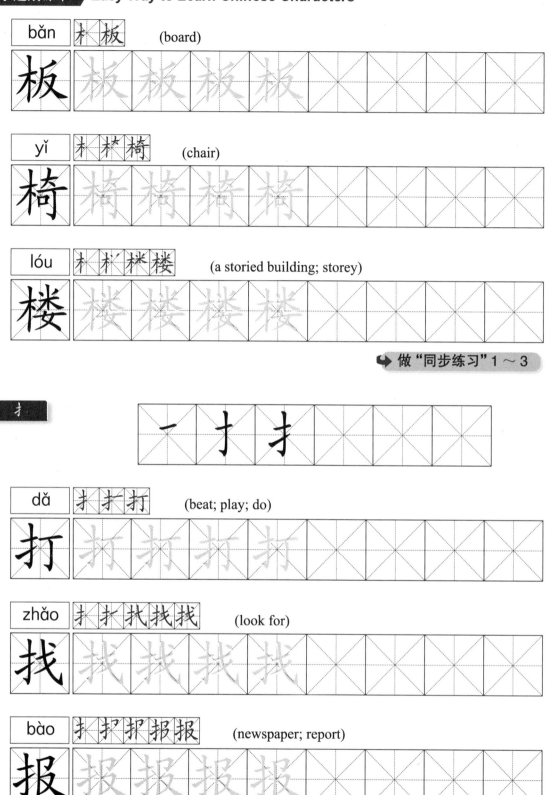

第十课 10 Lesson Ten

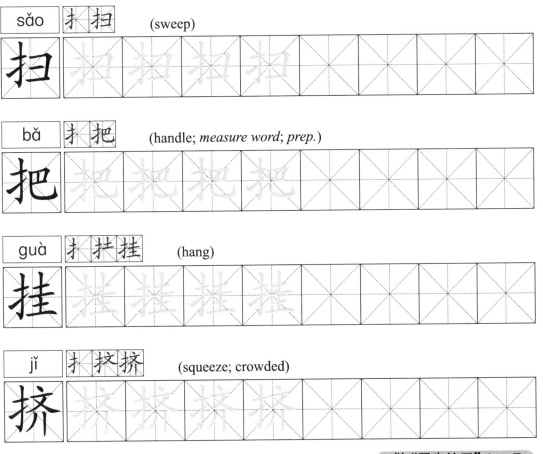

➡ 做"同步练习"4～7

纟：同"丝"，跟"丝"有关系　related to "silk"
　　红　绿　纸　经　给　绍

刂：同"刀"，跟"刀"有关系　related to "knife"
　　别　到　刮　刚

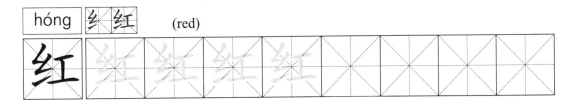

99

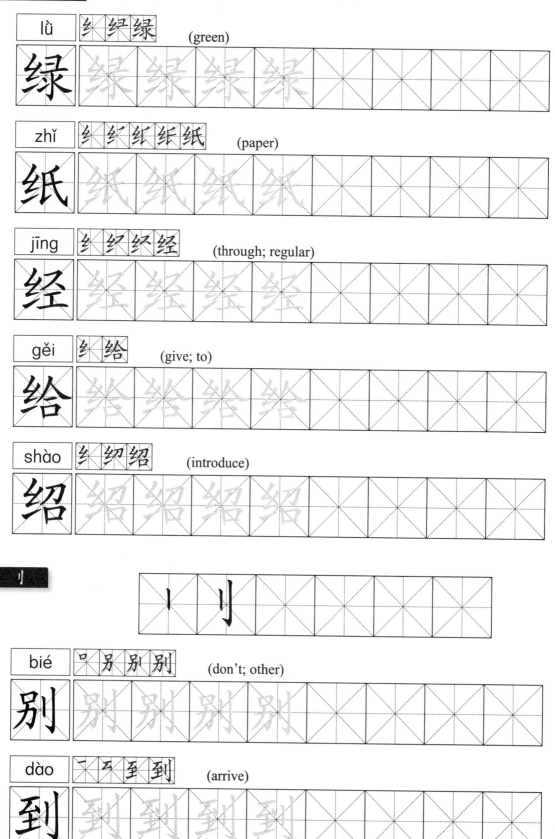

第十课 10 Lesson Ten

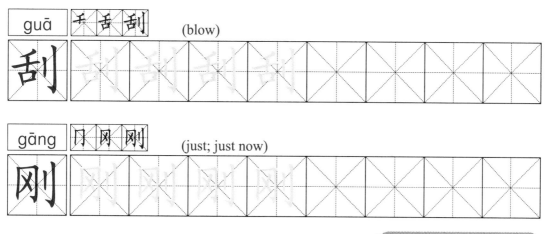

➡ 做"同步练习"8～11

心：跟"思想""心理"有关系　related to "thinking", "feeling"
　　忘　念　怎　思　志　急　感

火：跟"火"有关系　related to "fire"
　　灯　烧　烟

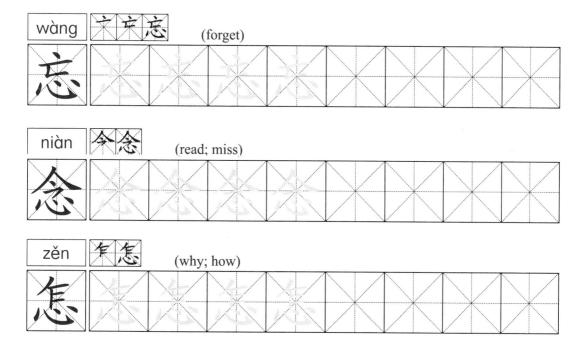

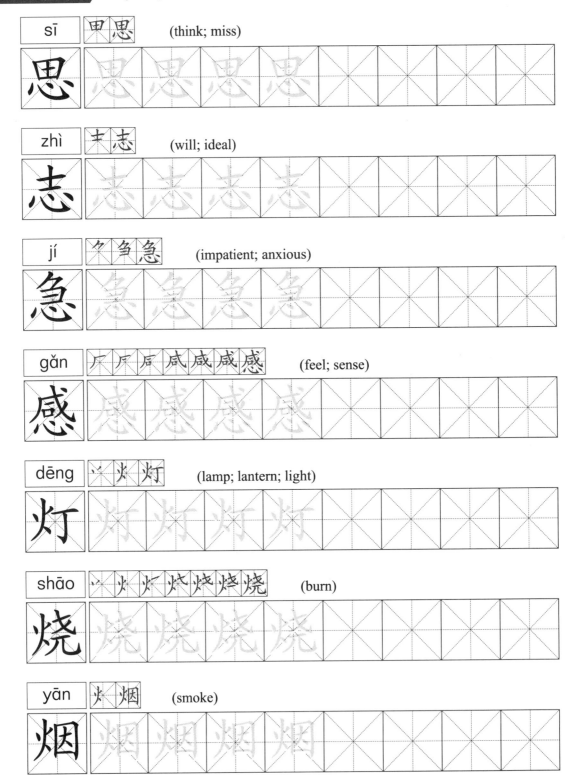

奇妙的汉字　The Wonder of Chinese Characters

义同形不同的形旁
Meaning radicals of the same meaning taking different forms

我们已经学过一些可以放在不同位置的形旁，在汉字里还有一些类似的形旁，两个或三个形旁意义完全一样，可它们的形不同，并且出现在不同的位置上。比如"人"和"亻"、"手"和"扌"，"刀"和"刂"等。请看下表：

We have learned that some meaning radicals can be positioned at different places. In Chinese there are some other meaning radicals that convey the same meaning but take different forms, e.g. "人" and "亻", "手" and "扌", "刀" and "刂", etc.

意义 Meaning	形旁 Meaning radical	位置 Position	例字 Example
手	手	字底 bottom	拿
	扌	左边 left	打、找
丝	纟	左边 left	红、给
	幺	字中 middle	系、紧
刀	刀	字底、右边 bottom, right	分、切
	刂	右边 right	到、刻
	勹	字头 top	色、象
心	心	字底 bottom	感、急
	忄	左边 left	忙、快、怕、懂、惯
火	火	左边 left	烧、烟
	灬	字底 bottom	热、照、黑

"刀""火""心"这些不同位置形旁的形差别很大；还有一些形旁，处于不同位置时，只有一点小小的变化，这也是我们在学习时要特别注意的。比如"女"，位于左边时，横比较短（"姓"），位于下边时，横比较长，撇不出头（"要"）；"火"在左边时，最后的一捺变成了点（"灯"）；"子"和"土"在左边时，最后的一横都

变成了提（"孩""地"）。这些小小的变化不容忽视，因为这种变化是为了汉字美观的，所以要先写得正确，才能写得漂亮。

本课学了两个汉字，声旁一样，形旁的意义也一样，只是形旁的形和位置不同，它们的意思因此完全不同，你能猜出这两个字是什么吗？（答案在本课找）

Some meaning radicals like "刀", "火" and "心" take quite different forms, while others just change a little with their relative position, which demands our close attention. For example, when "女" is positioned on the left, the horizontal line is shortened (as in "姓"); when at bottom, the same line will be lengthened (as in "要"). "火" is more or less the same: when on the left, the last stroke becomes a dot (as in "灯"). When "子" and "土" are on the left, the last horizontal line becomes an upward dot (as in "孩" and "地"). These small changes should be noticed, for they contribute to the beauty of Chinese characters.

There are two characters that share the same meaning radical and phonetic radical. The only difference is the form and relative position of the radicals, which makes the meaning entirely different. Can you guess the two characters? (The key can be found within this lesson.)

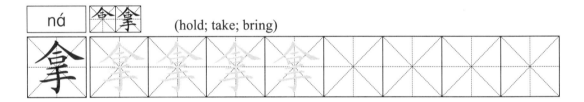

(hold; take; bring)

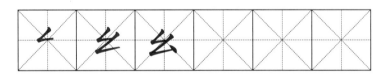

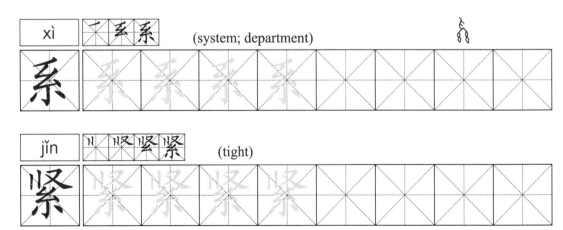

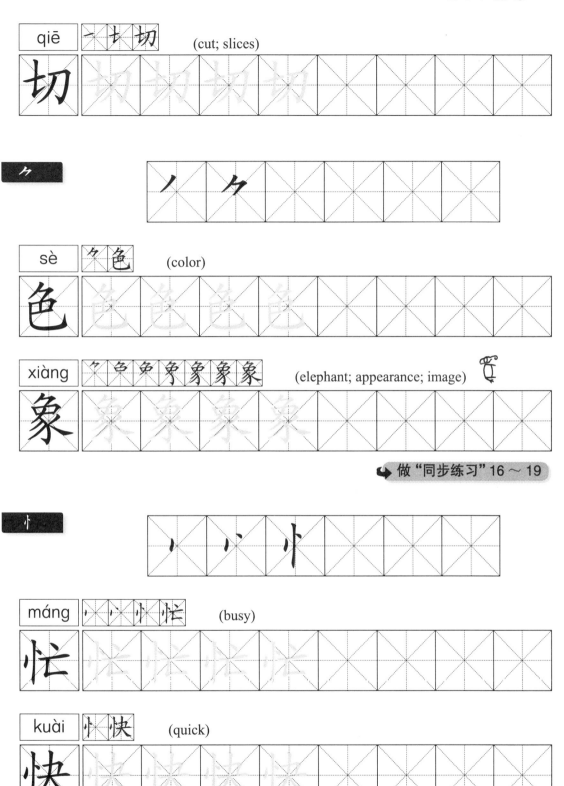

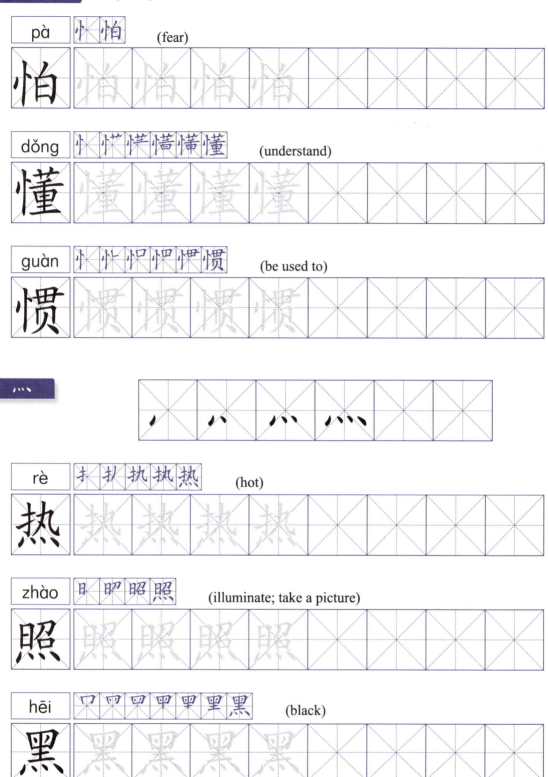

学习策略 Learning Strategy

怎样记汉字 (6)
——利用关键部件

How to memorize Chinese characters (6)
— Using key component

我们每一课都要介绍一些汉字知识,这是为了让大家了解汉字,掌握汉字的一些规律,然后利用这些知识记忆汉字。**在学习汉字时,要尽可能地利用所学知识。**比如,学习了部件后,记汉字时就可以利用部件的知识,以部件为单位来记,而不必以笔画为单位。

不仅要知道利用部件,还要考虑怎样利用部件更方便,对记忆更有帮助,比如"想"字,通过记三个部件"木""目""心"一定比一笔一画地记容易;如果把它看作是由两个不同的"mù"(木、目)和一个"心"组成的,似乎记起来更容易些;如果已经学过了"相"字,那么你又可以利用形旁、声旁的知识来记汉字,这样"想"就只有两部分了,一是声旁"相",一是形旁"心"。你对哪个部件更熟悉,就把哪个部件作为记忆汉字的关键。

因此,了解一些基本的汉字知识有助于记汉字。随着学习的汉字数量和知识的增多,记汉字的方法也会越来越简便。

The reason we introduce the information about Chinese characters is to help you become familiar with Chinese characters, learn the rules governing the construction of them and remember them. **So you should make full use of such knowledge in your learning process**. For instance, when you have learned the knowledge about components, you should remember the characters on basis of the components rather than the strokes.

But how to use such knowledge more efficiently? The example "想" can be quite illustrative. First we can divide it into its three components, "木", "目" and "心", rather than remember the character stroke by stroke. Then the task will be further reduced if you know the first two components are of the same sound. If you have come to know the character "相", you can remember it according to its radicals, where "相" is the phonetic radical and "心" the meaning radical. Make the part you are more familiar with a key component for memorizing the character.

So you can see how useful this knowledge is in remembering the characters, and the more knowledge you have, the easier the task will be.

"奇妙的汉字" 答案 Key to "The Wonder of Chinese Characters"

忙　忘

11 第十一课
Lesson Eleven

汉字知识　Knowledge about Chinese Characters

形旁（4） Meaning radicals (4)

辶、口、钅、饣、犭、目、足、艹、竹

辶：跟"走；路"有关系　related to "walk, road"
边　过　进　送　迟　还　迎　适　道　远

辶

ˋ	辶	辶			

biān 力 ナ 边 边　(side)

边

guò 寸 过　(pass; past; aspect particle for past experience)

过

jìn 井 进　(move ahead; enter)

进

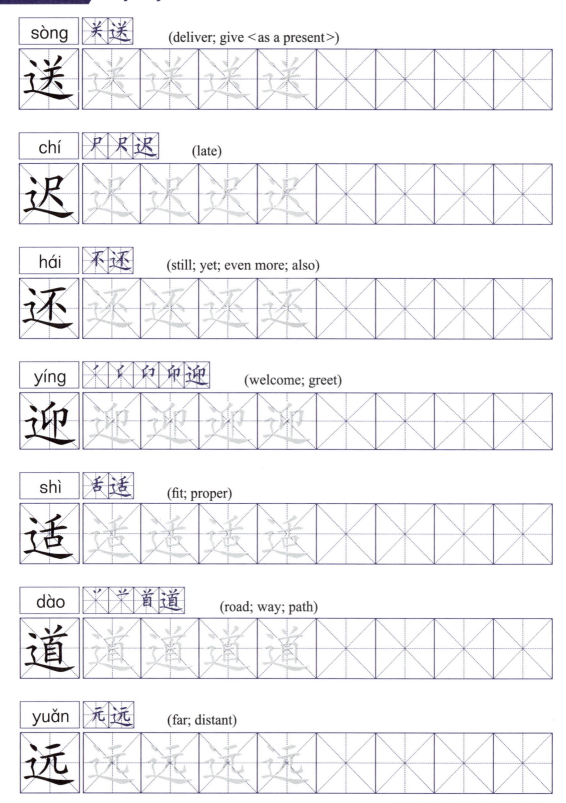

口：跟"周围、边界"有关系　related to "surroundings, border"
　　园　图　围

钅：同"金"；跟"金属"有关系　related to "metal"
　　钱　钟　钢　错　锻

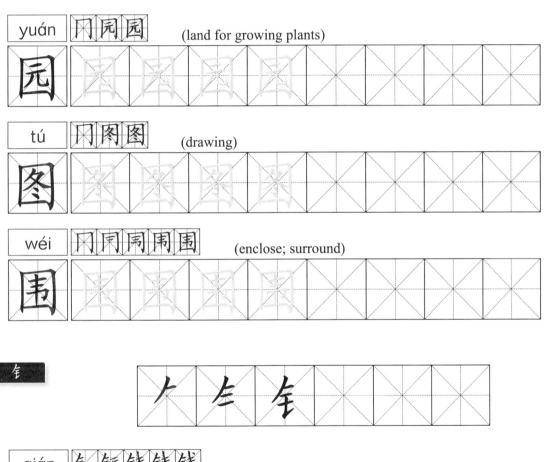

汉字速成课本 Easy Way to Learn Chinese Characters

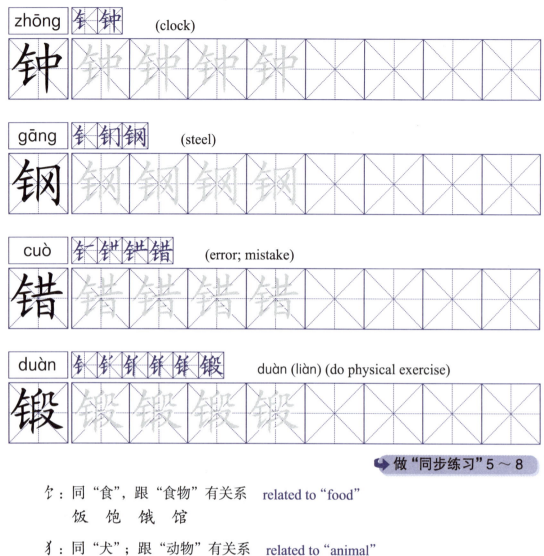

做"同步练习"5～8

饣：同"食"，跟"食物"有关系 related to "food"
　　饭　饱　饿　馆

犭：同"犬"；跟"动物"有关系 related to "animal"
　　猫　狗　猪　猜

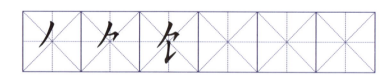

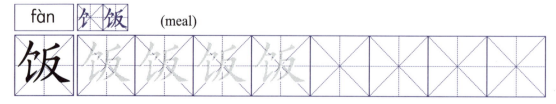

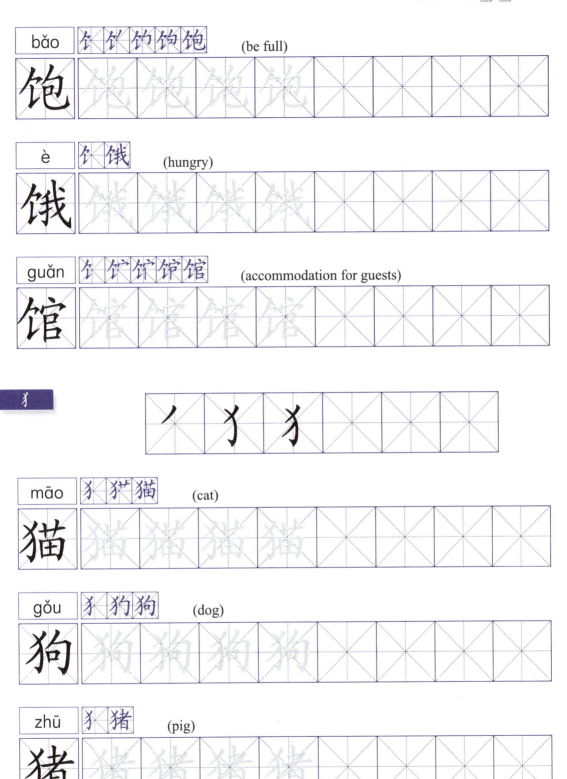

| cāi | 犭 犭 犭 犭 猜 | (guess) |

猜

➡ 做"同步练习"9～12

目：跟"眼睛"有关系　related to "eyes"
　　眼　睛　睡

足：同"足"，跟"脚"有关系　related to "feet"
　　跑　跳　踢　路　跟

目

丨 冂 月 目

| yǎn | 目 眼 | yǎn (jing) (eye) |

眼

| jīng | 目 睛 | (yǎn) jing (eye) |

睛

| shuì | 目 目' 目千 目千 目千 目千 睡 睡 | (sleep) |

睡

足

口 卫 乒 足 足

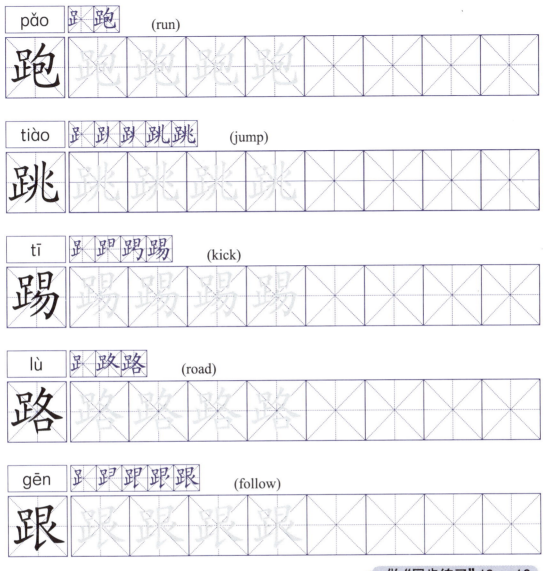

艹: 跟"草"有关系　related to "grass"
花　草　英　茶　菜　药　节

竹: 同"竹",跟"竹子"有关系　related to "bamboo"
笔　简　第　答　等

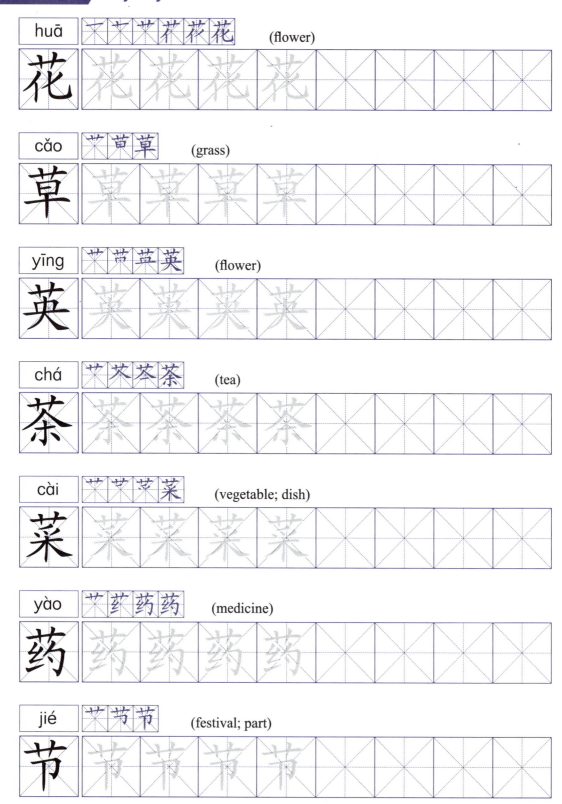

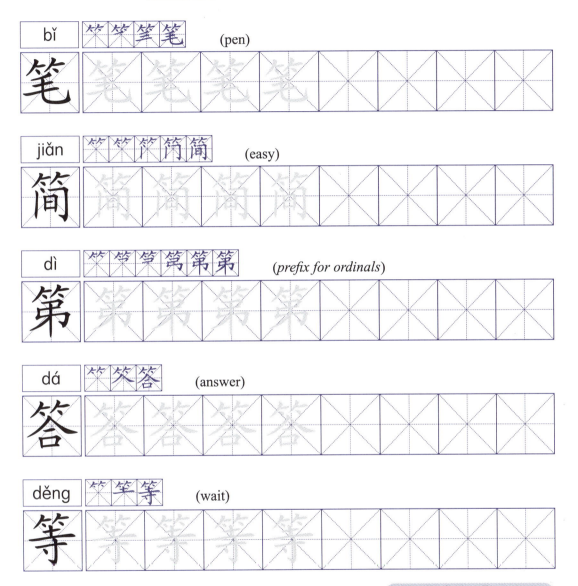

奇妙的汉字　The Wonder of Chinese Characters

形象字
Graphic characters

　　有些汉字非常像它所代表的事物或动作，有的因为是古象形字，至今还保留着事物的基本轮廓、形状，比如"伞""网"等；也有的不是古象形字，但字的部件的组合却非常形象化，比如"哭"，好像一滴眼泪从眼中流出，流到了嘴边，"笑"也可以被想象成一张高兴的脸。这样的字是不是很形象呢？

　　Some Chinese characters resemble very much the object or the action they indicate. The reason is multifold: characters like "伞" and "网" evolve from ancient Chinese, maintaining the basic shape of the thing; characters like "哭" and "笑" have nothing to do with ancient characters. It is the combination of the components that makes them so graphic: "哭" resembles a drop of tear flowing down to the mouth while "笑" makes people think of a smiling face. Aren't they very vivid renderings of the actions?

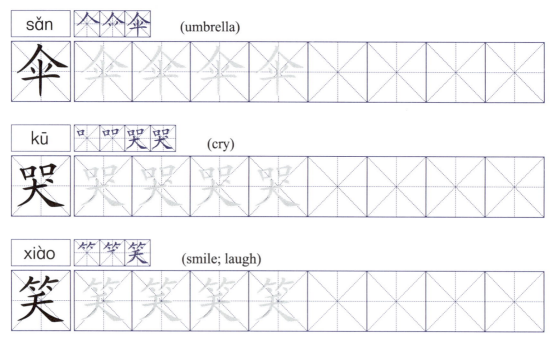

做"同步练习"24～26

学习策略 Learning Strategy

怎样记汉字（7）
——联想法

How to memorize Chinese characters（7）
— Association strategy

学习汉字，有时我们很难一下记住它的部件、结构或者意义什么的，这时可以通过联想来帮助记忆。

记汉字可以利用各种各样有关汉字形、音、义的联想，如"左"和"右"，这两个字很容易记住，但是又很容易混淆。为了将两者区别开，可以把"左"中的"工"与发音的声母"Z"联系起来，把"右"中的"口"联想成"人们常用右手吃饭"，从而加深记忆。

我们可以利用学过的各种汉字知识进行联想，有的联想可以打破汉字的部件和结构，比如"宿"（sù, lodge for the night; stay overnight），我们可以把它看作是"一百个人住在房子里"。虽然这种联想与"宿"字的本源有些不同，但是并不会产生什么后果。

汉字的结构是客观的，写汉字时我们不能任意改变，但是记忆汉字时，却可以大胆想象，因为我们的最终目的就是把学过的汉字记住，并且是轻松、愉快地记住。因此，为了记忆的方便，你可以尽情地发挥想象。

Sometimes it is hard for us to remember the components, structure and meaning of a character all at once. In this case, mental association can be called upon for help.

When memorizing a character, we can draw support from anything associated with the character in form, sound or meaning. For example , "左" and "右" are just as easy to remember as get mixed up. To distinguish them, we can associate "工" in "左" with its sound (the first letter is "Z", which is similar in shape with "工"), and "口" in "右" with the fact that the Chinese people usually eat with their right hand handling the chopsticks skillfully.

Mental asssociation can go beyond the component and struture. Take "宿" (sù, lodge for the night; stay overnight) for example, where we can interpret it as "one hundred people live in one house". (Translator: the character can somewhat give us this kind of impression with its particular construction.) Despite the deviation of this interpretation from its original meaning, no negative effect will be thus incurred.

The structure of Chinese characters is objective existence and we should write them accordingly. But it is quite another matter when we attempt at memorization. So long as we can remember the character, preferrably with ease and joy, our imagination can be brought to full play, for our ultimate goal is to learn the character by heart.

第十二课
Lesson Twelve

汉字知识　Knowledge about Chinese Characters

形旁（5） Meaning radicals (5)

宀、穴；广、疒；尸、户；礻、衣（衤）；欠、攵

有的偏旁看起来差不多一样，很容易弄混，其实它们在意义或笔画结构上都是不一样的。如果知道它们的意义，就可以知道什么字用什么偏旁。下面我们就学习几组形近的偏旁。

Some radicals look much alike, so you may get confused. In fact, they differ in meanings as well as in structure. If you know the meaning of the radicals, you will surely know when to use what. Following are several groups of such radicals:

宀：跟"屋顶"有关系　related to "roof"
　　安　客　家　室　宿　完　容　宽

穴：跟"洞穴"有关系　related to "cave"
　　空　窗　穿　穷　究　窄

宀

丶　丷　宀

ān　宀安　(safe)

安

kè　宀客　(guest)

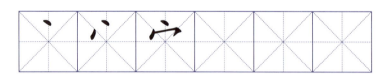

客

第十二课 Lesson Twelve

| jiā | 宀宀宁宇家家家 | (home; family) |

家

| shì | 宀室 | (room) |

室

| sù | 宀宀宿 | (lodge for the night; stay overnight) |

宿

| wán | 宀完 | (finish) |

完

| róng | 宀宀容 | (permit; contain) |

容

| kuān | 宀宀宽 | (wide) |

宽

➡ 做 "同步练习" 1～3

穴

宀穴

| kòng/kōng | 宀空 | kòng (empty space or free time); kōng (empty) |

空

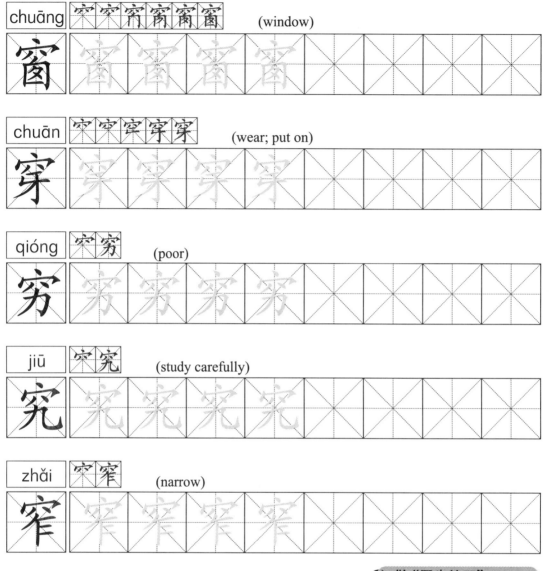

做"同步练习"4～7

广：跟"房屋"有关系 related to "room"
　　床　店　座

疒：跟"疾病"有关系 related to "illness"
　　病　疼　瘦

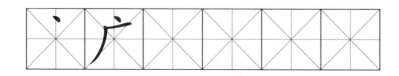

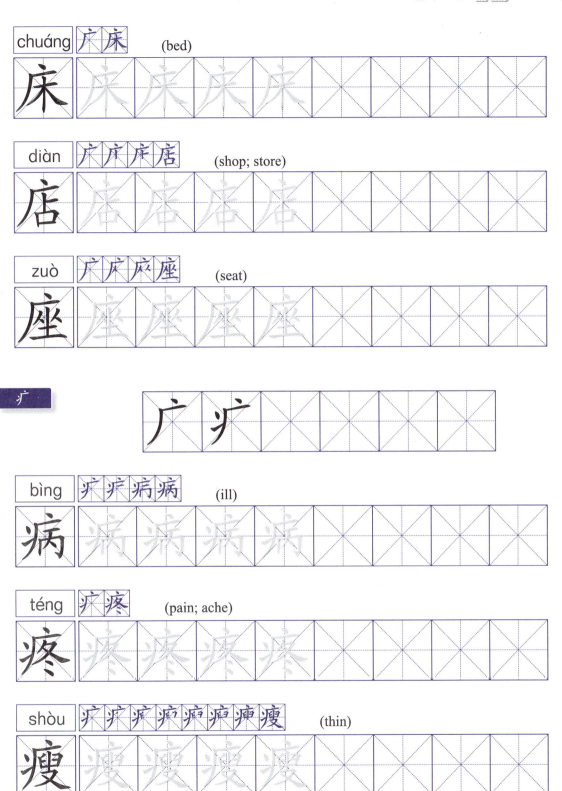

尸：跟"房屋"或"人、动物体"有关系　related to "room" or "body"
　　屋　层　局　展

户：跟"门"有关系　related to "door"
　　房　扇

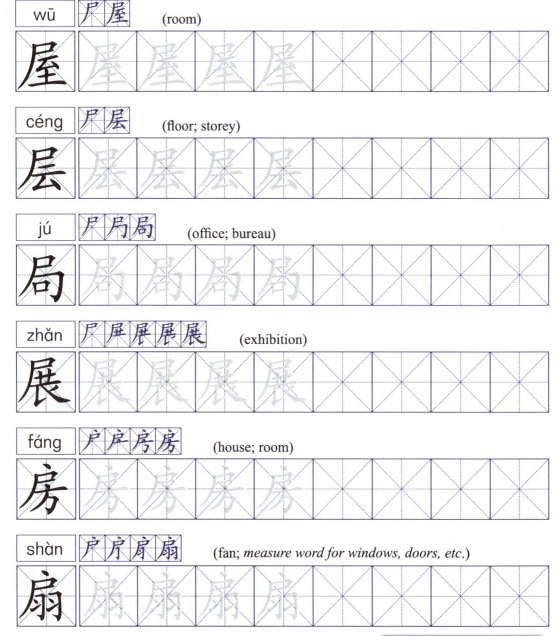

礻：同"示"，跟"祈祷、祝福"有关系 related to "pray", "bless"
　　视　礼　祝

衤：同"衣"，跟"衣服"有关系 related to "clothes"
　　衣　衬　衫　被　袜　裤；袋

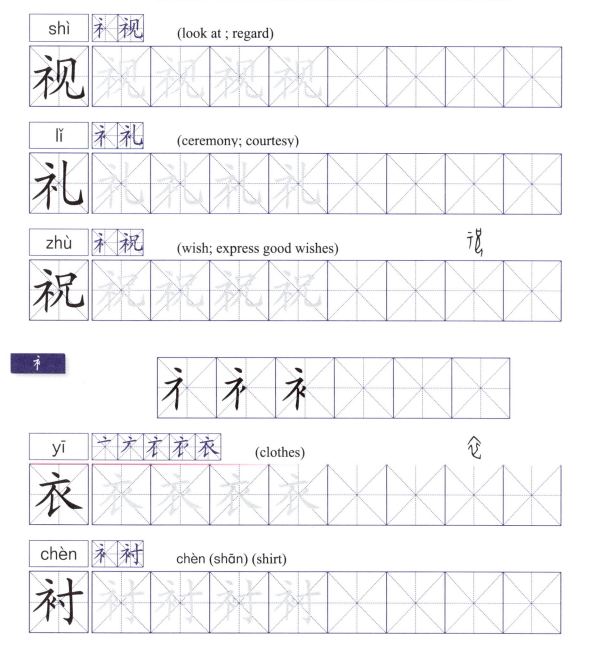

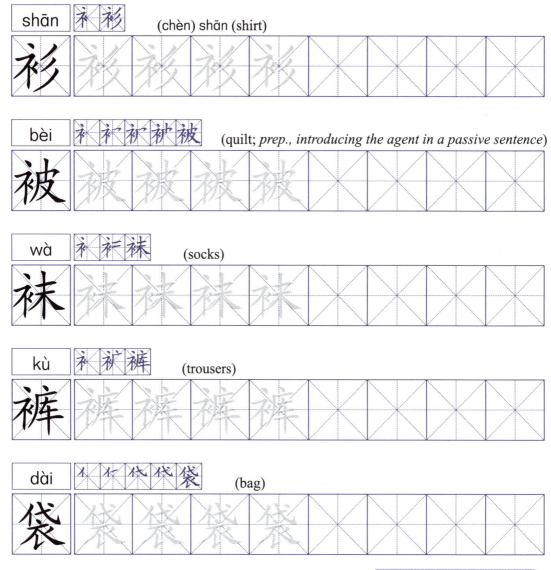

欠：跟"口"及"心情"有关系　related to "mouth", "mood"
　　欢　歌

攵：多数跟"动作"有关系　often indicating actions
　　收　放　教　数

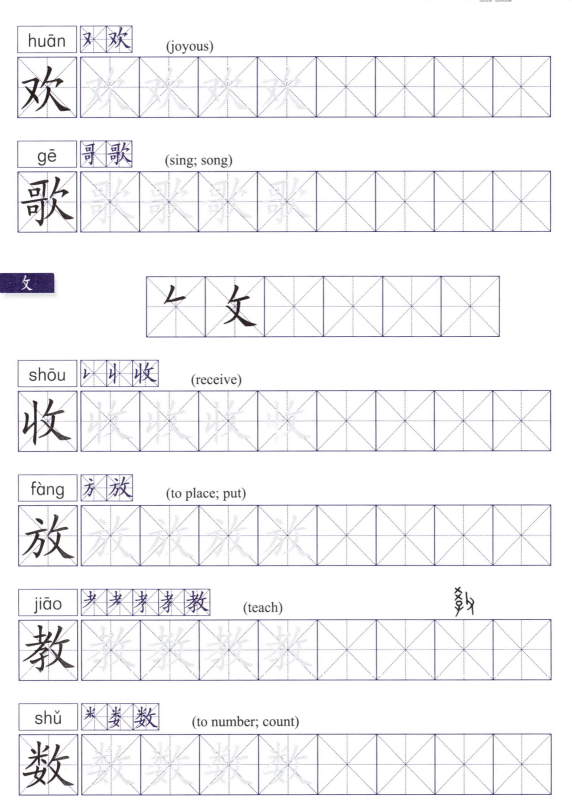

奇妙的汉字 The Wonder of Chinese Characters

夹心字
Sandwich characters

我们曾经学习过有两个相同部件的汉字，比如"从""行"等。汉语里还有一种类似的有趣汉字，我们可以称它们是"夹心字"，它们是由两个或几个相同的部件夹杂着另一个部件组成的，就像三明治一样。比如"班""街""咖""器""坐"等。这类汉字也比较容易记忆。

We have learned characters composed of two identical components, like "从" and "行". In Chinese there is another group of characters that are quite interesting. We refer to them as sandwich characters. Such characters have two or more identical components enclosing another one, in a similar manner to sandwich. For example, "班", "街", "咖", "器" and "坐". It is comparatively easy to remember these characters.

学习策略 Learning Strategy

怎样记汉字（8）
——自制汉字卡片

How to memorize Chinese characters（8）
— Making flashcards

记汉字有很多方法，每个人应该选择最适合自己的方法。有的同学很喜欢用汉字卡片，这也是一个好方法。卡片使用起来比较方便、直观，但是制作、使用卡片也有学问，比如卡片上应该写什么，写在哪儿，怎么写，使用起来有哪些方法等。

我们自己制作卡片时，最重要的是卡片上的汉字不要写错。制作卡片的纸不一定要很大，也不一定要很硬。一般来说，如果你认读汉字有困难，使用卡片只是为了提高字词的认读能力，那么在卡片的正面写汉字或词，背面写拼音和翻译。如果只写字的话，最好在字的下面、卡片的下角写上一两个提示词（见下）；如果写的是词，卡片的下角可写上一两个短语。

There are many ways to remember a Chinese character and everyone has his own method. A good method favored by some students is to use cards with Chinese characters. Card are convenient to use and characters can be directly perceived. But there are some know-hows in making and using the cards. You may wonder what and where to be written on the card, how to write and use the card.

When we are preparing a card, the most important is to write characters correctly. The paper for the card does not have to be very large, nor very hard. If you have difficulty for recognizing and reading Chinese characters, you want to use the flashcards for improving your reading ability, the usual practice is to write the character on the front side and *pinyin* and translation on the back. If you just prepare the character, it is desirable to write one or two example words below the character (as illustrated below); if it is a word, one or two phrases are preferred.

正面
the front of the card

guàn   be used to;
xíguàn habit

背面
the back of the card

如果你制作卡片是为了提高汉语的综合能力，那么请把字词和拼音写在卡片的同一面，但是分列于两边，大小以拇指能够遮盖住为宜，而把翻译单独写在另一面（见下）。这样，可以用拇指遮住拼音，只看汉字想意思来练习阅读；或者遮住汉字，只读拼音想意思来练习听力；还可以看着翻译，练习说出或写出字词来。

If you make flashcards to strengthen your comprehensive ability of Chinese, you need to write the character and *pinyin* on the same side of the card, but put them respectively on the left and right, each in the size of your thumb, and write the translation on the other side of the card (see below). In this way, you can use your thumb to cover the *pinyin*, and just look at the character to think of the meaning, which will help you practice reading; or you can cover the character and think of the meaning through reading out the *pinyin*, this will help practice listening; or you can just look at the translation for practicing speaking and writing.

惯   guàn
习惯 xíguàn

be used to;
habit

正面
the front of the card

背面
the back of the card

使用卡片时，可以用"排除法"学习，也就是学习卡片一两次后，把记住的（或容易的）和没记住的（或难的）分开，以后常复习没记住的，隔段时间再看看记住的，看是否有忘了的。这样有重点、有计划地反复学习，学习的效率会比较高。

When you are using the cards, you can divide them into two groups after reviewing the characters once or twice. One group is the harder characters for frequent reference and the other easier ones for reference at longer intervals to check if you can remember the characters. If you can learn with emphasis and regularly, your efficiency will be improved.

13 第十三课
Lesson Thirteen

汉字知识 Knowledge about Chinese Characters

形旁（6） Meaning radicals (6)

土、石、山、身、耳、页、马、牛、羊、虫、鱼、鸟

在汉语里，有些形旁本身就是汉字，这些形旁的意义也就是该汉字的本义。

In Chinese, some meaning radicals are characters themselves and in turn the meaning of the radical is that of the character.

土：跟"泥土"有关系   related to "soil"

地　场　城　墙　垃　圾；基

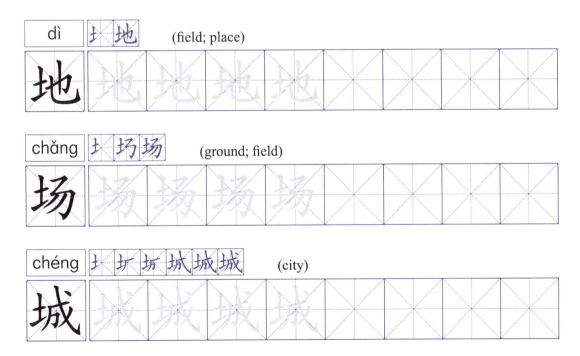

汉字速成课本 Easy Way to Learn Chinese Characters

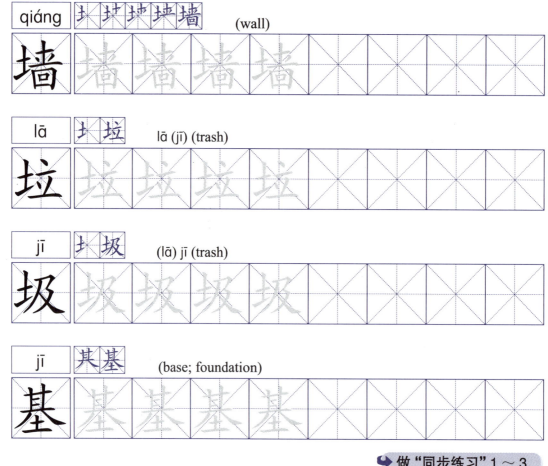

➜ 做"同步练习"1～3

石：跟"石头"有关系　related to "stone"
　　研　础　破

山：跟"山"有关系　related to "mountain", "hill"
　　岸　岁；岛

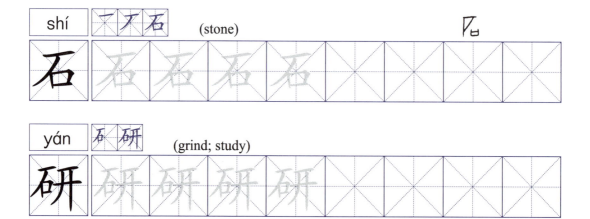

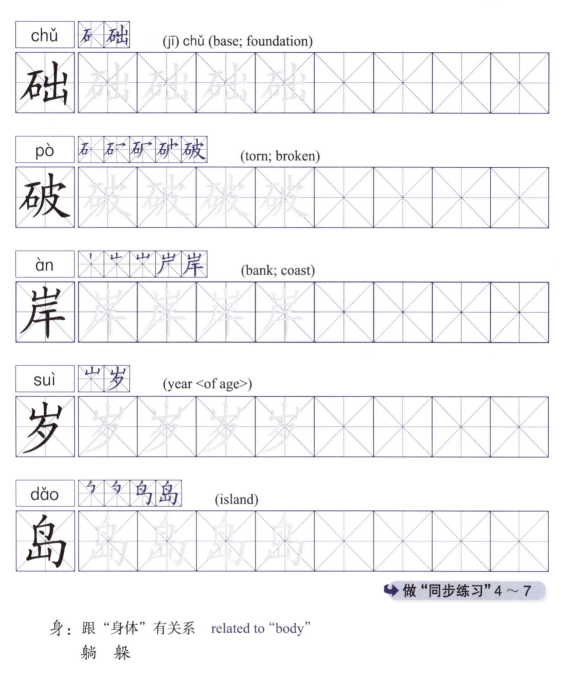

身：跟"身体"有关系　related to "body"
躺　躲

耳：跟"耳朵"或"听"有关系　related to "ear", "listen"
闻； 取　聪　联　职

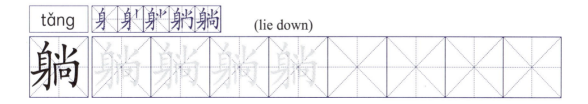

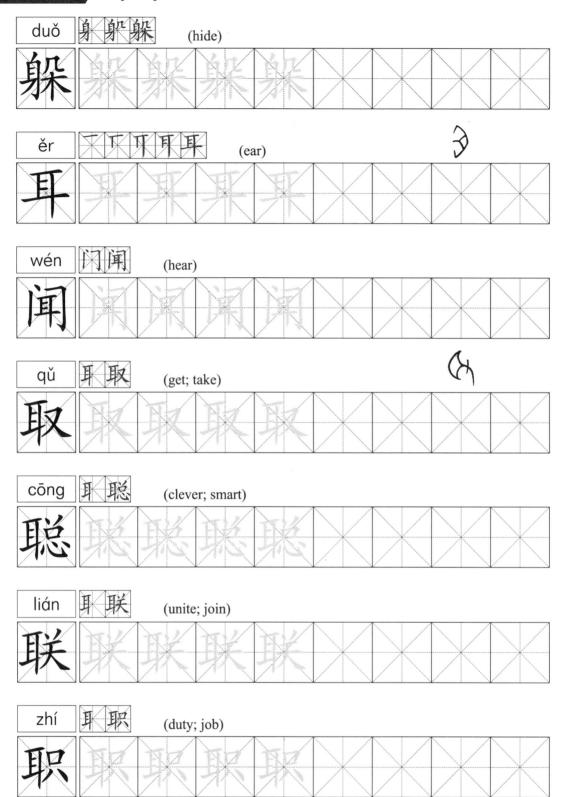

页：跟"人的头"有关系 related to "head"
　　顶　预　顾　颜　题

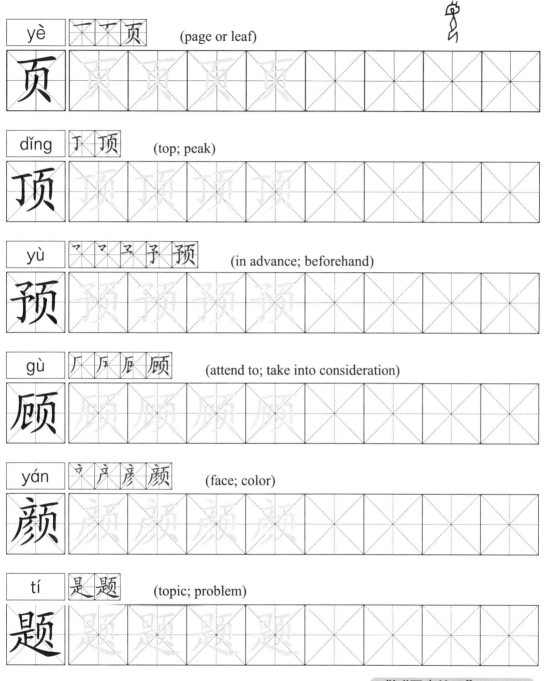

做"同步练习"11～14

马：跟"马"有关系 related to "horse"
　　骑　骗

牛：跟"牛"有关系 related to "ox"
　　特　物；告

羊：跟"羊"有关系　related to "sheep, goat"
群；着　差

| qí | 马 驴 骑 | (ride) |

| piàn | 马 驴 骗 骗 骗 骗 | (cheat) |

| tè | 牛 牪 特 | (special) |

| wù | 牛 物 | (thing) |

| gào | 牛 告 | (tell) |

| yáng | 丷 ⺷ 羊 | (sheep; goat) |

| qún | フ ⺕ ヨ 尹 君 群 | (crowd; group) |

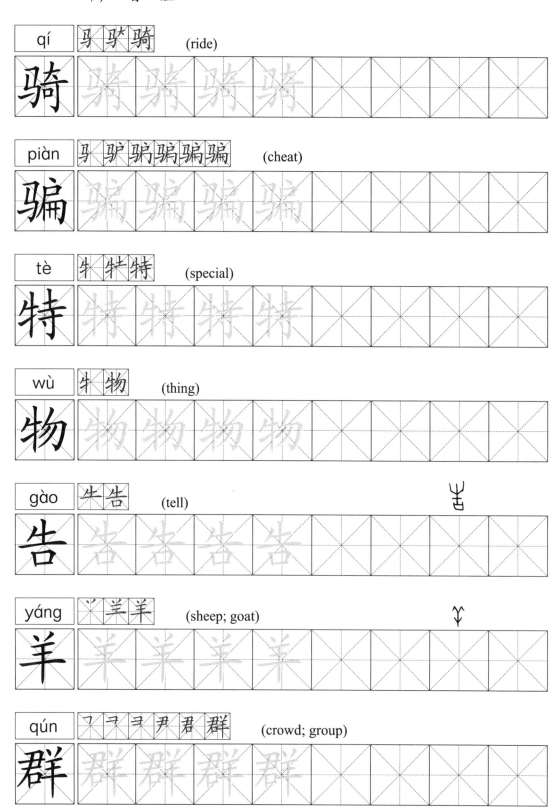

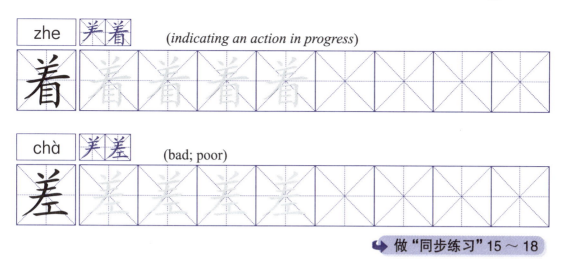

虫：跟"昆虫"或其他一些动物有关系 related to "insect"
　　虾　蛇

鱼：跟"鱼类"有关系 related to "fish"
　　鲜

鸟：跟"鸟类"有关系 related to "bird"
　　鸡　鸭

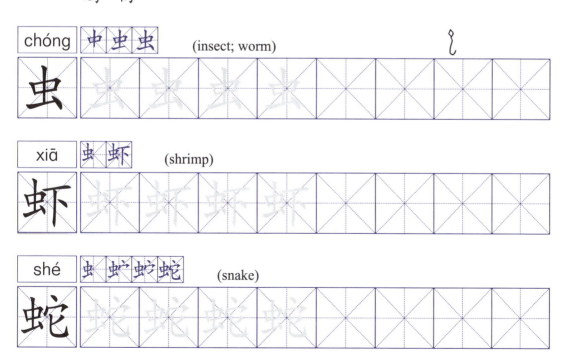

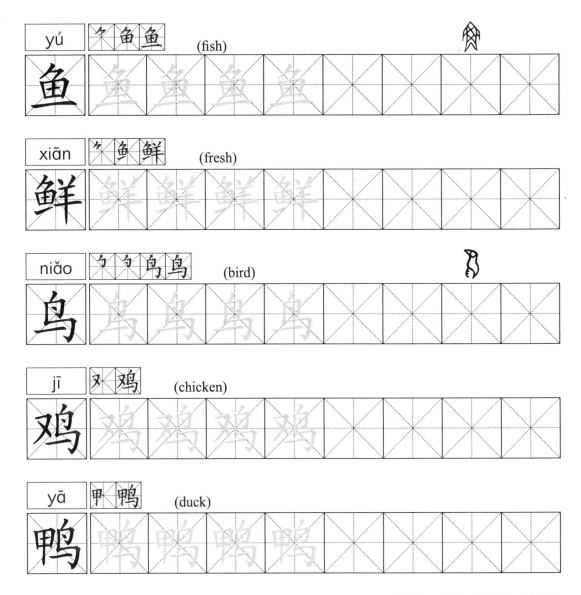

第十三课 13 Lesson Thirteen

奇妙的汉字 The Wonder of Chinese Characters

合 字
Compound characters

汉语里还有一种奇特的字，是由两个字组成的，意义就是这两个字的合成意义，有时候读音也是这两个字的合音，如"俩""甭""歪"。这样的字在汉语里并不多，但是很独特。

There are some fancy characters in Chinese in that they are composed of two characters both in makeup and in meaning. And sometimes the sound is the combination of the two components, too. For example, "俩", "甭" and "歪". The number of such characters is not large but they are of fancy characteristics.

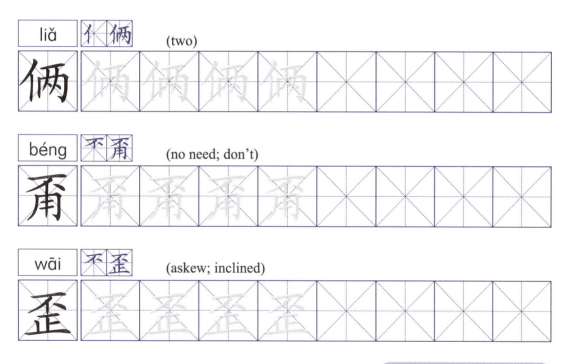

➡ 做"同步练习"23～24

学习策略 Learning Strategy

怎样记汉字（9）
——利用科技工具和网络资源

How to memorize Chinese characters (9)
— Using technology tools and online resources

随着电脑和网络成为生活必不可少的一部分，如今学习的方式也在发生着变化。不仅学习的材料变得多种多样，学习的工具也今非昔比。网络上出现了很多汉字学习的软件和工具，包括各种电子字典、笔画笔顺的动画演示、电子字卡词卡、汉字语音朗读、汉字书写助手和汉字练习游戏等等。这些网络资源和工具大多是免费的，只需要上网搜索一下就可以找到很多，选择一种适合自己的就可以了。

网络上除了可以找到汉字学习工具以外，还可以找到很多汉字教学的视频。有的是教授中国孩子学习汉字的动画，有的是学过中文的外国人自拍的视频来教授汉语汉字。如果感兴趣的话，可以搜索这些动画和视频来观看和学习。

最方便的工具可能要算手机上下载的一些汉字学习应用程序了。有的程序不仅有字典，还附带有个人化字卡，为你量身定做字表并设计复习计划，帮助你定时复习生字生词，还能把你有问题的生字检索出来，累积成下次复习的字表。如果找到一款适合你的应用程序，就可以随时随地轻松地学习汉字了。

如果能够巧妙地利用各种高科技工具和网络资源，不仅可以提高你的汉字学习效率，还可以带来一些学习的乐趣，让你的学习更轻松愉快。

Since computers and networks have now become an indispensable part of life, learning approaches are also changing. Not only has learning material become more diverse, but the learning instruments also differ a lot from before. Many software and tools for learning Chinese characters have appeared on the internet, including a variety of electronic dictionaries, stroke order animations, electronic flashcards, character reading assistants, character writing assistants, and Chinese character games. Most of these online resources and tools are free. You can find a lot if you search on the internet, you just need to select a suitable one for yourself.

In addition to the learning software and tools, you can also find many teaching videos for Chinese characters. Some are animations for Chinese kids to learn characters, some are made by foreigners who learned Chinese. If you are interested in watching them, you can search and learn from them.

The most convenient tools may be smart phone applications. Some programs not only have a dictionary, but also attach personalized flashcards, which can help you regularly review characters and pick out those that you have trouble recognizing for your review the next time. If you find a suitable application, you can easily learn Chinese characters anywhere.

If you can make good use of a variety of high-tech tools and online resources, it can not only improve the efficiency of your learning of Chinese characters, but also make your learning more enjoyable.

14 第十四课
Lesson Fourteen

汉字知识　Knowledge about Chinese Characters

形旁（7） Meaning radicals (7)

王、贝、皿、酉、车、舟、田、米、走、见、力、巾

王：跟"玉石"有关系　related to "jade"
　　玩　现　球　理；望

贝：跟"钱"有关系　related to "money"
　　贵　货　费　贺

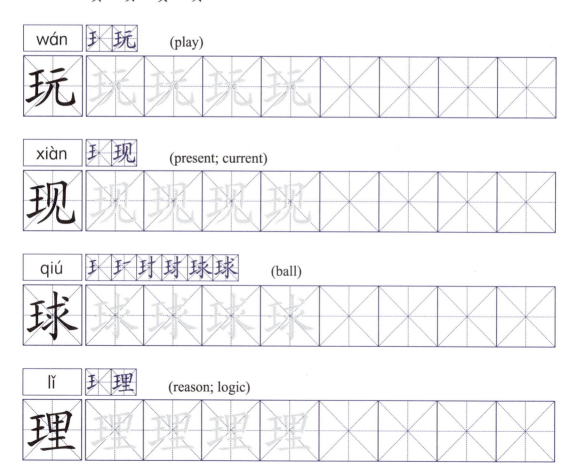

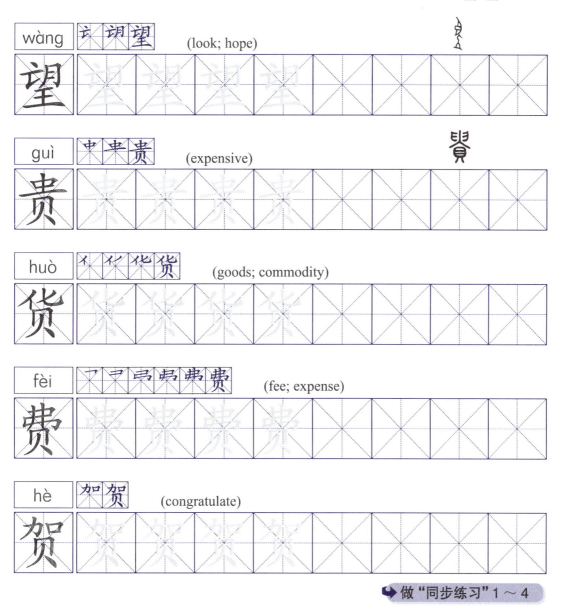

皿: 跟"器皿"有关系　related to "vessel"
　　盒　盆　益

酉: 跟"酒"有关系　related to "alcohol, wine"
　　醉　醒　配

皿

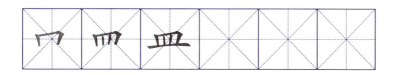

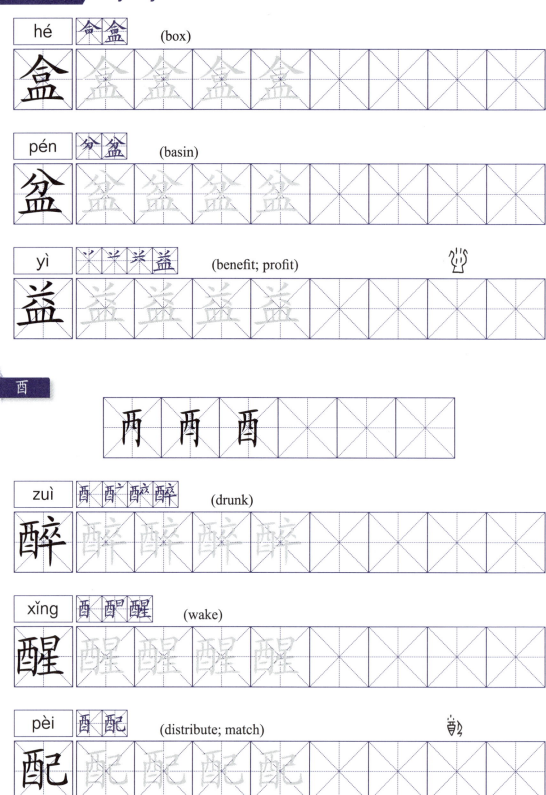

车：跟"车"有关系　related to "vehicle"
　　轻　辆　较　辅　输

舟：跟"船"有关系　related to "boat"
　　船　般；盘

| qīng | 车 轻 | (light) |

| liàng | 车 辆 | (measure word for cars or bikes) |

| jiào | 车 较 | (compare) |

| fǔ | 车 车 轫 轫 辅 辅 | (assist) |

| shū | 车 轮 轮 输 输 | (lose) |

| zhōu | 丿 凢 舟 舟 舟 | (boat) 舟

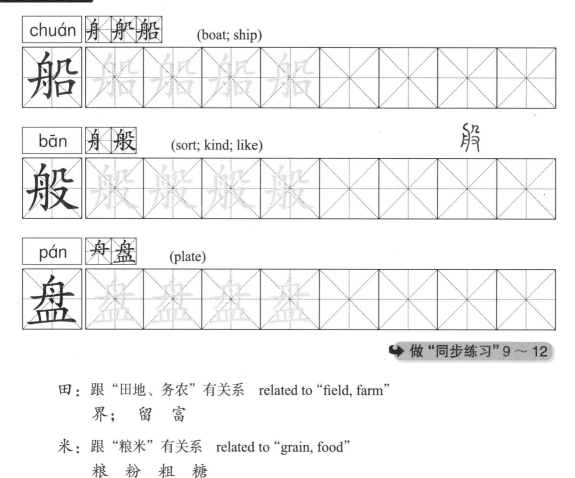

田：跟"田地、务农"有关系 related to "field, farm"
　　界； 留 富

米：跟"粮米"有关系 related to "grain, food"
　　粮 粉 粗 糖

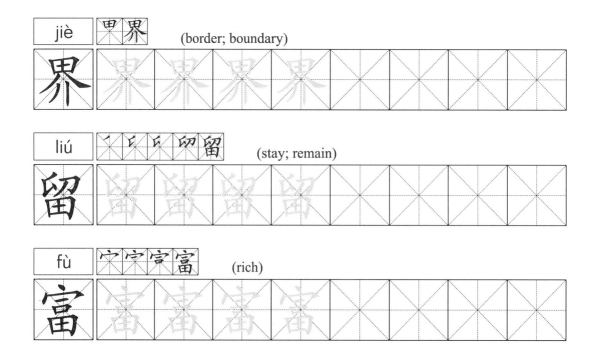

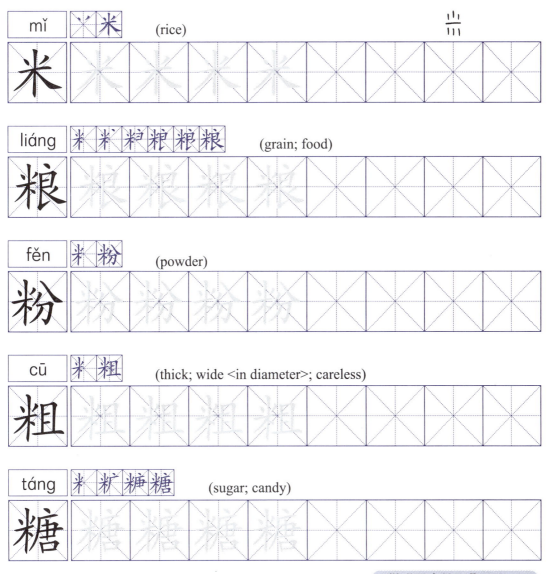

走：跟"急走、跑去"有关系 related to "running"
　　赶　越　超　趋

见：跟"看"有关系 related to "see"
　　览　观　规

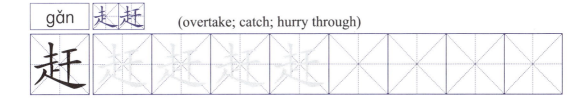

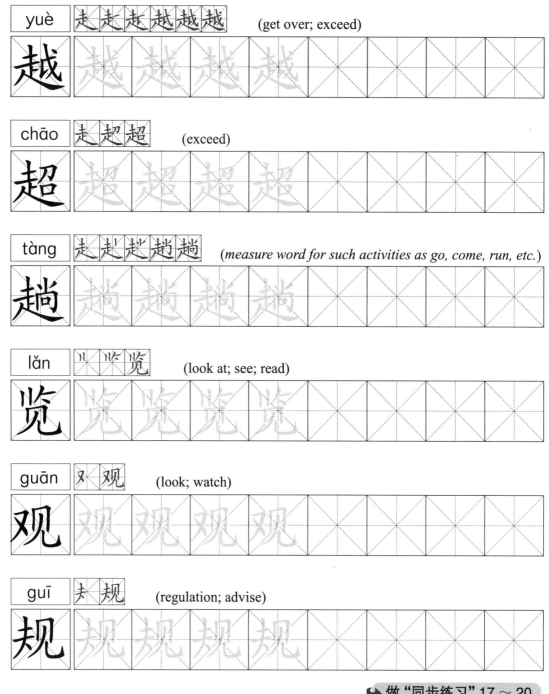

做"同步练习" 17～20

力：跟"力气"有关系　related to "strength"
　　动　助

巾：跟"布"有关系　related to "cloth"
　　带　帮　希

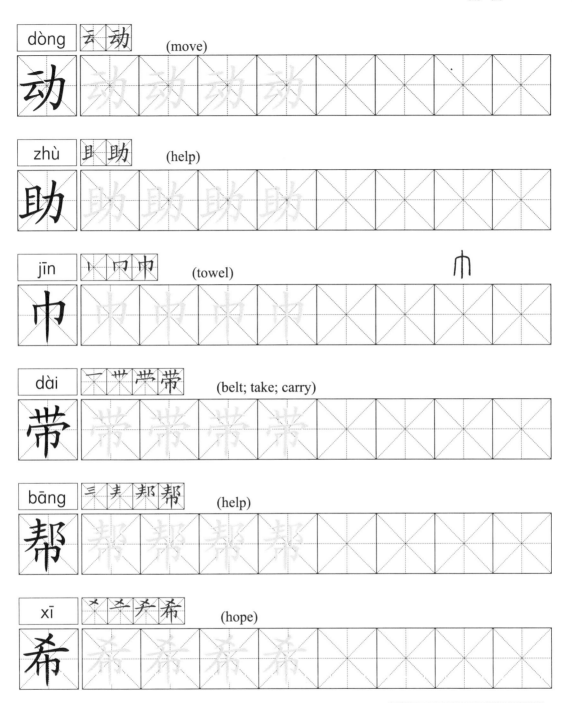

奇妙的汉字 The Wonder of Chinese Characters

"品"形字
Pyramid-shaped characters

我们已经学习过由两个相同部件构成的汉字，汉语里还有由三个相同的部件构成的汉字，它们的结构好像金字塔一样，和汉字"品"的结构一样，比如"众"和"森"等。这样的汉字不是特别多，但在人们的日常生活中却也经常能遇到。

We have learned characters with two identical components, and in Chinese there are characters with three identical components, which take the shape of a pyramid, such as "品", "众" and "森". They are not many in number but frequently used in daily life.

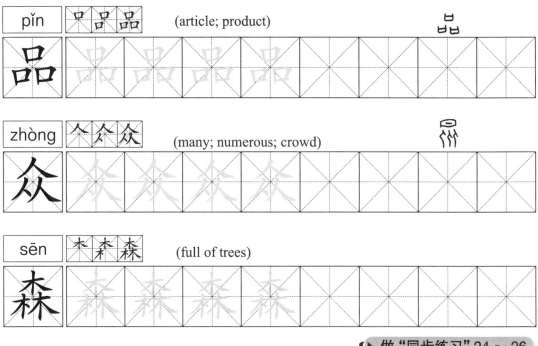

➡ 做"同步练习"24～26

学习策略 Learning Strategy

怎样记汉字（10）
——复习

How to memorize Chinese characters（10）
— Review

学习汉字是一个记忆的过程，不仅需要写、念等记忆的方法，也需要有反复的过程，就是复习。复习要注意时机，时机适宜的话，常常可以收到事半功倍的效果。

最有效的复习是及时复习，就是在学习的汉字还没有完全忘记时就复习，可以是当天复习，也可以过一两天复习。为了记忆的巩固，还需要间隔复习，也就是在学习了一段时间以后进行复习，把忘记的重新学习一下。能够做到及时复习和间隔复习的话，将会提高记忆的效果。

复习是记忆很重要的一部分，也是提高记忆效果的重要手段。有时候由于时间有限，不能做大量的复习。其实每天只要有几分钟的时间就可以复习，每次复习的内容不必很多，时间不必很长，但是复习的次数却是越多越好。复习汉字最适宜的时机是在忘记这个汉字之前，此时复习汉字就可以起到事半功倍的效果。

Learning Chinese characters is a process of memorization. You need not only reading and writing, but also repetition of such activities, which can be simply referred to as review. Review at the right moment will greatly enhance your learning.

The most efficient review is timely review, i.e. review before you forget the characters completely. It can be done on the same day, or one or two days after. But if you want to strengthen your memory, you need to review the characters from time to time. Timely review and review from time to time will help you reinforce your memory.

Although review is of great importance in enhancing your memory, you may not have that much time to do a lot of such exercises. In fact, however, you do not have to spend too much time. A few minutes each day will do. Try to limit the content of memorization for each time. So the time need not be long, but the more often you review the characters, the better the result will be. The best time to review characters is before forgetting the characters, reviewing the characters at that time can play a multiplier effect.

第十五课
Lesson Fifteen

汉字知识 Knowledge about Chinese Characters

声旁（1） Phonetic radicals (1)

> 巴、马、圣、可、方、青、及、艮、交、己、夬、舌、采、生、其

汉语的表音功能并不强，但是在形声字中，声旁在很大程度上可以传递出所组成汉字的近似或相同的读音。因此，学习一些声旁对记忆汉字也有很大的帮助。

Chinese characters do not have a strong function of sound representation, but in pictophonetic characters, the phonetic radical can, to a large extent, transmit information about the sound of the character. So it will help you learn Chinese characters if you know something about the phonetic radicals.

巴： 爸（bà）　　爸爸　dad; father
　　 爬（pá）　　爬山　climb the mountain

马： 码（mǎ）　　号码　number
　　 骂（mà）　　骂人　swear at people

圣： 经（jīng）　已经　already
　　　　　　　　经常　often
　　　　　　　　经理　manger
　　 轻（qīng）　年轻　young

可： 河（hé）　　黄河　the Yellow River　　（黄　huáng　yellow）
　　 何（hé）　　何时　when

方： 访（fǎng）　访问　visit
　　 旁（páng）　旁边　side

➦ 做"同步练习"1～3

青： 青*（qīng） 青草 green grass
　　 清（qīng） 清楚（chu） clear　　　（楚 chǔ　clear; neat）
　　 晴（qíng） 晴天 sunny day
　　 情（qíng） 事情 thing; matter
　　 请（qǐng） 请坐 please sit down
　　　　　　　 请问 may I ask
　　 精（jīng） 精神（shen） spirit; vigorous　（神 shén　spirit; god）

及： 及（jí）　 及时 in time
　　　　　　　 来得及 still have time
　　　　　　　 来不及 no enough time
　　 级（jí）　 班级 class
　　 极（jí）　 好极了 great; wonderful
　　　　　　　 热极了 extremely hot

艮： 跟（gēn）　我跟你 you and I
　　 根（gēn）　树根 root of a tree

▶ 做"同步练习"4～6

交： 郊（jiāo）　郊区 suburb
　　 饺（jiǎo）　饺子 dumpling

己： 记（jì）　记得 remember; keep in memory
　　 纪（jì）　纪念 commemorate

夬： 快（kuài） 快乐 happy　　　　（乐 lè　happy; smile）
　　 块（kuài） 一块糖 a piece of candy
　　 筷（kuài） 筷子 chopsticks

舌： 话（huà）　说话 speak; talk
　　 活（huó）　生活 live; life
　　　　　　　 活动 activity; exercise

▶ 做"同步练习"7～9

---

*部分声旁本身为常用字，所以作为生字出现，但不属于形声字。
Some phonetic radicals are characters themselves and are among those of frequent usage. Therefore, they will be introduced as new characters but not to be regarded as pictophonetic characters.

采：采（cǎi） 采茶 pick tea-leaves
　　彩（cǎi） 彩色 many colors; colorful
　　　　　　 精彩 wonderful
　　菜（cài） 点菜 order dishes

生：星（xīng） 星星 star
　　性（xìng） 性别 gender
　　　　　　 男性 male
　　　　　　 女性 female
　　胜（shèng）胜利 victory; triumph
　　甥（shēng）外甥 sister's son

其：其（qí） 其他 other; others
　　　　　　 其它 other; others（for things or animals） （它 tā it）
　　期（qī） 星期 week
　　　　　　 日期 date
　　　　　　 学期 term
　　棋（qí） 下棋 play chess
　　旗（qí） 彩旗 colorful flags
　　　　　　 红旗 red flags

➡ 做"同步练习"10～12

第十五课 Lesson Fifteen

奇妙的汉字　The Wonder of Chinese Characters

一旁多音
One phonetic radical with more than one sound

形声字中，有的声旁在现代汉字中可以表示多个读音，比如："工""丁""分"等，由它们充当声旁的汉字的发音并不相同，请看：

Some phonetic radicals can have more than one sound, such as "工"，"丁" and "分". The characters with such radicals are pronounced differently. Look at the following examples:

工：江（jiāng）　　长江　the Yangtze River
　　红（hóng）　　红色　red
　　空（kōng）　　空气　air
　　功（gōng）　　功课　schoolwork; lesson

丁：订（dìng）　　预订　to book
　　顶（dǐng）　　山顶　mountain top
　　厅（tīng）　　客厅　sitting room
　　灯（dēng）　　电灯　electric lamp
　　打（dǎ）　　　打球　play ball games

分：份（fèn）　　　一份菜　a dish
　　盼（pàn）　　　盼望　hope for; long for
　　贫（pín）　　　贫穷　poor

➡ 做"同步练习"13～15

学习策略 Learning Strategy

声旁与汉字的关系（1）
The relationship between the phonetic radical and the character (1)

形声字的声旁和形旁一样，从古代发展到现代，已经有了很大的变化。声旁与形声字的关系也比较复杂，存在一旁多音、一音多旁的现象。这些字，有的是在历史发展中，读音发生了改变，有的是比较现代的形声字。这种一旁多音现象的存在提醒我们，不能看到形声字，就以声旁判定读音。因此，学习声旁最大的意义还在于帮助记忆汉字，而不是用来确定汉字的读音。

Like the meaning radical in pictophonetic characters, the phonetic radical has also experienced great changes with its development from ancient time to today. So the relationship between the radical and the character is complicated, where one radical can have more than one sound and one sound can be represented by more than one radical. Some of these characters are the descendants of ancient ones whose sound has been changed, while others are coinages with a shorter history. The very existence of multi-sound radicals reminds us that we cannot decide how to read a character just according to its phonetic radical. In this case, the phonetic radical is most efficient in helping you remember the character rather than deciding the sound.

16 第十六课
Lesson Sixteen

汉字知识 Knowledge about Chinese Characters

声旁（2）Phonetic radicals (2)

> 令、氏、监、羊、京、东、扁、乙、果、仑、争、平、包、比

令： 令（lìng） 命令 order （命 mìng order）
　　 领（lǐng） 领导 lead; leader （导 dǎo instruct）
　　 零（líng） 零钱 change
　　 铃（líng） 门铃 door bell
　　 邻（lín） 邻居 neighbor

氏： 低（dī） 高低 height
　　 底（dǐ） 底下 under; below

监： 蓝（lán） 蓝色 blue
　　 篮（lán） 篮球 basketball

➡ 做"同步练习"1～3

羊： 洋（yáng） 海洋 sea; ocean （海 hǎi sea）
　　 养（yǎng） 养狗 keep a dog
　　 氧（yǎng） 氧气 oxygen
　　 样（yàng） 样子 appearance; shape

京： 惊（jīng） 吃惊 be shocked; be amazed
　　 景（jǐng） 景色 scenery
　　 影（yǐng） 电影 film

东： 练（liàn） 练习 practice; do exercise
　　 炼（liàn） 锻炼 have physical training

157

扁： 遍（biàn） 说了两遍 have said twice
　　 篇（piān） 一篇文章 an article

> 做"同步练习"4～6

乙： 乙（yǐ）　 乙级　the second level
　　 艺（yì）　 艺术　art　　　　　　　（术 shù　art）
　　 亿（yì）　 一亿　a hundred million
　　 忆（yì）　 回忆　recall; recollect

果： 果（guǒ）　水果　fruit
　　 棵（kē）　 一棵树　a tree
　　 颗（kē）　 一颗心　a heart

仑： 轮（lún）　车轮　wheel（of a vehicle）
　　 论（lùn）　讨论　discuss　　　　（讨 tǎo　discuss; study）

> 做"同步练习"7～9

争： 争（zhēng）　争论　argument; dispute
　　 净（jìng）　　干净　clean; neat and tidy
　　 静（jìng）　　安静　quiet

平： 平（píng）　平等　equality
　　　　　　　　平常　ordinary
　　　　　　　　平时　in normal time
　　 评（píng）　评论　comment on
　　 苹（píng）　苹果　apple

包： 包（bāo）　书包　schoolbag
　　　　　　　　包饺子　make dumplings
　　 抱（bào）　抱孩子　carry a baby in one's arms
　　 炮（pào）　大炮　cannon

比： 毕（bì）　毕业　graduate
　　 批（pī）　批评　criticize
　　 屁（pì）　放屁　break wind

> 做"同步练习"10～12

158

奇妙的汉字　The Wonder of Chinese Characters

声旁位于形旁中间的形声字
Pictophonetic characters with the phonetic radical in the middle of the meaning radical

　　我们学习的形声字大部分都是左右结构、上下结构或者内外结构的，但是有一种形声字，它的声旁位于形旁的中间，如"裹"和"衷"，它们的形旁"衣"被声旁"果"和"中"分成了两部分，所以不是特别明显的形声字。这些字由于笔画稍多，不便于记忆，但如果认识到它们是形声字，记起来就容易多了。

Most pictophonetic characters we have learned so far are of left-right structure, top-bottom structure or enclosed structure. In addition, there is another type of pictophonetic characters whose phonetic radical is in the middle of the meaning radical. For example, the meaning radical "衣" in "裹" and "衷" is divided into two parts by "果" and "中" respectively. Since such characters are not quite typical and usually made up of more strokes, they seem difficult to remember. But when you come to know that they are pictophonetic characters, the task will be greatly reduced.

　　果：裹（guǒ）　　　　　包裹　parcel
　　中：衷（zhōng）　　　　衷心　sincerely

做"同步练习"13

学习策略 Learning Strategy

声旁与汉字的关系（2）
The relationship between the phonetic radical and the character（2）

虽然声旁与汉字的关系比较复杂，但是还是有一些规律的。声旁与汉字的音近关系体现在声、韵、调三个方面，具体如下：

Although the relationship between the phonetic radical and the character is variable, there are still some rules to follow. The phonetic radical is related to the character in three aspects, namely initial, final and tone.

	声 Initial	韵 Final	调 Tone	例字 Example
声旁与汉字读音相同的部分 The phonetic radical is related to the character in	√	√	√	洋、惊
	√	√		零、毕
	√			邻
			√	批、炮
				净、棵

声旁与汉字在声、韵、调三个方面的接近，决定了声旁对汉字具有一定的表音功能。

The fact that the phonetic radical is related to the sound of the character in the above three aspects determines the sound representation function of the radical.

17 第十七课
Lesson Seventeen

汉字知识 Knowledge about Chinese Characters

声旁（3） Phonetic radicals (3)

> 古、良、吉、票、戋、畐、居、正、廷、曼、兑、且、相、冈

古： 古（gǔ）　　　古时候（hou）in ancient times（候 hòu　time）
　　 故（gù）　　　故事　story; tale
　　 姑（gū）　　　姑娘　girl
　　　　　　　　　姑姑　aunt

良： 郎（láng）　　新郎　bridegroom　　　　（新 xīn　new; fresh）
　　 狼（láng）　　　　　wolf
　　 朗（lǎng）　　朗读　read aloud　　　　（读 dú　read）
　　 娘（niáng）　　新娘　bride

吉： 结（jié）　　　结婚　marry　　　　　　（婚 hūn　marriage）
　　 洁（jié）　　　清洁　clean

➡ 做"同步练习"1～3

票： 票（piào）　　门票　entrance ticket
　　　　　　　　　邮票　stamp
　　 飘（piāo）　　　　　float in the air
　　 漂（piào）　　漂亮（liang）beautiful　　（亮 liàng　bright）

戋： 浅（qiǎn）　　深浅　depth; deep or shallow
　　 线（xiàn）　　长线　long thread

畐： 福（fú）　　　幸福（happiness; will-being）（幸 xìng　good fortune）
　　 幅（fú）　　　一幅画儿　a picture
　　 副（fù）　　　一副手套　a pair of gloves　（套 tào　cover; case）

161

居：	剧（jù）	剧场 theater	
		京剧 Beijing opera	
	据（jù）	据说 it's said	

➡ 做"同步练习"4～6

正：	整（zhěng）	整齐 in good order; tidy	（齐 qí　neat）
	证（zhèng）	证书 certificate	
	政（zhèng）	政治 politics	（治 zhì　rule; govern）
廷：	庭（tíng）	家庭 family; household	
	挺（tǐng）	挺好的 very good	
曼：	慢（màn）	慢一点儿 a little slower	
	馒（mán）	馒头 steamed bread	
兑：	说（shuō）	说话 speak; talk	
	脱（tuō）	脱衣服 take off clothes	
	阅（yuè）	阅览室 reading room	

➡ 做"同步练习"7～9

且：	且（qiě）	而且 and; but also	（而 ér　but; yet）
	租（zū）	租房 rent a house	
	组（zǔ）	组织 organize; organization	（织 zhī　knit）
	祖（zǔ）	祖国 motherland	
相：	箱（xiāng）	箱子 case; big box	
	厢（xiāng）	车厢 railway carriage	
冈：	刚（gāng）	刚才 just now	
		刚刚 just	
	纲（gāng）	提纲 outline	（提 tí　carry in hand; draw out）

➡ 做"同步练习"10～12

奇妙的汉字　The Wonder of Chinese Characters

形似音近字
Characters with similar forms and sounds

有些声旁组成的几个形声字，读音都很接近，如"扬"和"杨"、"枪"和"抢"等，字形也比较相似，只是形旁有所不同，这样的字就是形似音近字。

Some phonetic radicals can be used to form characters with similar sounds, like "扬" and "杨"，"枪" and "抢". These characters are also of similar forms. Hence, we call them characters with similar forms and sounds.

昜：扬（yáng）　　　表扬　praise
　　杨（yáng）　　　杨树　poplar

仓：枪（qiāng）　　　手枪　pistol
　　抢（qiǎng）　　　抢东西　snatch; grab
　　　　　　　　　　抢购　rush to purchase　　（购 gòu　buy; purchase）

▶ 做"同步练习"13～14

学习策略　Learning Strategy

如何辨别形似音近字
How to distinguish characters from similar forms and sounds

形似音近字很容易混淆，辨别不同的形似音近字，可以从两个方面入手：一是根据形旁判定汉字的义类；二是根据汉字所在的上下文（词、短语或句子）来判断。

我们学习过很多形旁，知道了不同形旁所代表的义类，看到生字时，先确认是什么形旁、与它的意义是否有联系等再记。有几组特别容易混淆的形旁，需要特别注意，比如："扌"和"木"、"目"和"月"、"木"和"禾"等。

It is easy to mix up those characters with similar forms and sounds. Even so, distinction can be made from the following two aspects: one is to decide the meaning of the character according to its meaning radical; the other is to make your decision on basis of the context (a word, a phrase or a sentence).

We have learned many meaning radicals and come to know the meaning each radical represents. So when we come across a new character, we should first make sure what the meaning radical is and whether it is related to the meaning of the character before we try to remember it. There are several pairs of meaning radicals that are likely to get mixed up,"扌"and"木", "目"and"月", and"木"and"禾".

18 第十八课
Lesson Eighteen

汉字知识　Knowledge about Chinese Characters

声旁（4） Phonetic radicals (4)

> 隹、白、原、君、曷、竟、专、直、占、成、韦、㐱、尤、曹

隹：谁（shéi / shuí）　　你是谁　who are you
　　堆（duī）　　　　　一堆雪　a pile of snow
　　推（tuī）　　　　　推门　　push the door

白：伯（bó）　　伯伯　elder brother of father
　　怕（pà）　　害怕　be afraid; be scared　　（害 hài　harmful）
　　拍（pāi）　拍手　clap hands; applaud

原：原（yuán）　原来　original; former
　　源（yuán）　源头　source; fountainhead
　　愿（yuàn）　愿望　desire; wish

君：群（qún）　人群　crowd
　　裙（qún）　裙子　skirt

▶ 做"同步练习"1～3

曷：喝（hē）　喝水　drink water
　　渴（kě）　口渴　thirsty

竟：镜（jìng）　镜子　mirror
　　境（jìng）　环境　environment; surrounding
　　　　　　　　　　　　（环 huán　ring; hoop）

专：专（zhuān）　专心　be absorbed
　　　　　　　　专门　special

	传（zhuàn）	传记 biography	
	转（zhuǎn）	转身 turn round	

直： 植（zhí）　　　植树　plant trees
　　 值（zhí）　　　值班　be on duty
　　 置（zhì）　　　布置　arrange; assign

▶ 做"同步练习"4～6

占： 占（zhàn）　　　占少数　constitute the minority
　　 站（zhàn）　　　车站　station
　　 战（zhàn）　　　战争　war
　　 粘（zhān）　　　粘贴　stick; paste　　　（贴 tiē　stick; paste）

成： 成（chéng）　　成功　succeed
　　　　　　　　　　成为　become
　　 诚（chéng）　　诚实　honest　　　（实 shí　true; real; honest）
　　 盛（chéng）　　盛饭　fill a bowl with rice

韦： 伟（wěi）　　　伟大　great
　　 违（wéi）　　　违反　violate

▶ 做"同步练习"7～9

乡： 珍（zhēn）　　　珍珠　pearl　　　（珠 zhū　bead; pearl）
　　　　　　　　　　珍贵　rare and expensive
　　 诊（zhěn）　　　门诊　outpatient service (in a hospital)
　　 趁（chèn）　　　趁早　as early as possible

尤： 尤（yóu）　　　尤其　especially
　　 优（yōu）　　　优点　merit; virtue
　　 犹（yóu）　　　犹豫（yù）　hesitate

曹： 遭（zāo）　　　遭到　suffer; meet with
　　 糟（zāo）　　　糟糕　too bad　　　（糕 gāo　cake; pudding）

▶ 做"同步练习"10～12

第十八课 18 Lesson Eighteen

奇妙的汉字　The Wonder of Chinese Characters

形似字（1）
Characters similar in form (1)

汉语里有一部分形似音近字，还有一部分音不同的形似字。这些形似字的音不同，是由于其声旁不同，而形似也是由于其声旁的形相近，也就是说，这些形似字是由形似音不同的声旁构成的。这样的声旁有"未""末"和"朱"、"凡"和"凡"、"仓"和"仑"、"氏"和"氐"、"艮"和"良"等。它们常会构成形似字，例如：艮：跟、根；良：粮、(踉)等。

In addition to the characters with similar forms and sounds, there are also characters with similar forms but different sounds, which can be attributed to the phonetic radicals that are different in sound but similar in form. These phonetic radicals include "未", "末" and "朱", "凡" and "凡", "仓" and "仑", "氏" and "氐", "艮" and "良". For example: 艮：跟，根；良：粮，(踉).

未（wèi）	未来　future	
末（mò）	末尾　tail; end 月末　the end of the month	（尾 wěi　tail）
朱（Zhū）	surname	

➡ 做"同步练习"13

学习策略　Learning Strategy

如何辨别形似字
How to distinguish characters from similar forms

形似字的辨别可以从以下几个方面入手：一是字形，声旁相同、形旁不同的形似字，要注意分辨不同形旁的意义，意义不同，其形不同；二是字音，声旁不同，尽管其形相似，读音也是不同的，要注意不同读音的声旁的形；三是字义，不论声旁相近还是形旁相近，形似字的意义都不同，要注意形似字代表不同意义的形旁。总而言之，要注意形声字的声旁和形旁，准确地使用每一个字。

One can make distinction between characters with similar forms from the following aspects. First is the form of the character: when such characters have the same phonetic radical, you should examine the meaning radical carefully; the form varies with the meaning. Second is the sound: when the phonetic radical is different, the sound will differ; you should pay attention to the form of the phonetic radical. Third is the meaning of the character: despite the similarity in form or sound, different characters have different meanings; you should focus your attention on the meaning radical. To put it in short, a careful examination upon the phonetic and meaning radicals will be of great help in using the character correctly.

19 第十九课
Lesson Nineteen

汉字知识 Knowledge about Chinese Characters

多义字 Multi-meaning characters

随着社会的不断发展，人们对事物的描绘越来越细，需要表达的新事物、新现象也越来越多，但是汉语并没有因此而造出很多新字，而是用原有的字来代替，延伸原来汉字的意思，所以大多数的汉字都有两个或两个以上的意义，这也就形成了汉语中大量的多义字。这些多义字的各意义之间大都有着某种联系。

With the development of society, people describe things in more details and there are more and more new things and phenomena to be represented. The Chinese language solves the problems not by coining new characters but by extending the meaning of the already existent characters. This is why most Chinese characters have more than one meaning and make the language rich in multi-meaning characters. The different meanings of a character are usually interrelated.

> 日　打　表

日：	sun	日出	sunrise	
	day	日子	day	
	daytime	日夜	day and night	（夜 yè　night）
	daily	日报	daily paper	

打：	beat	打人	beat a person	
	break	花瓶打了	the vase is broken	（瓶 píng　bottle）
	knit	打毛衣	knit a sweater	
	raise	打伞	hold up an umbrella	
	make	打电话	make a phone call	
	play	打篮球	play basketball	

（"打"一共有24种意思，这里只选了6种。）

（There are altogether 24 meanings to "打" character, only 6 out of which are listed here.）

表： surface　　　　　　表面　outside appearance
　　 show; express　　　表示　show; express; indicate　（示 shì　show; instruct）
　　　　　　　　　　　 表演　perform　　　　　　　　（演 yǎn　perform; play）
　　　　　　　　　　　 表扬　praise
　　 form　　　　　　　 填表　fill in a form　　　　　（填 tián　write; fill in）
　　 watch　　　　　　　手表　wrist watch
　　 model; example　　 代表　representative; delegate（代 dài　take the place of;
　　　　　　　　　　　　　　　　　　　　　　　　　　　　　　act for）

▶ 做"同步练习"1～3

成 交 节

成： become　　　　　　成为　become
　　 success　　　　　　成功　success; succeed
　　 complete　　　　　 成绩　achievement　　　　　（绩 jì　achievement; merit）
　　 turn into　　　　　成人　adult

交： hand in　　　　　　交费　pay dues
　　 make friends with　交朋友　make friends
　　 associate with　　 交往　contact; intercourse
　　 mutual　　　　　　 交换　exchange　　　　　　　（换 huàn　exchange）
　　　　　　　　　　　　交流　exchange　　　　　　　（流 liú　flow; spread）
　　 cross; intersect　交通　traffic　　　　　　　　（通 tōng　open; through）

节： part; division　　 音节　syllable
　　 section; length　 两节课　two sections of classes
　　 festival　　　　　 节日　festival
　　　　　　　　　　　　过节　celebrate a festival
　　　　　　　　　　　　节目　program
　　 economize　　　　　节约　economize; save
　　　　　　　　　　　　　　　　　　　　　　　　　　（约 yuē　brief; approximately）

▶ 做"同步练习"4～6

第十九课 19 Lesson Nineteen

> 生 发 安

生：be born　　　　　　　　出生　be born
　　existence; life　　　　　一生　all one's life
　　unripe; green　　　　　 生瓜　unripe watermelon　（瓜 guā　melon）
　　raw; uncooked　　　　　生肉　raw meat　　　　　（肉 ròu　meat）
　　unfamiliar; strange　　 生词　new word　　　　　（词 cí　word）
　　pupil; student　　　　　师生　teacher and student
　　get; have　　　　　　　 生病　get ill; fall ill

发（fā）：feel; have a feeling　　发烧　have a fever
　　　　　occur　　　　　　　　　发生　happen; take place
　　　　　expand　　　　　　　　 发展　develop
　　　　　send out; deliver　　　发电子邮件　to e-mail
　　　　　　　　　　　　　　　　　　　　（件 jiàn　*measure word*）
　　　　　utter; express　　　　发言　speak; make a statement
　　　　　　　　　　　　　　　　　　　　（言 yán　word; say）
　　　　　show one's feeling　　发笑　laugh
　　　　　start　　　　　　　　　出发　start; set out

安：quiet　　　　　　　　　　　　安静　quiet; peaceful
　　place in a suitable position　安排　arrange
　　　　　　　　　　　　　　　　　　　　（排 pái　line up; arrange）
　　safe; secure　　　　　　　　　安全　safe; secure
　　set (sb's feeling) at ease　　安慰　comfort; console
　　　　　　　　　　　　　　　　　　　　（慰 wèi　console）
　　peaceful; calm　　　　　　　　安心　feel at ease; be relieved

➡ 做"同步练习" 7~9

奇妙的汉字　The Wonder of Chinese Characters

形似字（2）
Characters similar in form (2)

除了有些形声字因形旁或声旁的相近造成了形似字外，非形声字中也有一些形似字。这些形似字主要是由于笔画或部件的相似造成的。例如：

Characters with similar sounds or forms include not only pictophonetic characters but also non-pictophonetic ones, which are the result of similar stroke(s) or component(s). For example:

爪 zhuǎ	爪子	claw; paw
瓜 guā	西瓜	watermelon
	黄瓜	cucumber

历 lì	历史	history
厉 lì	厉害	terrible; fierce

今 jīn	今天	today
	今年	this year
令 lìng	命令	order

爱 ài	爱情	love	
	爱人	husband or wife	
受 shòu	接受	accept	（接 jiē　receive）
	受不了	unbearable	

折 zhé	折断	break	（断 duàn　break; cut）
	骨折	fracture	（骨 gǔ　bone）
拆 chāi	拆开	open; take apart	
析 xī	分析	analysis; analyse	

➡ 做"同步练习"10～11

172

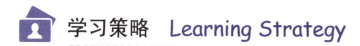

学习策略 Learning Strategy

上下文的重要性
The importance of the context

汉语中大部分的汉字都是多义字，学习和使用汉字时，就会遇到给多义字确定意义的问题。确定多义字的意义，最主要的依据是上下文，这里说的"上下文"包括多义字组合成的词，也包括它所在的短语、句子甚至语段。所以学习时，最好不要孤立地学习单个汉字，而是通过学习字所在的词和短语或句子来学习。运用汉字时也是如此，我们常会遇到一些没学过的，或是学过但没记住的字和词，必要时，可以通过上下文来确定或猜测其意义。

Since most characters in Chinese are multi-meaning characters, you will surely be faced with the difficulty of choosing the proper meaning for a character when you are learning and using Chinese. Your decision should be mainly based on the context, ranging from words and phrases consisting of the character to sentences or even paragraphs. So the best way to learn a Chinese character is to put it in the context, rather than learn it separately. This principle also applies to the case of using the character. The context can also help us guess and determine the meaning of characters that are new or have eluded our memory.

20 第二十课
Lesson Twenty

汉字知识 Knowledge about Chinese Characters

多音多义字 Multi-phonetic and meaning characters

有些多义字只有一个读音,而有些多义字有两个(或两个以上的)读音,其中一些字的两种读音之间没有什么关系,而另一些字两种读音的意义基本相同,有两个读音常是为区别词性的。

Some multi-meaning characters have only one sound while others have two or more sounds. And the different sounds of some such characters are not related at all while others have basically the same meaning. Different sounds are usually used for the purpose of differentiating word classes.

了　着　干　好

了:	le	*particle*	他去商店了	He has gone to a shop.
	liǎo	finish	吃不了	cannot eat all
			拿不了	cannot take all
		know	了解	know; understand
				(解 jiě　understand)
着:	zhe	*particle*	坐着看书	sit there reading a book
	zháo	*indicating result*	睡着了	be asleep
干:	gān	dry	干净	clean
	gàn	do	干什么	What do you want?
好:	hǎo	a.	好书	a good book
	hào	v.	爱好	hobby; love doing sth.

➤ 做"同步练习"1～2

长　教　背　空

长：	cháng	长短	length	（短 duǎn　short）
	zhǎng	长大	grow up	

教：	jiāo	教课	give a lesson	
	jiào	教室	classroom	
		教师	teacher	（师 shī　teacher）

背：	bēi	背包	backpack	
	bèi	后背	back	

空：	kōng	空箱子	an empty box	
	kòng	有空儿	free time; spare time	

➡ 做"同步练习"3～4

少　数　种　处

少：	shǎo	多少	how many; how much	
	shào	少年	teenager	

数：	shǔ	数不清	uncountable	
	shù	数量	quantity	（量 liàng　amount; quantity）

种：	zhǒng	种类	sort; kind	（类 lèi　kind; type）
	zhòng	种树	plant trees	

处：	chǔ	相处	get along（with one another）	
	chù	处处	everywhere	

➡ 做"同步练习"5～7

还有一些多音多义字，它们两种读音的意义没有什么联系，常常是由于借音产生的。

The different sounds of the following characters are not related in meaning. They are the result of sound borrowing.

> 便 都 乐 假

便：biàn　　方便　　　convenient
　　pián　　便宜（yi）cheap　　　　　　（宜 yí　suitable; appropriate）

都：dū　　　首都　　　capital　　　　　　（首 shǒu　head）
　　dōu　　我们都去　We all go.

乐：yuè　　音乐　　　music
　　lè　　　快乐　　　happy

假：jiǎ　　　假话　　　lie; falsehood
　　jià　　　放假　　　have a holiday or vacation

➡ 做"同步练习"8～11

> 还 会 重 发

还：hái　　还是　　　still; or
　　huán　　还书　　　return the book

会：huì　　开会　　　have a meeting
　　kuài　　会计　　　accounting　　　　（计 jì　count; calculate）

重：chóng　重复　　　repeat
　　zhòng　重量　　　weight

发：fā　　　发现　　　discover
　　fà　　　理发　　　haircut; hairdressing　（理 lǐ　put in order; tidy up）

➡ 做"同步练习"12～13

第二十课 20 Lesson Twenty

> 系 差 的 得

系： xì   中文系   Chinese Department（in a university）
    jì   系带子   tie laces

差： chà   差不多   almost
    chāi   出差   be on a business trip

的： de   我的   my; mine
    dí   的确   really; indeed   （确 què   true; reliable）
    dī   打的   call a taxi

得： de   累得很   very tired
    dé   得到   get; gain
    děi   我得去   I should go.

➡ 做"同步练习"14～16

奇妙的汉字　The Wonder of Chinese Characters

多音同义字
Multi-phonetic characters with the same meaning

汉语里大部分的多音字是由于意义不同或词性不同形成的，还有小部分的多音字，只是与不同的字组合、搭配时才会读音不同，但意义、词性却是相同的。例如：

Most multi-phonetic characters are the result of different meanings and word classes. The rest small part, however, is due to the different combinations of characters or different collocations, while the meaning and word class remain unchanged. For example:

血：xiě	流血	bleed; shed blood	
xuè	血液	blood	（液 yè　liquid）
薄：báo	薄纸	thin paper	
	薄饼	thin pancake	（饼 bǐng　cake）
bó	薄弱	weak; frail	（弱 ruò　weak; inferior）
吓：xià	吓一跳	be scared	
hè	恐吓	threaten; frighten	（恐 kǒng　fear; terrify; intimidate）

➡ 做"同步练习"17～18

学习策略　Learning Strategy

怎样学习汉字（2）
How to learn Chinese characters（2）

学习汉字有一个过程，首先需要正确地认识汉字，其次是有效地记忆汉字，然后是准确地运用汉字。

正确地认识汉字，包括对汉字形、音、义的正确掌握，尤其是汉字的形，从笔画、部件到整字，要看清楚、看准确。

有效地记忆汉字，每个人都有不同的、适合自己的方法，但无论是什么方法，都需要多看、多写，反复记忆，才能有效地记住汉字。

准确地运用汉字，当有些汉字记得不十分清楚时，最好查字典。在必要时，可以猜字，如根据形旁猜字的意义等，但猜完之后还是需要查查字典来证实，并加强记忆。

在"学习策略"部分，我们介绍了一些学习方法，也介绍了一些学习汉字时需要注意的问题。希望这些建议对你有帮助，也希望你通过对这本书的学习，了解一些汉字的结构规律，从而轻松地学习汉字，并且取得好成绩。

Learning Chinese characters is a procedure of three steps: first, recognize the character correctly; second, remember it effectively; third, use it properly.

The first step, to recognize the character correctly, implies the mastery over the form, sound and meaning of the character, especially the form. You should examine the strokes and components carefully.

The second step varies with different learners, for everybody has his own method. But whatever method it is, more observation, more practice and repetitious memorization are among the prerequisites.

To use the character properly, you are advised to consult a dictionary when you are not quite sure of the character. Sometimes, you can make a guess based on the meaning radical and other knowledge you have learned about Chinese characters, but to enhance your memory, you still need to look it up.

In the section of "Learning Strategy", we have introduced some learning methods and at the same time highlight some points demanding your special attention during the course of Chinese character learning. We do hope that these suggestions can help you in your learning and that you come to know the basic rules governing the construction of Chinese characters, so that you can learn Chinese characters with ease and achievement.

生字总表

（括号内是课号）

A

1	爱	ài	(19)
2	安	ān	(12)
3	岸	àn	(13)

B

4	八	bā	(1)
5	把	bǎ	(10)
6	爸	bà	(15)
7	吧	ba	(8)
8	白	bái	(2)
9	百	bǎi	(2)
10	班	bān	(12)
11	般	bān	(14)
12	板	bǎn	(10)
13	办	bàn	(4)
14	半	bàn	(6)
15	帮	bāng	(14)
16	包	bāo	(16)
17	薄	báo	(20)
18	饱	bǎo	(11)
19	报	bào	(10)
20	抱	bào	(16)
21	背	bēi	(20)
22	北	běi	(7)
23	贝	bèi	(4)
24	背	bèi	(20)
25	被	bèi	(12)
26	本	běn	(2)
27	甭	béng	(13)
28	比	bǐ	(7)
29	笔	bǐ	(11)
30	毕	bì	(16)
31	边	biān	(11)
32	便	biàn	(20)
33	遍	biàn	(16)
34	表	biǎo	(19)
35	别	bié	(10)
36	冰	bīng	(9)
37	饼	bǐng	(20)
38	病	bìng	(12)
39	伯	bó	(18)
40	薄	bó	(20)
41	不	bù	(1)
42	部	bù	(9)

C

43	猜	cāi	(11)
44	才	cái	(4)
45	采	cǎi	(15)
46	彩	cǎi	(15)
47	菜	cài	(11)
48	参	cān	(8)
49	草	cǎo	(11)
50	层	céng	(12)
51	茶	chá	(11)
52	差	chà	(13)
53	拆	chāi	(19)
54	差	chāi	(20)
55	长	cháng	(3)
56	尝	cháng	(7)
57	常	cháng	(7)
58	厂	chǎng	(2)
59	场	chǎng	(13)
60	唱	chàng	(8)
61	超	chāo	(14)
62	朝	cháo	(9)
63	车	chē	(2)

64	衬	chèn	(12)		100	刀	dāo	(3)
65	趁	chèn	(18)		101	导	dǎo	(16)
66	成	chéng	(18)		102	岛	dǎo	(13)
67	诚	chéng	(18)		103	到	dào	(10)
68	城	chéng	(13)		104	道	dào	(11)
69	盛	chéng	(18)		105	得	dé	(20)
70	吃	chī	(8)		106	的	de	(4)
71	迟	chí	(11)		107	得	de	(8)
72	虫	chóng	(13)		108	得	děi	(20)
73	重	chóng	(20)		109	灯	dēng	(10)
74	出	chū	(2)		110	等	děng	(11)
75	除	chú	(9)		111	低	dī	(16)
76	处	chǔ	(20)		112	的	dī	(20)
77	础	chǔ	(13)		113	的	dí	(20)
78	楚	chǔ	(15)		114	底	dǐ	(16)
79	处	chù	(4)		115	地	dì	(13)
80	穿	chuān	(12)		116	弟	dì	(6)
81	船	chuán	(14)		117	第	dì	(11)
82	窗	chuāng	(12)		118	点	diǎn	(4)
83	床	chuáng	(12)		119	电	diàn	(3)
84	春	chūn	(9)		120	店	diàn	(12)
85	词	cí	(19)		121	顶	dǐng	(13)
86	次	cì	(9)		122	订	dìng	(15)
87	聪	cōng	(13)		123	东	dōng	(2)
88	从	cóng	(4)		124	冬	dōng	(7)
89	粗	cū	(14)		125	懂	dǒng	(10)
90	村	cūn	(8)		126	动	dòng	(14)
91	寸	cùn	(4)		127	都	dōu	(9)
92	错	cuò	(11)		128	都	dū	(20)
		D			129	读	dú	(17)
93	答	dá	(11)		130	肚	dù	(9)
94	打	dǎ	(10)		131	短	duǎn	(20)
95	大	dà	(1)		132	断	duàn	(19)
96	代	dài	(19)		133	锻	duàn	(11)
97	带	dài	(14)		134	堆	duī	(18)
98	袋	dài	(12)		135	队	duì	(9)
99	当	dāng	(7)		136	对	duì	(8)

#	汉字	拼音	页码
137	多	duō	(7)
138	躲	duǒ	(13)

E

#	汉字	拼音	页码
139	饿	è	(11)
140	儿	ér	(3)
141	而	ér	(17)
142	耳	ěr	(13)
143	二	èr	(1)

F

#	汉字	拼音	页码
144	发	fā	(19)
145	法	fǎ	(9)
146	发	fà	(20)
147	反	fǎn	(6)
148	饭	fàn	(11)
149	方	fāng	(7)
150	房	fáng	(12)
151	访	fǎng	(15)
152	放	fàng	(12)
153	飞	fēi	(3)
154	非	fēi	(7)
155	费	fèi	(14)
156	分	fēn	(4)
157	粉	fěn	(14)
158	份	fèn	(15)
159	丰	fēng	(1)
160	风	fēng	(5)
161	夫	fū	(1)
162	服	fú	(9)
163	幅	fú	(17)
164	福	fú	(17)
165	辅	fǔ	(14)
166	父	fù	(6)
167	附	fù	(9)
168	复	fù	(7)
169	副	fù	(17)
170	富	fù	(14)

G

#	汉字	拼音	页码
171	该	gāi	(8)
172	干	gān	(20)
173	赶	gǎn	(14)
174	感	gǎn	(10)
175	干	gàn	(4)
176	刚	gāng	(10)
177	纲	gāng	(17)
178	钢	gāng	(11)
179	高	gāo	(7)
180	糕	gāo	(18)
181	告	gào	(13)
182	哥	gē	(7)
183	歌	gē	(12)
184	个	gè	(1)
185	各	gè	(4)
186	给	gěi	(10)
187	根	gēn	(15)
188	跟	gēn	(11)
189	工	gōng	(1)
190	公	gōng	(6)
191	功	gōng	(15)
192	共	gòng	(6)
193	狗	gǒu	(11)
194	购	gòu	(17)
195	够	gòu	(9)
196	姑	gū	(17)
197	古	gǔ	(17)
198	骨	gǔ	(19)
199	故	gù	(17)
200	顾	gù	(13)
201	瓜	guā	(19)
202	刮	guā	(10)
203	挂	guà	(10)
204	关	guān	(6)
205	观	guān	(14)

#	字	拼音	页
206	馆	guǎn	(11)
207	惯	guàn	(10)
208	广	guǎng	(2)
209	规	guī	(14)
210	贵	guì	(14)
211	国	guó	(5)
212	果	guǒ	(16)
213	裹	guǒ	(16)
214	过	guò	(11)

H

#	字	拼音	页
215	还	hái	(11)
216	孩	hái	(5)
217	海	hǎi	(16)
218	害	hài	(18)
219	汉	Hàn	(4)
220	好	hǎo	(4)
221	号	hào	(9)
222	好	hào	(20)
223	喝	hē	(18)
224	禾	hé	(5)
225	合	hé	(9)
226	何	hé	(15)
227	和	hé	(5)
228	河	hé	(15)
229	盒	hé	(14)
230	吓	hè	(20)
231	贺	hè	(14)
232	黑	hēi	(10)
233	很	hěn	(8)
234	红	hóng	(10)
235	后	hòu	(6)
236	候	hòu	(17)
237	户	hù	(2)
238	花	huā	(11)
239	画	huà	(2)
240	话	huà	(8)
241	欢	huān	(12)
242	还	huán	(20)
243	环	huán	(18)
244	换	huàn	(19)
245	黄	huáng	(15)
246	回	huí	(7)
247	会	huì	(8)
248	婚	hūn	(17)
249	活	huó	(15)
250	火	huǒ	(2)
251	货	huò	(14)

J

#	字	拼音	页
252	圾	jī	(13)
253	机	jī	(5)
254	鸡	jī	(13)
255	基	jī	(13)
256	及	jí	(15)
257	级	jí	(15)
258	极	jí	(15)
259	急	jí	(10)
260	几	jǐ	(3)
261	己	jǐ	(3)
262	挤	jǐ	(10)
263	计	jì	(20)
264	记	jì	(15)
265	纪	jì	(15)
266	系	jì	(20)
267	绩	jì	(19)
268	家	jiā	(12)
269	假	jiǎ	(20)
270	架	jià	(10)
271	假	jià	(20)
272	间	jiān	(5)
273	简	jiǎn	(11)
274	见	jiàn	(4)
275	件	jiàn	(19)
276	江	jiāng	(9)
277	交	jiāo	(7)

#	字	pinyin	( )
278	郊	jiāo	(15)
279	教	jiāo	(12)
280	饺	jiǎo	(15)
281	叫	jiào	(8)
282	较	jiào	(14)
283	教	jiào	(20)
284	接	jiē	(19)
285	街	jiē	(12)
286	节	jié	(11)
287	洁	jié	(17)
288	结	jié	(17)
289	姐	jiě	(8)
290	解	jiě	(20)
291	介	jiè	(8)
292	界	jiè	(14)
293	巾	jīn	(14)
294	斤	jīn	(2)
295	今	jīn	(8)
296	紧	jǐn	(10)
297	进	jìn	(11)
298	近	jìn	(5)
299	京	Jīng	(7)
300	经	jīng	(10)
301	惊	jīng	(16)
302	睛	jīng	(11)
303	精	jīng	(15)
304	景	jǐng	(9)
305	净	jìng	(16)
306	境	jìng	(18)
307	静	jìng	(16)
308	镜	jìng	(18)
309	究	jiū	(12)
310	九	jiǔ	(3)
311	酒	jiǔ	(9)
312	旧	jiù	(4)
313	局	jú	(12)
314	剧	jù	(17)
315	据	jù	(17)
316	决	jué	(9)
317	觉	jué/jiào	(7)

K

#	字	pinyin	( )
318	咖	kā	(12)
319	开	kāi	(2)
320	看	kàn	(4)
321	考	kǎo	(7)
322	棵	kē	(16)
323	颗	kē	(16)
324	可	kě	(5)
325	渴	kě	(18)
326	克	kè	(6)
327	刻	kè	(4)
328	客	kè	(12)
329	课	kè	(8)
330	恐	kǒng	(20)
331	空	kòng/kōng	(12)
332	口	kǒu	(2)
333	哭	kū	(11)
334	裤	kù	(12)
335	会	kuài	(20)
336	块	kuài	(15)
337	快	kuài	(10)
338	筷	kuài	(15)
339	宽	kuān	(12)

L

#	字	pinyin	( )
340	垃	lā	(13)
341	来	lái	(6)
342	蓝	lán	(16)
343	篮	lán	(16)
344	览	lǎn	(14)
345	郎	láng	(17)
346	狼	láng	(17)
347	朗	lǎng	(17)
348	老	lǎo	(7)
349	乐	lè	(15)

350	了	le	(2)
351	类	lèi	(20)
352	累	lèi	(8)
353	冷	lěng	(9)
354	礼	lǐ	(12)
355	里	lǐ	(3)
356	理	lǐ	(14、20)
357	力	lì	(3)
358	历	lì	(5)
359	厉	lì	(19)
360	立	lì	(6)
361	俩	liǎ	(13)
362	联	lián	(13)
363	脸	liǎn	(9)
364	练	liàn	(16)
365	炼	liàn	(16)
366	凉	liáng	(9)
367	粮	liáng	(14)
368	两	liǎng	(7)
369	亮	liàng	(17)
370	辆	liàng	(14)
371	量	liàng	(20)
372	了	liǎo	(20)
373	邻	lín	(16)
374	林	lín	(7)
375	铃	líng	(16)
376	零	líng	(16)
377	领	lǐng	(16)
378	令	lìng	(16)
379	留	liú	(14)
380	流	liú	(19)
381	六	liù	(2)
382	楼	lóu	(10)
383	路	lù	(11)
384	绿	lǜ	(10)
385	轮	lún	(16)
386	论	lùn	(16)

		M	
387	妈	mā	(5)
388	马	mǎ	(3)
389	码	mǎ	(15)
390	骂	mà	(15)
391	吗	ma	(5)
392	买	mǎi	(2)
393	卖	mài	(6)
394	馒	mán	(17)
395	慢	màn	(17)
396	忙	máng	(10)
397	猫	māo	(11)
398	么	me	(6)
399	没	méi	(9)
400	每	měi	(6)
401	美	měi	(4)
402	妹	mèi	(8)
403	门	mén	(3)
404	们	men	(5)
405	米	mǐ	(14)
406	面	miàn	(3)
407	名	míng	(4)
408	明	míng	(4)
409	命	mìng	(16)
410	末	mò	(18)
411	母	mǔ	(6)
412	木	mù	(1)
413	目	mù	(2)
		N	
414	拿	ná	(10)
415	哪	nǎ	(8)
416	那	nà	(9)
417	奶	nǎi	(8)
418	男	nán	(5)
419	南	nán	(6)
420	呢	ne	(8)
421	能	néng	(9)

#	字	拼音	页	#	字	拼音	页
422	你	nǐ	(4)	458	瓶	píng	(19)
423	年	nián	(3)	459	破	pò	(13)
424	念	niàn	(10)			**Q**	
425	娘	niáng	(17)	460	七	qī	(3)
426	鸟	niǎo	(13)	461	期	qī	(9)
427	您	nín	(5)	462	齐	qí	(17)
428	牛	niú	(3)	463	其	qí	(15)
429	努	nǔ	(5)	464	骑	qí	(13)
430	女	nǚ	(3)	465	棋	qí	(15)
		P		466	旗	qí	(15)
431	爬	pá	(15)	467	起	qǐ	(5)
432	怕	pà	(10)	468	气	qì	(3)
433	拍	pāi	(18)	469	汽	qì	(5)
434	排	pái	(19)	470	器	qì	(12)
435	盘	pán	(14)	471	千	qiān	(1)
436	盼	pàn	(15)	472	前	qián	(6)
437	旁	páng	(15)	473	钱	qián	(11)
438	胖	pàng	(9)	474	浅	qiǎn	(17)
439	跑	pǎo	(11)	475	枪	qiāng	(17)
440	炮	pào	(16)	476	墙	qiáng	(13)
441	陪	péi	(9)	477	抢	qiǎng	(17)
442	配	pèi	(14)	478	切	qiē	(10)
443	盆	pén	(14)	479	且	qiě	(17)
444	朋	péng	(7)	480	青	qīng	(15)
445	批	pī	(16)	481	轻	qīng	(14)
446	屁	pì	(16)	482	清	qīng	(15)
447	篇	piān	(16)	483	情	qíng	(15)
448	便	pián	(20)	484	晴	qíng	(15)
449	骗	piàn	(13)	485	请	qǐng	(8)
450	飘	piāo	(17)	486	穷	qióng	(12)
451	票	piào	(17)	487	秋	qiū	(5)
452	漂	piào	(17)	488	球	qiú	(14)
453	贫	pín	(15)	489	区	qū	(5)
454	品	pǐn	(14)	490	取	qǔ	(13)
455	平	píng	(16)	491	去	qù	(6)
456	评	píng	(16)	492	全	quán	(8)
457	苹	píng	(16)	493	确	què	(20)

494	裙	qún	(18)		528	师	shī	(20)
495	群	qún	(13)		529	十	shí	(1)
		R			530	石	shí	(13)
496	让	ràng	(8)		531	时	shí	(9)
497	热	rè	(10)		532	识	shí	(8)
498	人	rén	(1)		533	实	shí	(18)
499	认	rèn	(8)		534	食	shí	(8)
500	日	rì	(2)		535	史	shǐ	(5)
501	容	róng	(12)		536	始	shǐ	(8)
502	肉	ròu	(19)		537	士	shì	(3)
503	弱	ruò	(20)		538	示	shì	(19)
		S			539	市	shì	(7)
504	三	sān	(1)		540	事	shì	(3)
505	伞	sǎn	(11)		541	试	shì	(8)
506	扫	sǎo	(10)		542	视	shì	(12)
507	色	sè	(10)		543	是	shì	(4)
508	森	sēn	(14)		544	适	shì	(11)
509	山	shān	(2)		545	室	shì	(12)
510	衫	shān	(12)		546	收	shōu	(12)
511	扇	shàn	(12)		547	手	shǒu	(2)
512	上	shàng	(1)		548	首	shǒu	(20)
513	烧	shāo	(10)		549	受	shòu	(19)
514	少	shǎo	(2)		550	瘦	shòu	(12)
515	少	shào	(20)		551	书	shū	(3)
516	绍	shào	(10)		552	输	shū	(14)
517	蛇	shé	(13)		553	数	shǔ	(12)
518	舍	shè	(8)		554	术	shù	(16)
519	谁	shéi/shuí	(18)		555	树	shù	(8)
520	身	shēn	(3)		556	数	shù	(20)
521	深	shēn	(9)		557	双	shuāng	(7)
522	什	shén	(6)		558	水	shuǐ	(3)
523	神	shén	(15)		559	睡	shuì	(11)
524	生	shēng	(1)		560	说	shuō	(8)
525	甥	shēng	(15)		561	思	sī	(10)
526	胜	shèng	(15)		562	四	sì	(3)
527	尸	shī	(2)		563	送	sòng	(11)
					564	宿	sù	(12)

汉字速成课本 Easy Way to Learn Chinese Characters

565	岁	suì	(13)			W	
566	孙	sūn	(5)	600	袜	wà	(12)
		T		601	歪	wāi	(13)
567	他	tā	(8)	602	外	wài	(4)
568	它	tā	(15)	603	完	wán	(12)
569	她	tā	(8)	604	玩	wán	(14)
570	太	tài	(1)	605	晚	wǎn	(9)
571	堂	táng	(7)	606	王	wáng	(3)
572	糖	táng	(14)	607	网	wǎng	(7)
573	躺	tǎng	(13)	608	往	wǎng	(8)
574	趟	tàng	(14)	609	忘	wàng	(10)
575	讨	tǎo	(16)	610	望	wàng	(14)
576	套	tào	(17)	611	违	wéi	(18)
577	特	tè	(13)	612	围	wéi	(11)
578	疼	téng	(12)	613	伟	wěi	(18)
579	踢	tī	(11)	614	尾	wěi	(18)
580	提	tí	(17)	615	为	wèi	(4)
581	题	tí	(13)	616	未	wèi	(18)
582	体	tǐ	(8)	617	位	wèi	(8)
583	天	tiān	(1)	618	慰	wèi	(19)
584	田	tián	(2)	619	文	wén	(1)
585	填	tián	(19)	620	闻	wén	(13)
586	条	tiáo	(7)	621	问	wèn	(5)
587	跳	tiào	(11)	622	我	wǒ	(2)
588	贴	tiē	(18)	623	屋	wū	(12)
589	厅	tīng	(5)	624	五	wǔ	(2)
590	听	tīng	(8)	625	午	wǔ	(1)
591	庭	tíng	(17)	626	务	wù	(7)
592	挺	tǐng	(17)	627	物	wù	(13)
593	通	tōng	(19)			X	
594	同	tóng	(5)	628	西	xī	(3)
595	头	tóu	(6)	629	希	xī	(14)
596	图	tú	(11)	630	析	xī	(19)
597	土	tǔ	(1)	631	息	xī	(4)
598	推	tuī	(18)	632	习	xí	(5)
599	脱	tuō	(17)	633	洗	xǐ	(9)

634	系	xì	(10)
635	虾	xiā	(13)
636	下	xià	(1)
637	吓	xià	(20)
638	夏	xià	(7)
639	先	xiān	(6)
640	鲜	xiān	(13)
641	现	xiàn	(14)
642	线	xiàn	(17)
643	相	xiāng	(8)
644	香	xiāng	(5)
645	厢	xiāng	(17)
646	箱	xiāng	(17)
647	想	xiǎng	(8)
648	象	xiàng	(10)
649	小	xiǎo	(2)
650	校	xiào	(10)
651	笑	xiào	(11)
652	些	xiē	(9)
653	写	xiě	(4)
654	血	xiě	(20)
655	谢	xiè	(8)
656	心	xīn	(2)
657	新	xīn	(17)
658	信	xìn	(8)
659	星	xīng	(15)
660	行	xíng	(7)
661	醒	xǐng	(14)
662	兴	xìng	(7)
663	幸	xìng	(17)
664	性	xìng	(15)
665	姓	xìng	(8)
666	兄	xiōng	(6)
667	休	xiū	(4)
668	学	xué	(7)
669	血	xuè	(20)

	Y		
670	鸭	yā	(13)
671	烟	yān	(10)
672	言	yán	(19)
673	研	yán	(13)
674	颜	yán	(13)
675	眼	yǎn	(11)
676	演	yǎn	(19)
677	扬	yáng	(17)
678	羊	yáng	(13)
679	阳	yáng	(9)
680	杨	yáng	(17)
681	洋	yáng	(16)
682	养	yǎng	(16)
683	氧	yǎng	(16)
684	样	yàng	(16)
685	药	yào	(11)
686	要	yào	(8)
687	也	yě	(3)
688	业	yè	(2)
689	页	yè	(13)
690	夜	yè	(19)
691	液	yè	(20)
692	一	yī	(1)
693	衣	yī	(12)
694	医	yī	(5)
695	宜	yí	(20)
696	乙	yǐ	(16)
697	已	yǐ	(3)
698	以	yǐ	(4)
699	椅	yǐ	(10)
700	亿	yì	(16)
701	艺	yì	(16)
702	忆	yì	(16)
703	易	yì	(9)
704	益	yì	(14)
705	意	yì	(8)

706	因	yīn	(5)
707	阴	yīn	(9)
708	音	yīn	(8)
709	应	yīng	(5)
710	英	yīng	(11)
711	迎	yíng	(11)
712	影	yǐng	(16)
713	泳	yǒng	(9)
714	用	yòng	(7)
715	优	yōu	(18)
716	尤	yóu	(18)
717	由	yóu	(4)
718	邮	yóu	(9)
719	犹	yóu	(18)
720	游	yóu	(9)
721	友	yǒu	(6)
722	有	yǒu	(6)
723	又	yòu	(3)
724	右	yòu	(6)
725	于	yú	(4)
726	鱼	yú	(13)
727	雨	yǔ	(6)
728	语	yǔ	(8)
729	育	yù	(9)
730	预	yù	(13)
731	豫	yù	(18)
732	元	yuán	(6)
733	园	yuán	(11)
734	原	yuán	(18)
735	圆	yuán	(9)
736	源	yuán	(18)
737	远	yuǎn	(11)
738	院	yuàn	(9)
739	愿	yuàn	(18)
740	约	yuē	(19)
741	月	yuè	(3)
742	乐	yuè	(20)
743	阅	yuè	(17)
744	越	yuè	(14)
745	云	yún	(2)

Z

746	在	zài	(6)
747	遭	zāo	(18)
748	糟	zāo	(18)
749	早	zǎo	(9)
750	澡	zǎo	(9)
751	怎	zěn	(10)
752	窄	zhǎi	(12)
753	粘	zhān	(18)
754	展	zhǎn	(12)
755	占	zhàn	(18)
756	战	zhàn	(18)
757	站	zhàn	(18)
758	长	zhǎng	(20)
759	着	zháo	(20)
760	找	zhǎo	(10)
761	照	zhào	(10)
762	折	zhé	(19)
763	者	zhě	(7)
764	这	zhè	(5)
765	着	zhe	(13)
766	珍	zhēn	(18)
767	诊	zhěn	(18)
768	争	zhēng	(16)
769	整	zhěng	(17)
770	正	zhèng	(3)
771	证	zhèng	(17)
772	政	zhèng	(17)
773	支	zhī	(6)
774	知	zhī	(9)
775	织	zhī	(17)
776	直	zhí	(6)
777	值	zhí	(18)
778	职	zhí	(13)

779	植	zhí	(18)	800	住	zhù	(8)
780	只	zhǐ/zhī	(6)	801	祝	zhù	(12)
781	纸	zhǐ	(10)	802	爪	zhuǎ	(19)
782	志	zhì	(10)	803	专	zhuān	(18)
783	治	zhì	(17)	804	转	zhuǎn	(18)
784	置	zhì	(18)	805	传	zhuàn	(18)
785	中	zhōng	(2)	806	桌	zhuō	(10)
786	钟	zhōng	(11)	807	仔	zǐ	(2)
787	衷	zhōng	(16)	808	自	zì	(2)
788	种	zhǒng	(20)	809	字	zì	(4)
789	众	zhòng	(14)	810	租	zū	(17)
790	种	zhòng	(20)	811	组	zǔ	(17)
791	重	zhòng	(20)	812	祖	zǔ	(17)
792	舟	zhōu	(14)	813	最	zuì	(9)
793	周	zhōu	(7)	814	醉	zuì	(14)
794	朱	Zhū	(18)	815	昨	zuó	(9)
795	珠	zhū	(18)	816	左	zuǒ	(6)
796	猪	zhū	(11)	817	作	zuò	(8)
797	竹	zhú	(7)	818	坐	zuò	(12)
798	主	zhǔ	(1)	819	座	zuò	(12)
799	助	zhù	(14)	820	做	zuò	(8)

补充生字总表

（括号内是课号）

821	步	bù	（11）		840	商	shāng	（12）
822	晨	chén	（9）		841	社	shè	（8）
823	抽	chōu	（10）		842	世	shì	（14）
824	磁	cí	（14）		843	诉	sù	（13）
825	导	dǎo	（14）		844	台	tái	（12）
826	典	diǎn	（4）		845	舞	wǔ	（11）
827	啡	fēi	（12）		846	误	wù	（11）
828	封	fēng	（8）		847	向	xiàng	（7）
829	互	hù	（8）		848	相	xiàng	（10）
830	寄	jì	（8）		849	赢	yíng	（14）
831	加	jiā	（8）		850	永	yǒng	（11）
832	举	jǔ	（7）		851	运	yùn	（14）
833	旅	lǚ	（7）		852	杂	zá	（10）
834	毛	máo	（11）		853	再	zài	（4）
835	冒	mào	（10）		854	张	zhāng	（10）
836	内	nèi	（12）		855	注	zhù	（8）
837	啤	pí	（9）		856	总	zǒng	（4）
838	浅	qiǎn	（9）		857	走	zǒu	（3）
839	亲	qīn	（6）		858	足	zú	（9）

形旁总表

偏旁 Radical	义类 Meaning	例字 Example	位置 Position	偏旁 Radical	义类 Meaning	例字 Example	位置 Position
亻	person	他	L*	穴	cave	空	T
彳	street	往	L	广	room	床	T、L
口	mouth	叫和号	F	疒	illness	病	T、L
讠	speaking;	说	L	尸	room; body	屋尾	T、L
	knowledge	识	L	户	door	房	T、L
女	female	姐要	F	衣	cloth	袋	B
人	person	会	T	衤	cloth	裤	L
冫	cold	冰	L	礻	pray, bless	祝	L
氵	water	江	L	欠	mood	歌	R
日	sun; time	晚早春	F	攵	action	放	R
月	time; light	期	R	土	soil	地基走	L、B、T
	body	肚肾	L、B	石	stone	破	L、B、T
阝	fenced	院	L	山	hill	岸岛岭	F
	city; area	那	R	身	body	躺	L
木	trees	楼桌	F	耳	ear	闻取聂	F
手	hand	拿	B	页	head	顶	R
扌	hand	打	L	马	horse	骑驾	L、B、R
纟	silk	纸	L	牛	ox	物	L
幺	silk	累	M	羊	sheep; goat	群着	R、T
刀	knife	分切	B、R	虫	insect	虾	L、B、R
刂	knife	到	R	鱼	fish	鲜鲨	L、B、R
夕	knife	色	T	鸟	bird	鸡	R、B、L
火	fire	烧炎	L、B、R	王	jade	玩望	L、B
灬	fire	热	B	贝	money	贵购	L、B
心	thinking	忘	B	皿	vessel	盒	B
忄	feeling	忙	L	酉	alcohol	酒醉酱	L、B、R
辶	walk; road	进远	L、B	车	vehicle	辆	L
囗	border	图	O	舟	boat	船盘	L、T
钅	metal	钱	L	田	farm	界留略	L、B
饣	food	饭	L	米	grain	粮	L、B、T
犭	animal	狗	L	走	run	赶	L、B
目	eyes	眼看泪	L、B、R	见	look	览观	R、B
足	feet	跑	L	力	strength	动务加	R、B、L
艹	grass	花	T	巾	cloth	带	L、B
竹	bamboo	笔	T				
宀	roof	家	T				

* 注：B—bottom, F—free, L—left, M—middle, O—outside, R—right, T—top

声旁总表

偏旁 Radical	例字 Example	字音 Pronunciation	偏旁 Radical	例字 Example	字音 Pronunciation
巴	爸吧把 / 爬	ba / pa	比	毕 / 批屁	bi / pi
马	吗妈码骂	ma	古	故姑	gu
圣	经 / 轻	jing / qing	良	郎狼朗 / 娘	lang / niang
可	河何	he	吉	结洁	jie
方	访 / 旁	fang / pang	票	飘漂	piao
青	清请情晴 / 精	qing / jing	戋	浅 / 线	qian / xian
及	级极	ji	畐	福幅副	fu
艮	跟根	gen	居	剧据	ju
交	较郊饺 / 校	jiao / xiao	正	整证政	zheng
己	记纪	ji	廷	庭挺	ting
夬	快块筷	kuai	曼	慢馒	man
舌	话 / 活	hua / huo	兑	说 / 脱 / 阅	shuo / tuo / yue
采	彩菜	cai	且	租组祖	zu
生	姓星性 / 胜甥	xing / sheng	相	箱厢	xiang
其	期棋旗	qi	冈	刚纲	gang
工	江 / 红 / 空 / 功	jiang / hong / kong / gong	易	扬杨	yang
丁	订顶 / 厅 / 灯	ding / ting / deng	仓	枪抢	qiang
分	份 / 盼 / 贫	fen / pan / pin	隹	谁 / 堆 / 推	shei、shui / dui / tui
令	领零铃 / 邻	ling / lin	白	伯 / 怕 / 拍	bo / pa / pai
氐	低底	di	原	源愿	yuan
监	蓝篮	lan	君	群裙	qun
羊	洋养氧样	yang	曷	喝 / 渴	he / ke
京	惊景 / 影	jing / ying	竟	镜境	jing
东	练炼	lian	专	传转	zhuan
扁	遍 / 篇	bian / pian	直	植值置	zhi
乙	艺亿忆	yi	占	站战粘	zhan
果	课棵颗	ke	成	诚盛	cheng
仑	轮论	lun	韦	伟违	wei
争	净静	jing	㐱	珍诊 / 趁	zhen / chen
平	评苹	ping	尤	优犹	you
包	抱 / 炮	bao / pao	曹	遭糟	zao

SECOND EDITION

EASY WAY TO LEARN CHINESE CHARACTERS

柳燕梅　编著
刘林军　翻译

汉字速成课本 | 第 2 版

汉字练习本
WORKBOOK

目 录 CONTENTS

1 第一课　Lesson One
　　一、同步练习　Synchronous exercises ·········· 1
　　二、本课复习　Review ·········· 6

2 第二课　Lesson Two
　　一、同步练习　Synchronous exercises ·········· 8
　　二、本课复习　Review ·········· 15

3 第三课　Lesson Three
　　一、同步练习　Synchronous exercises ·········· 17
　　二、本课复习　Review ·········· 24

4 第四课　Lesson Four
　　一、同步练习　Synchronous exercises ·········· 26
　　二、本课复习　Review ·········· 33

5 第五课　Lesson Five
　　一、同步练习　Synchronous exercises ·········· 35
　　二、本课复习　Review ·········· 41

6 第六课　Lesson Six
　　一、同步练习　Synchronous exercises ·········· 44
　　二、本课复习　Review ·········· 50

7 第七课　Lesson Seven
　　一、同步练习　Synchronous exercises ·········· 53
　　二、本课复习　Review ·········· 60

8	第八课	Lesson Eight	
	一、同步练习	Synchronous exercises	62
	二、本课复习	Review	72
9	第九课	Lesson Nine	
	一、同步练习	Synchronous exercises	74
	二、本课复习	Review	83
10	第十课	Lesson Ten	
	一、同步练习	Synchronous exercises	86
	二、本课复习	Review	96
11	第十一课	Lesson Eleven	
	一、同步练习	Synchronous exercises	98
	二、本课复习	Review	109
12	第十二课	Lesson Twelve	
	一、同步练习	Synchronous exercises	111
	二、本课复习	Review	121
13	第十三课	Lesson Thirteen	
	一、同步练习	Synchronous exercises	123
	二、本课复习	Review	133
14	第十四课	Lesson Fourteen	
	一、同步练习	Synchronous exercises	135
	二、本课复习	Review	145
15	第十五课	Lesson Fifteen	
	一、同步练习	Synchronous exercises	147
	二、本课复习	Review	155

目 录 CONTENTS

16 第十六课 Lesson Sixteen
一、同步练习 Synchronous exercises ·········· 158
二、本课复习 Review ·········· 166

17 第十七课 Lesson Seventeen
一、同步练习 Synchronous exercises ·········· 169
二、本课复习 Review ·········· 178

18 第十八课 Lesson Eighteen
一、同步练习 Synchronous exercises ·········· 181
二、本课复习 Review ·········· 189

19 第十九课 Lesson Nineteen
一、同步练习 Synchronous exercises ·········· 191
二、本课复习 Review ·········· 197

20 第二十课 Lesson Twenty
一、同步练习 Synchronous exercises ·········· 199
二、本课复习 Review ·········· 205

第一课
Lesson One

一、同步练习　Synchronous exercises

① 根据拼音写笔画　Write the strokes according to the *pinyin*

Héng　(　　)　　　　　　Piě　(　　)
Diǎnr　(　　)　　　　　　Shù　(　　)
Nà　(　　)　　　　　　　Tí　(　　)

② 用拼音写出下列笔画的名称　Give the *pinyin* for the following strokes

丶 _____　　一 _____　　丶 _____

丿 _____　　丨 _____　　㇀ _____

③ 写一写　Writing exercise

yī 一

èr 二

sān 三

shí 十

gōng 工

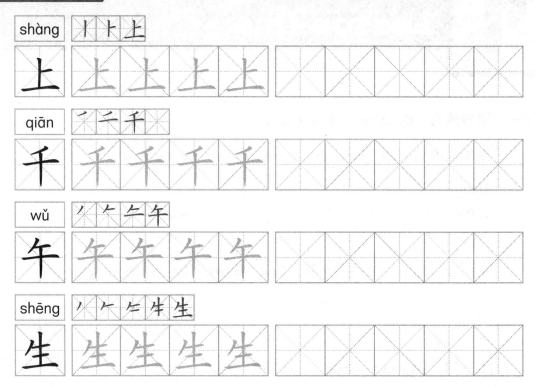

4. 大声朗读下面的词语　Read aloud the following words

十一（11）　　十三（13）　　二十（20）　　三十（30）

二十一（21）　三十二（32）　一千（1000）　三千（3000）

5. 用汉字写出下列数字　Rewrite the following figures in Chinese characters

10（　　　　）　12（　　　　）　22（　　　　）

23（　　　　）　31（　　　　）　33（　　　　）

6. 根据拼音写汉字　Write the Chinese characters according to the *pinyin*

7. 写一写　Writing exercise

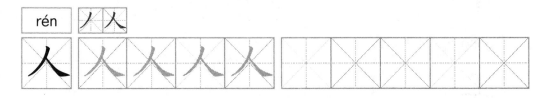

第一课 Lesson One

⑧ 大声朗读下面的词和短语，并记住它们的意思
Read aloud the following words and phrases and remember their meanings

上午（morning） 工人（worker）
下午（afternoon） 主人（host）
一个（one ...） 一个人（one person）
八个（eight ...） 八个人（eight people）

⑨ 把下面的英语翻译成汉语，并用汉字写出来
Translate the following into Chinese

three workers（　　　） one morning（　　　）
eight workers（　　　） one afternoon（　　　）

⑩ 根据拼音写汉字　Write the Chinese characters according to the *pinyin*

shàngwǔ　　　　　　zhǔrén　　　　　　xiàwǔ

Easy Way to Learn Chinese Characters · Workbook

⑪ 写一写　Writing exercise

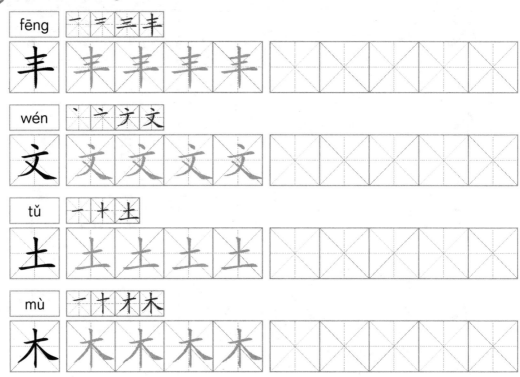

⑫ 按笔画顺序写出下面的汉字，想一想笔顺是否合规律

Write the following characters according to the rules of stroke order

下 _____　　个 _____

工 _____　　主 _____

千 _____

⑬ 写一写　Writing exercise

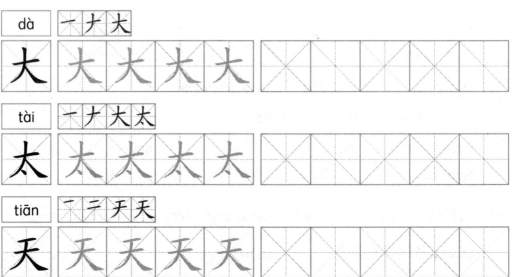

4

第一课 Lesson One

fū	一 二 ヲ 夫

夫 夫 夫 夫 夫

⑭ 大声朗读下面的词和短语，并记住它们的意思
Read aloud the following words and phrases and remember their meanings

大人（adult）　　　　一天（one day）　　　太大（too big）

夫人（madam）　　　三天（three days）　　不大（not big）

大夫 dàifu（doctor）　八天（eight days）　　不太大（not too big）

⑮ 把下面的英语翻译成汉语，并用汉字写出来
Translate the following into Chinese

10 days （　　　　　　）　　11 doctors （　　　　　　）

18 days （　　　　　　）　　12 doctors （　　　　　　）

88 days （　　　　　　）　　30 adults （　　　　　　）

⑯ 按笔画顺序写出下面的汉字，并写出笔画数
Write the following characters in proper stroke order and give the number of strokes

例（For example）：木（4画）<u>一 十 才 木</u>

太（　画）_____　　　夫（　画）_____

天（　画）_____　　　文（　画）_____

⑰ 用拼音写出下面汉字中第二笔的笔画名称
Write in *pinyin* the name of the second stroke in each of the following characters

例（For example）：木（Shù）

上（　　　　）　　个（　　　　）　　不（　　　　）

土（　　　　）　　丰（　　　　）　　太（　　　　）

Easy Way to Learn Chinese Characters · Workbook

二、本课复习　Review

一	二	三	十	工	上	千	午
生	人	八	个	下	不	主	丰
文	土	木	大	太	天	夫	

① 按笔画数量把上面的汉字写在下面的括号里
Write the above characters in the following brackets according to the number of strokes

1 画（　　　　　　　　　　　　　　）

2 画（　　　　　　　　　　　　　　）

3 画（　　　　　　　　　　　　　　）

4 画（　　　　　　　　　　　　　　）

5 画（　　　　　　　　　　　　　　）

② 用拼音写出下列笔画的名称，并将含有下列笔画的汉字写在相应的括号里，每个括号里至少写四个
Write in *pinyin* the names of the strokes below and write at least four Chinese characters consisting of the strokes in the corresponding brackets

例（For example）：一　Héng　（一、二、三、十、工）

丨　_____（　　　　　　　　　　　　　　）

丿　_____（　　　　　　　　　　　　　　）

丶　_____（　　　　　　　　　　　　　　）

㇏　_____（　　　　　　　　　　　　　　）

③ 用拼音写出下列笔画的名称，并将笔顺中第三笔是如下笔画的汉字写在相应的括号里
Write the name of the strokes in *pinyin* and write in the corresponding brackets the characters whose third strokes are the same as given

一　_____（　　　　　　　　　　　　　　）

丨　_____（　　　　　　　　　　　　　　）

ノ＿＿＿＿（　　　　　　　）
丶＿＿＿＿（　　　　　　　）
、＿＿＿＿（　　　　　　　）

④ 给下面的汉字注音并写出英文（或你的母语）意思

Write the *pinyin* transcription and the meaning in English or your native language for each of the following characters

例（For example）：人 <u>rén</u>（person）

午＿＿＿＿（　　　　　）　　千＿＿＿＿（　　　　　）
主＿＿＿＿（　　　　　）　　丰＿＿＿＿（　　　　　）
文＿＿＿＿（　　　　　）　　夫＿＿＿＿（　　　　　）

⑤ 根据拼音写汉字，并想想它们的意思

Write the Chinese characters according to the *pinyin* and think about their meanings

shàngwǔ ▭▭▭▭　　gōngrén ▭▭▭▭　　dàifu ▭▭▭▭
xiàwǔ ▭▭▭▭　　zhǔrén ▭▭▭▭　　bā tiān ▭▭▭▭

2 第二课
Lesson Two

一、同步练习　Synchronous exercises

① 写一写　Writing exercise

běn　一十才木本
本　本本本本

shǎo　丨卜小少
少　少少少少

liù　丶一六六
六　六六六六

jīn　丿厂斤斤
斤　斤斤斤斤

kāi　一二于开
开　开开开开

② 根据拼音写笔画　Write the strokes according to the *pinyin*

Zuǒdiǎnr （　　　　　）　　　Chángdiǎnr （　　　　　）
Píngpiě　（　　　　　）　　　Shùpiě　　（　　　　　）

③ 把下面的英语翻译成汉语，并用汉字写出来
Translate the following into Chinese

six days　　　　（　　　　　）　　half a kilogram （　　　　　）
sixty-two persons（　　　　　）　　three kilograms （　　　　　）

not little （　　　　　）　　　too little　　（　　　　　）
not open　（　　　　　）　　　not too little　（　　　　　）

4 按笔画顺序写出下面的汉字，并写出笔画数
Write the following characters in proper stroke order and give the number of strokes

例（For example）：太（4画）一ナ大太

本（　画）_____　　开（　画）_____

少（　画）_____　　斤（　画）_____

5 写一写　Writing exercise

| kǒu | 丨 冂 口 |
| 口 | 口 口 口 口 |

| wǔ | 一 丆 五 五 |
| 五 | 五 五 五 五 |

| shān | 丨 凵 山 |
| 山 | 山 山 山 山 |

| chū | 𠃍 屮 中 出 出 |
| 出 | 出 出 出 出 |

| chē | 一 𠂇 车 车 |
| 车 | 车 车 车 车 |

| yún | 一 二 云 云 |
| 云 | 云 云 云 云 |

6 大声朗读下面的词和短语，并记住它们的意思
Read aloud the following words and phrases and remember their meanings

五口人（five persons in a family）　　出口（exit; export）

六口人（six persons in a family）　　出生（be born）

上山（go up the hill）　　上车（get on a car）

下山（go down the hill）　　下车（get off a car）

山上（on the hill）　　车上（on the car）

山下（on the foot of the hill）　　车下（under the car）

7 用汉字写出下面的数字
Rewrite the following figures in Chinese characters

15（　　　　　）　　61（　　　　　）
55（　　　　　）　　66（　　　　　）
58（　　　　　）　　60（　　　　　）

8 用拼音写出下面汉字中第二笔的笔画名称
Write in *pinyin* the names of the second stroke in each of the following characters

例（For example）：大（Piě）

口（　　　　）　　山（　　　　）　　云（　　　　）

斤（　　　　）　　少（　　　　）　　五（　　　　）

9 写一写　Writing exercise

dōng	一 𠃍 车 东 东
东	东 东 东 东

le	乛 了
了	了 了 了 了

mǎi	一 𠃍 乛 乛 乛 买 买
买	买 买 买 买

wǒ	一 二 于 于 我 我 我
我	我 我 我 我

xīn	丶 心 心 心
心	心 心 心 心

⑩ 大声朗读下面的词和短语，并记住它们的意思
Read aloud the following words and phrases and remember their meanings

小心（careful）　　　买了（bought）
开心（happy）　　　买不买（buy or not）

⑪ 把下面的英语翻译成汉语，并用汉字写出来
Translate the following into Chinese

small car　（　　）　　small hand　（　　）
big car　（　　）　　big hand　（　　）
not happy　（　　）　　be happy or not　（　　）
not careful　（　　）

⑫ 根据拼音写笔画　Write the strokes according to the *pinyin*

Chángdiǎnr（　　）　Píngpiě（　　）　Wāngōu（　　）
Piězhé（　　）　Xiégōu（　　）　Shùpiě（　　）

Easy Way to Learn Chinese Characters · Workbook

⑬ 用拼音写出下列笔画的名称，并将含有下列笔画的汉字写在相应的括号里，每个括号里至少写四个

Write in *pinyin* the names of the strokes below and write at least four Chinese characters consisting of the strokes in the corresponding brackets

例（For example）： 一 __Héng__ （一、二、三、十、工）

丨 _____ (   )

丿 _____ (   )

㇏ _____ (   )

丶 _____ (   )

⑭ 写一写　Writing exercise

| rì | 丨 冂 日 日 |
| 日 |

| tián | 丨 冂 日 田 田 |
| 田 |

| huà | 一 ｢ 厂 雨 画 画 画 |
| 画 |

| yè | 丨 丨丨 丨丨丨 业 业 |
| 业 |

| zhōng | 丨 冂 口 中 |
| 中 |

| zǐ | ㇇ 了 子 |
| 子 |

| huǒ | 丶 丷 火 火 |

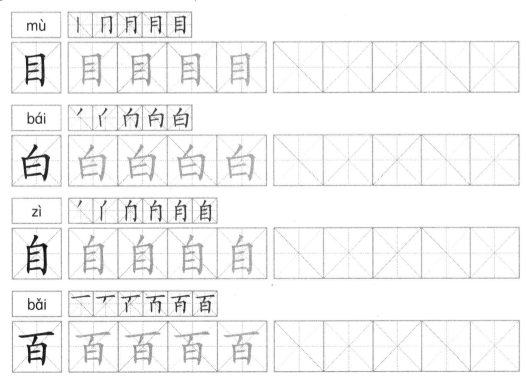

⑮ 大声朗读下面的词和短语，并记住它们的意思
　　Read aloud the following words and phrases and remember their meanings

个子（height; stature）　　画了（drew）
本子（notebook）　　　　　不画（not draw）
生日（birthday）　　　　　　画不画（draw or not）
日本（Japan）

⑯ 按笔画顺序写出下面的汉字，并写出笔画数
　　Write the following characters in proper stroke order and give the number of strokes

五（　　画）_____　　买（　　画）_____
出（　　画）_____　　我（　　画）_____
车（　　画）_____　　心（　　画）_____

⑰ 写一写　Writing exercise

| mù | 丨 冂 冃 月 目 |

| bái | 丿 亻 白 白 白 |

| zì | 丿 亻 冂 自 自 自 |

| bǎi | 一 丆 刁 百 百 百 |

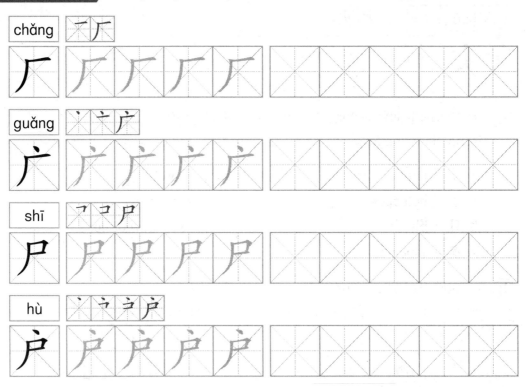

18 大声朗读下面的词和短语，并记住它们的意思
Read aloud the following words and phrases and remember their meanings

白天（daytime）　　　　　工厂（factory）

自己（oneself）　　　　　广大（vast）

* 己 jǐ（self）

一百一十（110）　　　　　三百一十六（316）

一百零四（104）　　　　　九百七十二（972）

* 零 líng（zero）

19 用汉字写出下面的数字　Rewrite the following figures in Chinese

583（　　　　　　　）　　820（　　　　　　　）

610（　　　　　　　）　　605（　　　　　　　）

20 给下面的汉字添一笔，使它成为另一个字，看看你能写出几个

Add one stroke and make each character a different one. How many can you get for each?

例（For example）：十——土

口——   日——

头——   大——

二、本课复习　Review

本	少	六	斤	开	口	五	山
出	车	云	小	手	东	了	买
我	心	日	田	画	业	中	子
火	目	白	自	百	厂	广	户
户							
(*己)①		(*零)					

① 把上面汉字中符合下列笔画数的写在相应的括号里，至少写四个

Write in the corresponding brackets at least four characters listed above that have the same number of strokes as indicated

3 画（　　　　　　　）　　4 画（　　　　　　　）

② 用拼音写出笔画的名称，并把含有下列笔画的汉字写在相应的括号里，至少写三个

Write the name of the stroke in *pinyin* and write the characters consisting of the stroke in the corresponding brackets

㇇：＿＿＿＿（　　　　）　　乚：＿＿＿＿（　　　　）

一：＿＿＿＿（　　　　）　　丿：＿＿＿＿（　　　　）

---

① 加＊的为"补充生字"；加括号表示这些字会在以后的课文中正式学习，因此不列入"补充生字总表"；不加括号的将列入"补充生字总表"。

③ 按笔画顺序写出下面的汉字，并写出笔画数
Write the following characters in proper stroke order and give the number of strokes

自（　画）_____　　田（　画）_____
买（　画）_____　　手（　画）_____
心（　画）_____　　我（　画）_____

④ 给下面的汉字注音并写出英文（或你的母语）意思
Write the *pinyin* transcription and the meaning in English or your native language for each of the following characters

例（For example）：大　<u>dà</u>　（ big ）

车_____（　　　）　　买_____（　　　）
我_____（　　　）　　出_____（　　　）
田_____（　　　）　　心_____（　　　）

⑤ 按要求给下面的汉字添笔画，使它变成另一个汉字
Add strokes to the following characters as required and make them different characters

例（For example）：一（2笔）　<u>三　大　千　工</u>

二（2笔）_____
人（2笔）_____
日（2笔）_____
厂（1笔）_____

⑥ 根据拼音写汉字，并想想它们的意思
Write the Chinese characters according to the *pinyin* and think about their meanings

liù jīn　▭　　chūkǒu　▭　　shàng chē　▭
bù shǎo　▭　　chūshēng　▭　　xià chē　▭
xiǎoxīn　▭　　shēngrì　▭　　gōngchǎng　▭
kāixīn　▭　　běnzi　▭　　báitiān　▭

3 第三课
Lesson Three

一、同步练习 Synchronous exercises

① 根据已经学过的笔画名称，用拼音写出下面复合笔画的名称
Write in *pinyin* the names of the following complex strokes

㇆（   ）　　　㇄（   ）
㇇（   ）　　　㇆（   ）
㇉（   ）　　　㇋（   ）

② 数一数下面的汉字一共有多少画
Count the number of strokes in each of the following Chinese characters

马（   画）　女（   画）　及（   画）　乃（   画）
专（   画）　队（   画）　水（   画）　计（   画）

③ 写一写 Writing exercise

yòu 又
水 shuǐ
月 yuè
门 mén

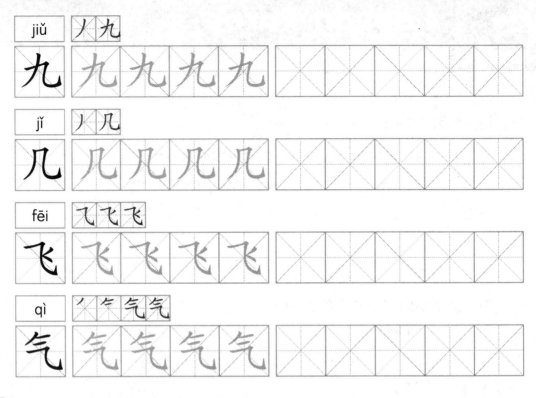

4 大声朗读下面的词和短语，并记住它们的意思
Read aloud the following words and phrases and remember their meanings

九月（September）　　　　门口（entrance; doorway）
几月（which month）　　　 大门（gate; front door）
九个月（nine months）　　　天气（weather）
几个月（a few months）　　 生气（angry）
上个月（last month）　　　 又飞了（flew away again）
下个月（next month）　　　 又买了（bought again）

5 把下面的英语翻译成汉语，并用汉字写出来
Translate the following into Chinese

January　　（　　　　）　　June　　　（　　　　）
February　（　　　　）　　November（　　　　）
May　　　 （　　　　）　　December（　　　　）

one month　　（　　　　）　　drew again　　（　　　　）
five months　（　　　　）　　bought again　（　　　　）
six months　　（　　　　）　　opened again　（　　　　）

18

6 用拼音写出下面汉字中第二笔的笔画名称
Write in *pinyin* the name of the second stroke in each of the following characters

车（　　　）　　水（　　　）　　月（　　　）
心（　　　）　　门（　　　）　　九（　　　）

7 给下面的汉字注音，并写出笔画数
Write the *pinyin* and number of strokes for each of the following characters

例（For example）：我　wǒ　（7画）

又　　　（　　画）　　几　　　（　　画）　　出　　　（　　画）
手　　　（　　画）　　田　　　（　　画）　　气　　　（　　画）

8 写一写　Writing exercise

| sì | 丨 冂 冂 四 四 |
| 四 | 四 四 四 四 |

| xī | 一 丆 冂 两 两 西 |
| 西 | 西 西 西 西 |

| ér | 丿 儿 |
| 儿 | 儿 儿 儿 儿 |

| qī | 一 七 |
| 七 | 七 七 七 七 |

| mǎ | 𠃍 马 马 |
| 马 | 马 马 马 马 |

Easy Way to Learn Chinese Characters · Workbook

cháng 丿 一 长 长
长 长 长 长 长

nǚ 〈 女 女
女 女 女 女 女

⑨ 大声朗读下面的词和短语，并记住它们的意思
Read aloud the following words and phrases and remember their meanings

儿子（son）　　画儿（drawing）　　画画儿（draw a picture）
女儿（daughter）　东西（thing）　　买东西（buy something）
女人（woman）　　马上（at once）　　马上走（go at once）
　　　　　　　　　　　　　　　　　＊走 zǒu（walk; go）

⑩ 根据拼音写汉字，并想想它们的意思
Write the characters according to the *pinyin* and think about their meanings

kāi mén　　　　　　mǎi huàr　　　　　　xiǎo mǎ
guān mén　　　　　　mǎshàng　　　　　　bái mǎ

jǐ ge nǚrén　　　　　xīmén
jǐ ge érzi　　　　　　dōngmén

⑪ 用拼音写出下面汉字中第三笔的笔画名称
Write in *pinyin* the name of the third stroke in each of the following characters

西（　　）　　水（　　）　　长（　　）
女（　　）　　门（　　）　　气（　　）

⑫ 按笔画顺序写出下面的汉字，并写出笔画数
Write the following characters in proper stroke order and give the number of strokes

四（　画）_____　　九（　画）_____
长（　画）_____　　女（　画）_____
月（　画）_____　　水（　画）_____

13 写一写 Writing exercise

shū 乛 乛 书 书
书 书 书 书 书

yě 乛 乛 也
也 也 也 也 也

diàn 丨 冂 冂 日 电
电 电 电 电 电

nián 丿 丿 ⺅ ⺅ 乍 年
年 年 年 年 年

lǐ 丨 冂 冂 日 甲 甲 里
里 里 里 里 里

shēn 丿 丿 冂 冃 身 身 身
身 身 身 身 身

miàn 一 丆 丆 丆 丙 而 而 面 面
面 面 面 面

shì 一 丆 丆 亘 亘 写 写 事
事 事 事 事 事

⑭ 大声朗读下面的词和短语，并记住它们的意思
Read aloud the following words and phrases and remember their meanings

一年（one year）　　　东面（east）
三年（three years）　　里面（inside）

大事（important matter）　电车（trolley）
小事（trifling matter）　　一本书（one book）

⑮ 根据拼音写汉字，并想想它们的意思
Write the characters according to the *pinyin* and think about their meanings

sì nián　　　　　　　shàngmiàn
qī nián　　　　　　　xiàmiàn
shísì nián　　　　　　sìmiàn
shíqī nián　　　　　　xīmiàn

⑯ 按笔画顺序写出下面的汉字，并写出笔画数
Write the following characters in proper stroke order and give the number of strokes

年（　画）_____　　面（　画）_____
里（　画）_____　　事（　画）_____
身（　画）_____

⑰ 写一写　Writing exercise

(18) 大声朗读下面的词和短语，并记住它们的意思
Read aloud the following words and phrases and remember their meanings

自己（oneself） 刀子（knife）
正门（main gate, front gate） 力气（strength）

(19) 根据拼音写汉字，并想想它们的意思
Write the characters according to the *pinyin* and think about their meanings

wǒ zìjǐ   xiǎo dāo   Xiǎo Wáng

lìqi dà   lìqi xiǎo

20 根据括号里的数目给汉字添笔画，使它成为另一个字，看看你能写出几个
Add one or two strokes as indicated to the character given below to make it different. How many characters can you get?

十（1笔）_____   十（2笔）_____

二、本课复习　Review

又	水	月	门	九	几	飞	气
四	西	儿	七	马	长	女	书
也	电	年	里	身	面	事	正
士	己	已	王	牛	刀	力	
*走							

1 用拼音写出下列笔画的名称，并将含有下列笔画的汉字写在相应的括号里
Write in *pinyin* the name of the stroke below and list the characters with the stroke in the corresponding brackets

例（For example）：㇆ Héngzhé （ 口 日 ）

丿 _____ （　　　　　）　　㇆ _____ （　　　　　）
乙 _____ （　　　　　）　　㇆ _____ （　　　　　）
㇏ _____ （　　　　　）　　亅 _____ （　　　　　）

2 按笔画顺序写出下面的汉字，并写出笔画数
Write the following characters in proper stroke order and give the number of strokes

水（　　画）_____　　电（　　画）_____
也（　　画）_____　　身（　　画）_____
门（　　画）_____　　事（　　画）_____

③ 给下列汉字注音并写出英文（或你的母语）意思
Write the *pinyin* transcription and the meaning in English or your native language for each of the following characters

刀_____（   ）　　力_____（   ）
午_____（   ）　　牛_____（   ）
土_____（   ）　　士_____（   ）
已_____（   ）　　己_____（   ）

④ 根据拼音写汉字，并想想它们的意思
Write the characters according to the *pinyin* and think about their meanings

tiānqì		nǚ'ér		zìjǐ	
shēngqì		ménkǒu		dōngxi	
diànchē		lǐmiàn		dāozi	
xiǎoshí		mǎshàng		lìqi	
jiǔ nián		shàng ge yuè			
zhèngmén		xià ge yuè			

⑤ 大声朗读下面的句子，并想想它们的意思
Read aloud the following sentences and think about their meanings

（1）我买了一斤水果（shuǐguǒ, fruit），我女儿又买了一斤。

（2）我画了一张（zhāng, *measure word for pictures*）画儿，小王也画了一张画儿。

（3）我女儿力气小，我儿子力气大。

（4）小王买了不少东西，我自己买了几本书。

第四课
Lesson Four

一、同步练习 Synchronous exercises

① 写一写 Writing exercise

měi	美
hǎo	好
xiū	休
kàn	看
cóng	从
míng	明
lín	林

fēn	ノ 八 分 分
分	分 分 分 分

② 大声朗读下面的词语，并记住它们的意思
Read aloud the following words and remember their meanings

美好（happy; fine） 明白（clear; understand） 身体（body）
好看（good-looking） 分开（separate） 明天（tomorrow）

③ 按笔画顺序写出下面的汉字，并写出笔画数
Write the following characters in proper stroke order and give the number of strokes

美（　画）_____　　看（　画）_____
好（　画）_____　　分（　画）_____

④ 写出下面的汉字有几个部件，分别是什么
Write components for each of the following characters and give the number of components

例（For example）：看（ 2 ）<u>手、目</u>

好（　）_____　　分（　）_____
明（　）_____　　体（　）_____

⑤ 写一写　Writing exercise

nǐ	ノ 亻 亻 你 你 你 你
你	你 你 你 你

Hàn	丶 丶 氵 汈 汉
汉	汉 汉 汉 汉

de	ノ 亻 白 白 白 的 的
的	的 的 的 的

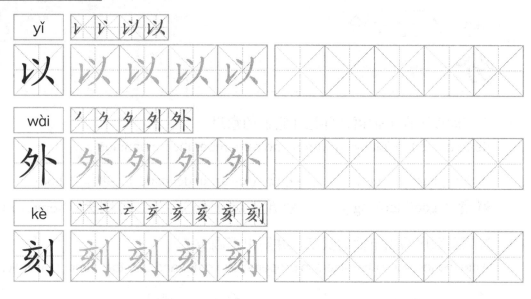

6 大声朗读下面的词和短语，并记住它们的意思
Read aloud the following words and phrases and remember their meanings

你的（your; yours） 一刻（one quarter）
我的（my; mine） 三刻（three quarters）

以上（above; over） 以外（beyond; outside）
以下（below; under） 外面（outside）

7 根据拼音写汉字，并想想它们的意思
Write the characters according to the *pinyin* and think about their meanings

nǐ zìjǐ   nǐ de érzi

wǒ zìjǐ   wǒ de nǚ'ér

sān ge yǐshàng   chē wàimiàn

wǔ ge yǐxià   dōngmén wàimiàn

8 按笔画顺序写出下面的汉字
Write the following characters in proper stroke order

你：_____   的：_____

以：_____   刻：_____

9 写一写 Writing exercise

zì	字
xiě	写
shì	是
míng	名
diǎn	点
xī	息

10 大声朗读下面的词和短语，并记住它们的意思
Read aloud the following words and phrases and remember their meanings

名字（name）　　　　　　一点儿（a little）
汉字（Chinese character）　点心（dessert; pastry）

大一点儿（a little bigger）　休息（have a rest）
小一点儿（a little smaller）　写好（finish writing）

总是（always）　　　　　　字典（dictionary）
* 总 zǒng（always）　　　 * 典 diǎn（standard work）

十一点（eleven o'clock） 三点一刻（three fifteen）
九点（nine o'clock） 四点三刻（four forty-five）
五点十八分（five eighteen） 六点半（six thirty）
七点四十分（seven forty） 十一点半（eleven thirty）
　　　　　　　　　　　　＊半 bàn（half）

⑪ 用汉字写出下面的时间　Write the time in Chinese characters

one fifteen　　（　　　）　　three twenty　　（　　　）
four forty-five　（　　　）　　five thirty　　（　　　）
six fifty　　　（　　　）　　seven fifty-eight（　　　）
eleven fifteen　（　　　）　　twelve thirty　　（　　　）

⑫ 根据拼音写汉字，并想想它们的意思
Write the characters according to the *pinyin* and think about their meanings

xiě Hànzì　　　　　　　　shǎo yìdiǎnr

xiě míngzi　　　　　　　cháng yìdiǎnr

xiūxi yíxià

xiūxi xiūxi

⑬ 写一写　Writing exercise

gàn　一二干
干 干干干干

yú　一二于
于 于于于于

bèi　丨冂贝贝
贝 贝贝贝贝

jiàn	丨 冂 见 见
见 见 见 见 见

cái	一 十 才
才 才 才 才 才

cùn	一 十 寸
寸 寸 寸 寸 寸

⑭ 大声朗读下面的词和短语，并记住它们的意思
Read aloud the following words and phrases and remember their meanings

看见 (see)　　　　见面 (meet)　　　　再见 (goodbye)
看见你 (see you)　　于是 (as a result; hence)　　*再 zài (again)

⑮ 根据括号里的要求给汉字添笔画，使它变成别的汉字，越多越好
Write as many characters as possible by adding two strokes to the strokes listed below

一（2笔）_____

亅（2笔）_____

⑯ 按笔画顺序写出下面的汉字，一边写，一边说出各笔画的名称
Write the following characters in proper stroke order, naming each stroke

贝：_____　　于：_____
见：_____　　才：_____

⑰ 写一写　Writing exercise

gè	丿 ク 夂 冬 各 各
各 各 各 各 各

chù	ノ ク 夂 处 处
处	处 处 处 处

bàn	ㄱ 力 办 办
办	办 办 办 办

wèi	丶 丿 为 为
为	为 为 为 为

jiù	丨 丨 旧 旧 旧
旧	旧 旧 旧 旧

yóu	丨 冂 日 由 由
由	由 由 由 由

⑱ 大声朗读下面的词和短语，并记住它们的意思
Read aloud the following words and phrases and remember their meanings

由于（since; due to）　　　各处（everywhere）
为了（in order to/that）　　各个（each; every）

⑲ 根据括号里的要求给汉字添笔画，使它变成别的汉字，越多越好
Write as many characters as possible by adding strokes as indicated in the brackets to the characters listed below

力（2笔）_____　　卜（3笔）_____
口（2笔）_____　　日（1笔）_____

⑳ 按笔画顺序写出下面的汉字
Write the following characters in proper stroke order

办：_____　　各：_____
为：_____　　处：_____

二、本课复习 Review

美	好	休	看	从	明	林	分
你	汉	的	以	外	刻	字	写
是	名	点	息	干	于	贝	见
才	寸	各	处	办	为	旧	由
*总	*典	(*半)	*再				

① 把上面的汉字写在下面相应的结构后
Group the above characters according to their structures

☐ : _____
☐ : _____
☐ : _____
☐ : _____
☐ : _____
☐ : _____

② 按笔画顺序写出下面的汉字，并写出笔画数
Write the following characters in proper stroke order and give the number of strokes

美（　　画）_____　　息（　　画）_____
好（　　画）_____　　外（　　画）_____
名（　　画）_____　　是（　　画）_____

③ 给下列汉字注音并写出英文（或你的母语）意思
Write the pinyin transcription and the meaning in English or your native language for each of the following characters

贝 _____ （　　　　） 　见 _____ （　　　　）
才 _____ （　　　　） 　寸 _____ （　　　　）
外 _____ （　　　　） 　处 _____ （　　　　）
为 _____ （　　　　） 　办 _____ （　　　　）

④ 根据拼音写汉字，并想想它们的意思

Write characters according to the *pinyin* and think about their meanings

hǎokàn　　　　　　shēntǐ　　　　　　xiūxi

míngbai　　　　　　míngtiān　　　　　míngzi

kànjiàn　　　　　　yóuyú

jiànmiàn　　　　　　wèile

⑤ 根据拼音写汉字，然后大声朗读，并想一想句子的意思

Write the characters according to the *pinyin* and read them aloud, paying attention to the meanings of the sentences

（1）Wǒ cái kànjiàn nǐ.

（2）Wǒ chūshēng yú yī jiǔ bā èr nián.

（3）Wǒ shíyī diǎn xiūxi.

（4）Nǐ jǐ diǎn xiūxi?

（5）Wǒ de shēngrì shì sìyuè shíjiǔ rì.

（6）Wǒ kànjiàn nǐ de jiù chē le.

（7）Wèile nǐ de shēntǐ, hǎohǎo xiūxi.

第五课
Lesson Five

一、同步练习 Synchronous exercises

1. 写一写 Writing exercise

mā	乚 ㄅ 女 奵 妈 妈

妈 妈 妈 妈 妈

men	ノ 亻 仃 仃 们

们 们 们 们 们

ma	丨 口 口 吖 吗 吗

吗 吗 吗 吗 吗

qì	丶 丶 氵 氵 汽 汽 汽

汽 汽 汽 汽 汽

jī	一 十 才 木 机 机

机 机 机 机 机

nín	ノ 亻 仃 仃 你 你 你 您 您 您

您 您 您 您 您

jìn	丶 厂 斤 斤 沂 近 近

近 近 近 近 近

② 大声朗读下面的词和短语，并记住它们的意思
Read aloud the following words and phrases and remember their meanings

飞机（plane）　　我们（we; us）　　太近了（too close）
汽车（car）　　　你们（you）　　　不近（not close）
妈妈（mom）　　　您好（Hello）

③ 根据拼音写汉字，然后大声朗读，并想一想句子的意思
Write the characters according to the *pinyin* and read them aloud, paying attention to the meanings of the sentences

（1）Nǐ māma de shēntǐ hǎo ma?

（2）Wǒ mǎi qìchē le.

（3）Nǐmen jǐ diǎn xiūxi?

④ 按笔画顺序写出下面的汉字，并写出笔画数
Write the following characters in proper stroke order and give the number of strokes

妈（　　画）_____　　您（　　画）_____
汽（　　画）_____　　近（　　画）_____

⑤ 写一写　Writing exercise

tīng

yīng

xí
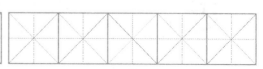

kě	一 丁 口 可

可 可 可 可 可

zhè	` 亠 亍 文 文 汶 这

这 这 这 这 这

qǐ	一 十 土 丰 丰 走 走 起 起 起

起 起 起 起 起

6 大声朗读下面的词语，并记住它们的意思
Read aloud the following words and remember their meanings

可以（can; may）　　这个（this）　　一起（together）
可是（but）　　　　这儿（here）　　大厅（hall）

7 根据拼音写汉字，然后大声朗读，并想一想句子的意思
Write the characters according to the *pinyin* and read them aloud, paying attention to the meanings of the sentences

（1）Zhè shì wǒ huà de huàr.

（2）Wǒ kěyǐ kànkan nǐ de shū ma?

（3）Wǒ mǎile qìchē, kěshì shì jiù chē.

8 写出符合下面结构的汉字　Write characters with the following structures

左上结构　⌐ : ＿＿＿＿＿＿＿＿＿＿＿＿
右上结构　┐ : ＿＿＿＿＿＿＿＿＿＿＿＿
左下结构　└ : ＿＿＿＿＿＿＿＿＿＿＿＿

9 写一写 Writing exercise

10 大声朗读下面的词语，并记住它们的意思

Read aloud the following words and remember their meanings

中国（China）　　　　　因为（because）
美国（United States）　　医生（doctor）
外国（foreign country）　大风（strong wind）
出国（go abroad）　　　　山区（mountain area）

⑪ 根据拼音写汉字，然后大声朗读，并想一想句子的意思

Write the characters according to the *pinyin* and read them aloud, paying attention to the meanings of the sentences

（1）Wǒ māma chū guó le.

（2）Wǒ bú shì yīshēng.

（3）Wǒmen yìqǐ kàn shū, xiě Hànzì.

（4）Nǐ shì Měiguó rén ma?

⑫ 写一写　Writing exercise

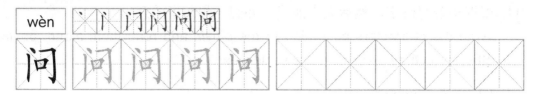

⑬ 大声朗读下面的词语，并记住它们的意思
Read aloud the following words and remember their meanings

男人（man） 努力（make great efforts）
历史（history） 中间（middle）

⑭ 按照结构给 12 题的汉字分类，并画出每类的结构图
Classify the characters in exercise 12 and draw the structure diagram

_____ _____

_____

⑮ 写一写　Writing exercise

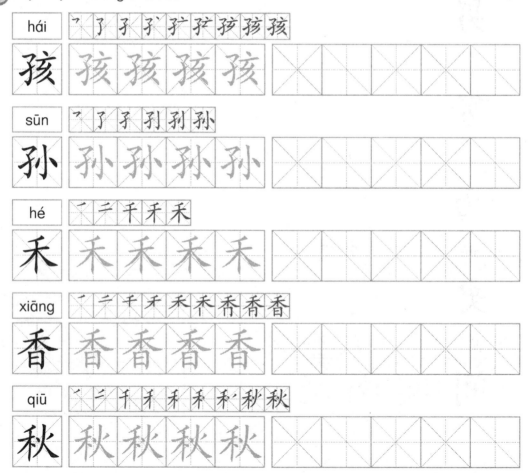

hé	丿 一 千 禾 禾 和 和 和

和 和 和 和 和

16 大声朗读下面的词和短语，并记住它们的意思
Read aloud the following words and phrases and remember their meanings

孩子（child） 女孩儿（girl） 秋天（autumn; fall）
孙子（grandson） 男孩儿（boy） 香山（the Fragrant Hills）

17 根据拼音写汉字，然后大声朗读，并想一想句子的意思
Write the characters according to the *pinyin* and read them aloud, paying attention to the meanings of the sentences

（1）Qiūtiān de tiānqì hǎo.

（2）Érzi de háizi shì sūnzi.

（3）Qiūtiān de Xiāng Shān měi bu měi?

（4）Zhè nánháir hé nǚháir zhōngjiān de rén shì wǒ.

18 按笔画顺序写出下面的汉字，并写出笔画数
Write the following characters in proper stroke order and give the number of strokes

男（　画）_____　　香（　画）_____
努（　画）_____　　秋（　画）_____
孩（　画）_____

二、本课复习 Review

妈	们	吗	汽	机	您	近	厅
应	习	可	这	起	风	同	医
区	国	因	男	努	历	史	间
问	孩	孙	禾	香	秋	和	

Easy Way to Learn Chinese Characters · Workbook

① 把上面的汉字写在下面相应的结构后
Group the above characters according to their structures

左右结构 ▯▯： _____

上下结构 ▭： _____

左上包围结构 ▯： _____

右上包围结构 ▯： _____

左下包围结构 ▯： _____

左上右包围结构 ▯： _____

四面包围结构 ▯： _____

② 给下列汉字注音并组词
Transcribe the character in *pinyin* and make up a word with it

例（For example）： 历 （lì） 　历史

汽（　　）_____　　可（　　）_____

医（　　）_____　　国（　　）_____

因（　　）_____　　努（　　）_____

孩（　　）_____　　秋（　　）_____

③ 按笔画顺序写出下面的汉字，并写出笔画数
Write the following characters in proper stroke order and give the number of strokes

近（　　画）_____　　医（　　画）_____

应（　　画）_____　　史（　　画）_____

风（　　画）_____　　起（　　画）_____

④ 在下面的方框中填上合适的部件，使它与中间的"口"字都能组成汉字
Write the proper component in the square so that it can make up a character with the component "口" in the middle

▯
+
▯ ＋ 口 ＋ ▯

5 根据拼音写汉字，并想想它们的意思
Write the characters according to the *pinyin* and think about their meanings

qìchē 　　　　　kěyǐ 　　　　　yìqǐ

yīshēng 　　　　kěshì 　　　　　nǔlì

nánháir 　　　　yīnwèi

qiūtiān 　　　　zhōngjiān

6 根据拼音写汉字，然后大声朗读，并想一想句子的意思
Write the characters according to the *pinyin* and read them aloud, paying attention to the meanings of the sentences

（1）Nǐ de shēntǐ hǎo ma?

（2）Wǒ kěyǐ kànkan nǐ de huàr ma?

（3）Wǒ mǎile qìchē, kěshì shì jiù chē.

（4）Wǒ tiāntiān nǔlì xiě Hànzì.

（5）Zhè nánháir hé nǚháir zhōngjiān de rén shì wǒ.

第六课
Lesson Six

一、同步练习 Synchronous exercises

1 写一写 Writing exercise

Pinyin	Stroke order	Character practice
me	丿 厶 么	么 么 么 么
gōng	丿 八 公 公	公 公 公 公
qù	一 十 土 去 去	去 去 去 去
zhī	一 十 步 支	支 支 支 支
nán	一 十 冂 冃 南 南 南 南	南 南 南 南
mài	一 十 丰 圥 产 卖 卖	卖 卖 卖 卖
zhí	一 十 广 market 古 直 直	直 直 直 直

第六课 6 Lesson Six

shén	ノ 亻 仁 什
什	什 什 什 什

② 大声朗读下面的词和短语，并记住它们的意思
Read aloud the following words and phrases and remember their meanings

公斤（kilogram）   公开（public）   什么（what）
公里（kilometer）   去年（last year）   为什么（why）
东南（southeast）   买卖（business）   一直（straight; always）
西南（southwest）   卖东西（sell something）

③ 根据拼音写汉字，并想想它们的意思
Write the characters according to the *pinyin* and think about their meanings

nánmén ____   mǎi shénme ____
dōngnán ____   yìzhí kàn shū ____
qùnián ____   sì gōnglǐ ____

④ 写出下面的汉字有几个部件，分别是什么
Write components for each of the following characters and give the number of components

例（For example）：什（2） 亻、十

公（　）_____   去（　）_____
支（　）_____   南（　）_____
卖（　）_____   直（　）_____

⑤ 写出含有下列部件的汉字，越多越好
Give the characters composed of the following components as many as you can

十：_____   厶：_____

⑥ 写一写 Writing exercise

zuǒ	一 ナ 九 左 左
左	左 左 左 左

Easy Way to Learn Chinese Characters · Workbook

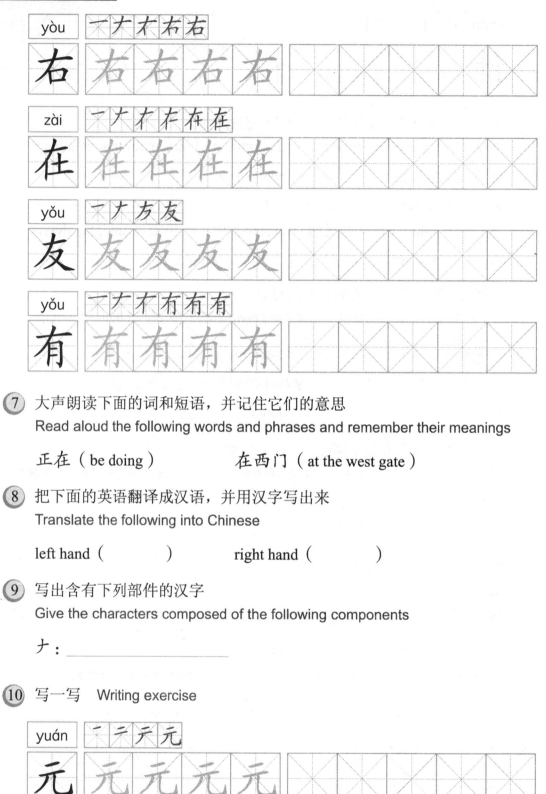

⑦ 大声朗读下面的词和短语，并记住它们的意思
Read aloud the following words and phrases and remember their meanings

正在（be doing）　　　　　　在西门（at the west gate）

⑧ 把下面的英语翻译成汉语，并用汉字写出来
Translate the following into Chinese

left hand（　　　　　）　　　right hand（　　　　　）

⑨ 写出含有下列部件的汉字
Give the characters composed of the following components

ナ：_____

⑩ 写一写　Writing exercise

xiān	丿 ㇒ 广 牛 生 牛 先
先	先 先 先 先

xiōng	丿 口 口 兄 兄
兄	兄 兄 兄 兄

kè	一 十 ナ 古 古 声 克
克	克 克 克 克

fǎn	一 厂 𠂆 反
反	反 反 反 反

hòu	一 厂 尸 斤 后 后
后	后 后 后 后

⑪ 大声朗读下面的词和短语，并记住它们的意思
   Read aloud the following words and phrases and remember their meanings

   先生（gentleman; sir）　　反应（reaction）　　后面（back）
   千克（kilogram）　　　　 反正（anyway）　　 以后（after; later）

   三千七百九十元（3,790 yuan）　　六个月以后（after six months）
   五千四百八十元（5,480 yuan）　　一年以后（after one year）

   先上后下（first up then down）
   我先买了马，又买了车。（I bought a horse first, then a cart.）

⑫ 写出下面的汉字有几个部件，分别是什么
   Write components for each of the following characters and give the number of components

   先（　　　）_____　　克（　　　）_____

反（　　　）_____　　后（　　　）_____

13 写出含有下列部件的汉字，越多越好
Write the characters composed of the following components as many as you can

儿：_____　　　　厂：_____

14 写一写　Writing exercise

| guān | 丶 丷 丷 关 关 |
| 关 | 关 关 关 关 |

| dì | 丶 丷 丷 弓 弟 弟 |
| 弟 | 弟 弟 弟 弟 |

| qián | 丶 丷 丷 广 广 广 前 前 前 |
| 前 | 前 前 前 前 |

| bàn | 丶 丷 丷 半 半 |
| 半 | 半 半 半 半 |

| lì | 丶 亠 亠 立 立 |
| 立 | 立 立 立 立 |

| lái | 一 丆 ⺈ 立 平 来 来 |
| 来 | 来 来 来 来 |

15 大声朗读下面的词和短语，并记住它们的意思
Read aloud the following words and phrases and remember their meanings

弟弟（younger brother）　　一半（half）
兄弟（brothers）　　　　　半天（half a day; a long time）

前面（in front; ahead）　　开关（switch）
以前（before; ago）　　　 关心（be concerned with; care for）
立刻（at once）　　　　　关门（close the door）

上来（come up）　　　　　上不来（cannot come up）
下来（come down）　　　　下不来（cannot come down）

16 把下面的英语翻译成汉语，并用汉字写出来
Translate the following into Chinese

come out　　　　（　　　　）　come down　　　　（　　　　）
go out　　　　　（　　　　）　go down　　　　　（　　　　）
cannot come out　（　　　　）　cannot come down　（　　　　）
cannot go out　　（　　　　）　cannot go down　　（　　　　）

17 写一写　Writing exercise

zhǐ/zhī　丶 口 口 尸 只
只

gòng　一 十 丗 共 共 共
共

tóu　丶 ˊ 二 头 头
头

yǔ　一 ㄧ 冂 币 雨 雨 雨
雨

mǔ　ㄥ 乜 母 母 母
母

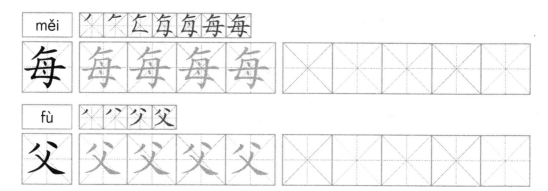

⑱ 大声朗读下面的词和短语，并记住它们的意思
Read aloud the following words and phrases and remember their meanings

只好（have to）　　　　一共（in all; altogether）
只是（only; just）　　　公共（public）

父亲（father）　　　　　每人（everyone）
母亲（mother）　　　　　每天（everyday）
* 亲 qīn（relative）　　下雨（rain）
父母（parents）　　　　　下雨了（It's rainning.）

⑲ 大声朗读下面的句子，并想想它们的意思
Read aloud the following sentences and think about their meanings

（1）我家一共有四口人：父亲、母亲、弟弟和我。
（2）你看，外面下大雨了。
（3）我们每人每天写二十个汉字。
（4）公共汽车来了，我们一起上了车。

二、本课复习　　Review

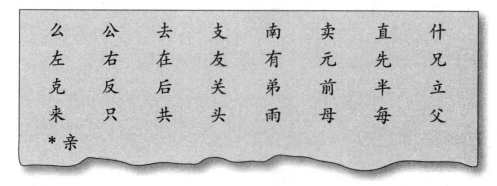

第六课 Lesson Six

① 写出含有下列部件的汉字
Write the characters composed of the following components

十：_____   厶：_____

厂：_____   儿：_____

② 按笔画顺序写出下面的汉字，并写出笔画数
Write the following characters in proper stroke order and give the number of strokes

在（　　画）_____　　雨（　　画）_____

弟（　　画）_____　　母（　　画）_____

半（　　画）_____

③ 写出下列汉字的部件　Write components for each of the following characters

卖（　　　　）　　　　南（　　　　）
前（　　　　）　　　　每（　　　　）

④ 给下列汉字注音并组词
Transcribe the character in *pinyin* and make up a word with it

只（　　　）_____　　前（　　　）_____
共（　　　）_____　　后（　　　）_____
父（　　　）_____　　立（　　　）_____

⑤ 根据拼音写汉字，并想想它们的意思
Write the characters according to the *pinyin* and think about their meanings

qùnián　　　　　xiānsheng　　　　　yìqǐ

yìzhí　　　　　　xiōngdì　　　　　　yǐhòu

lìkè　　　　　　 zhèngzài　　　　　 wèi shénme

yíbàn　　　　　　gōnggòng　　　　　měi tiān

6 根据拼音写汉字，然后大声朗读，并想一想句子的意思

Write the characters according to the *pinyin* and read them aloud, paying attention to the meanings of the sentences

（1）Wǒ guānxīn fùmǔ, fùmǔ yě guānxīn wǒ.

（2）Wǒ měi tiān shíyī diǎn xiūxi, nǐ jǐ diǎn xiūxi?

（3）Lái zhèr yǐqián, wǒ shì yí ge yīshēng.

（4）Wǒ dìdi zhèngzài kàn shū.

（5）Gōnggòng qìchē shang rén bù shǎo, wǒ shàng bu qù.

第七课 Lesson Seven

一、同步练习　Synchronous exercises

① 写一写　Writing exercise

fāng	方
jiāo	交
shì	市
Jīng	京
gāo	高
xìng	兴
xué	学

② 大声朗读下面的词和短语，并记住它们的意思
Read aloud the following words and phrases and remember their meanings

南京市（Nanjing City）　　方面（aspect）　　方向（direction）
东京市（Tokyo）　　　　　高兴（glad）　　　＊向 xiàng（direction）

高中（senior middle school）　　　学生（student）
学习（study）　　　　　　　　　 同学（classmate）

③ 大声朗读下面的句子，并想想它们的意思
Read aloud the following sentences and think about their meanings

（1）这方面的事，我不太明白。
（2）我的弟弟正在上高中。
（3）我父亲去南京买了不少书。

④ 写出下面的汉字有几个部件，分别是什么
Write components for each of the following characters and give the number of components

高（　　）_____　　　京（　　）_____
市（　　）_____　　　交（　　）_____

⑤ 写一写　Writing exercise

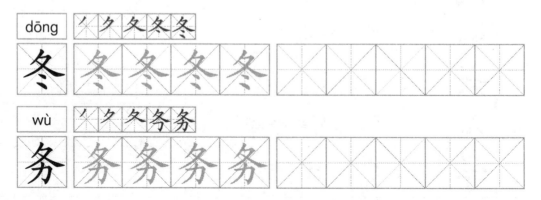

第七课 Lesson Seven

Character Practice

Pinyin	Character	Stroke Order
tiáo	条	丶 ク 夂 冬 条 条 条
xià	夏	一 丁 丁 丆 西 百 百 戸 夏 夏
fù	复	丿 ㇀ ㇀ 勹 勹 甸 旬 复 复
wǎng	网	丨 冂 冈 冈 网 网
liǎng	两	一 丁 丙 丙 丙 两 两
yòng	用	丿 冂 冂 月 用
zhōu	周	丿 冂 冂 冃 用 用 周 周

6 大声朗读下面的词和短语，并记住它们的意思

Read aloud the following words and phrases and remember their meanings

冬天（winter）　　复习（review）　　上网（go to internet）
夏天（summer）　　反复（again and again）　　网上（on the internet）

有用（useful）　　周日（Sunday）
用心（diligently）　　周二（Tuesday）

55

⑦ 把下面的英语翻译成汉语，并用汉字写出来
Translate the following into Chinese

Monday （　　　）　　　two persons （　　　）
Wednesday （　　　）　　　two thirty （　　　）
Thursday （　　　）　　　two days （　　　）
Friday （　　　）　　　two months （　　　）
Saturday （　　　）　　　two years （　　　）

⑧ 写出下面的汉字有几个部件，分别是什么
Write components for each of the following characters and give the number of components

务（　　　）_____　　　冬（　　　）_____
夏（　　　）_____　　　复（　　　）_____
学（　　　）_____　　　觉（　　　）_____

⑨ 写一写　Writing exercise

dāng　当
táng　堂
cháng　常
cháng　尝
lǎo　老

第七课 Lesson Seven

kǎo 一 十 土 耂 考
考

zhě 一 十 土 耂 ナ 耂 者 者
者

⑩ 大声朗读下面的词和短语，并记住它们的意思
Read aloud the following words and phrases and remember their meanings

老人（old person） 常常（often） 当医生（be a doctor）
老师（teacher） 尝尝（taste） 当老师（be a teacher）
* 师 shī（teacher）

⑪ 写出下面的汉字有几个部件，分别是什么
Write the components for each of the following characters and give the number of components

常（　）_____　　尝（　）_____
考（　）_____　　者（　）_____

⑫ 大声朗读下面的句子，并想想它们的意思
Read aloud the following sentences and think about their meanings

（1）这本书有用，你去买本吧（ba, *particle indicating a suggestion, a request or a mild command*）。
（2）我常常去南京。
（3）看见你也来了，我太高兴了。
（4）这两个月，我一直在学习。
（5）明天考汉字，你复习好了吗？

⑬ 写一写　Writing exercise

汉字速成课本·练习册 Easy Way to Learn Chinese Characters·Workbook

péng	丿 丌 月 月 朋 朋 朋 朋
朋	朋 朋 朋 朋

duō	' ク 夕 夕 多 多
多	多 多 多 多

gē	一 丆 可 可 哥 哥 哥 哥 哥 哥
哥	哥 哥 哥 哥

huí	㇆ 冂 冂 回 回 回
回	回 回 回 回

bǐ	一 ㇄ 比 比
比	比 比 比 比

xíng	' 彳 彳 行 行 行
行	行 行 行 行

zhú	丿 ㇇ 卜 ⺮ ⺮ 竹
竹	竹 竹 竹 竹

běi	丨 十 扌 扌 北
北	北 北 北 北

fēi	丨 丨 丨 亖 非 非 非 非
非	非 非 非 非

58

Lesson Seven

14 大声朗读下面的词和短语，并记住它们的意思
Read aloud the following words and phrases and remember their meanings

朋友（friend）　　　多少（how many）　　　回来（come back）
行人（pedestrian）　非常（very; extremely）　回去（go back）

两双手（two pairs of hands）　　去了两回（went for twice）
交朋友（make friends）　　　　　来了两回（came for twice）

举行（hold）　　　　　　　　旅行（travel）
* 举 jǔ（lift; raise; hold up）　* 旅 lǚ（travel）

我比你大。（I am older than you.）
十比八多两个。（Ten exceeds eight by two.）

15 把下面的英语翻译成汉语，并用汉字写出来
Translate the following into Chinese

（1）how many persons　　　　（　　　　　　　　　　）
（2）how many notebooks　　　（　　　　　　　　　　）
（3）how many days　　　　　　（　　　　　　　　　　）

16 根据拼音写汉字，然后大声朗读，并想一想句子的意思
Write the characters according to the *pinyin* and read them aloud, paying attention to the meanings of the sentences

（1）Nǐ jǐ diǎn huílai?

（2）Nǐ yǒu jǐ ge hǎo péngyou?

（3）Wǒ yǒu liǎng ge hǎo péngyou, shì wǒ de tóngxué.

（4）Wǒ bǐ nǐ dà.

汉字速成课本·练习册　Easy Way to Learn Chinese Characters·Workbook

二、本课复习　Review

方	交	市	京	高	兴	学	觉
冬	务	条	夏	复	网	两	用
周	当	堂	常	尝	老	考	者
双	朋	多	哥	回	比	行	竹
北	非						

*向　(*师)　*举　*旅

① 把上面的汉字写在下面相应的结构后
Group the characters according to their structures

▯▯ : _____

▭ : _____ (上下)

▯▯▯ : _____

▭ : _____ (上中下)

⧠ : _____

□ : _____

② 写出含有下列部件的汉字，越多越好
Write the characters composed of the following components as many as you can

又（　　　　）　　　月（　　　　）

木（　　　　）　　　夕（　　　　）

③ 按笔画顺序写出下面的汉字，并写出笔画数
Write the following characters in proper stroke order and give the number of strokes

北（　画）_____　　周（　画）_____

高（　画）_____　　考（　画）_____

④ 给下列汉字注音并组词
Transcribe the character in *pinyin* and make up a word with it

行（　　　）_____　　竹（　　　）_____

北（　　　）_____　　　比（　　　）_____
市（　　　）_____　　　周（　　　）_____

学（　　　）_____　　　高（　　　）_____

5 从"本课复习"的汉字框中找出合适的字，填在句子中的画线部分上
Fill in the blanks with appropriate characters given in the review box above

（1）我们每天_____习二十个汉字。
（2）_____日我们常常在家休息。
（3）我的身体_____你的身体好。
（4）我家有六口人，你家有四口人。我家比你家多_____口人。
（5）我有一个好_____友，是日本人。
（6）你来我非_____高兴。

6 根据拼音写汉字，并想想它们的意思
Write the characters according to the *pinyin* and think about their meanings

péngyou　　　　　gāoxìng　　　　　zhōurì

dōngtiān　　　　　fēicháng　　　　　tóngxué

7 根据拼音写汉字，然后大声朗读，并想一想句子的意思
Write the characters according to the *pinyin* and read them aloud, paying attention to the meanings of the sentences

（1）Wǒ zài Běijīng xuéxí.

（2）Wǒ zhōuliù qù Nánjīng.

（3）Xiàtiān wǒ zài Běijīng, dōngtiān wǒ zài Nánjīng.

（4）Wǒ de péngyou bǐ nǐ de shǎo.

（5）Nǐ yǒu duōshao ge běnzi?

第八课
Lesson Eight

一、同步练习 Synchronous exercises

① 写一写 Writing exercise

tā	他
tǐ	体
wèi	位
zhù	住
zuò	作
xìn	信
wǎng	往

第八课 8 Lesson Eight

hěn	很
很	很很很

de	得
得	得得得得

② 大声朗读下面的词和短语，并记住它们的意思
Read aloud the following words and phrases and remember their meanings

他们（they; them）　　　　写信（write a letter）
作业（homework）　　　　回信（write back; a letter in reply）
工作（work; job）　　　　　来信（send a letter here）

很近（very close）　　　　觉得（feel）
很努力（very hard）　　　　上得去（can go up）
很高兴（very happy）　　　下得来（can come down）
　　　　　　　　　　　　 回得来（can come back）

一封信（a letter）　　　　　寄信（mail letter）
* 封 fēng（measure word for letters）　　* 寄 jì（post; mail）

③ 根据拼音写汉字，并想想句子的意思
Write the characters according to the *pinyin* and think about the meanings of the sentences

（1）我学习_____（hěn）努力，我父母_____（hěn）高兴。
（2）这山不太高，我们_____（shàng de qù）。
（3）今天我们的汉字_____（zuòyè）不多。
（4）他的_____（gōngzuò）是看信。
（5）我_____（juéde）住在这儿比在家好。

④ 写出带有下列偏旁的汉字
Write the characters consisting of the following radicals

亻:_____　　　　彳:_____

5 写一写 Writing exercise

6 大声朗读下面的词语，并记住它们的意思

Read aloud the following words and remember their meanings

听见（hear） 好吃（delicious）

听写（dictation） 好听（pleasing to the ear）

7 根据拼音写汉字，并想想句子的意思

Write the characters according to the *pinyin* and think about the meanings of the sentences

（1）我_____（jiào）王林，你_____（jiào）什么？

第八课 8 Lesson Eight

（2）这个很香，你＿＿＿＿＿（chī）一点儿尝尝＿＿＿＿＿（ba）。

（3）我去买点儿什么＿＿＿＿＿（ne）？

（4）我＿＿＿＿＿（chàng）得不＿＿＿＿＿（hǎotīng）。

8 写一写 Writing exercise

shuō	说
yǔ	语
huà	话
rèn	认
shí	识
qǐng	请
kè	课

Easy Way to Learn Chinese Characters · Workbook

shì 试
ràng 让
gāi 该

9 大声朗读下面的词和短语，并记住它们的意思
Read aloud the following words and phrases and remember their meanings

听说（hear of） 认识（know sb.） 课文（text）
应该（should） 考试（examine） 说明（explain; instruction）

说话（speak） 汉语（Chinese） 上课（attend class）
电话（telephone） 日语（Japanese） 下课（finish class）

10 根据拼音写汉字，并想想句子的意思
Write the characters according to the *pinyin* and think about the meanings of the sentences

（1）你的_____（Hànyǔ）说得很好。

（2）我听见有人在_____（shuō huà）。

（3）我没看见_____（shuōmíng），不会（huì, can）用这个机子。

（4）下午有汉字_____（kǎoshì），我_____（yīnggāi）好好复习。

（5）我们每天八点_____（shàng kè），十二点_____（xià kè）。

（6）我的_____（diànhuà）是62375698。

11 写出带有下列偏旁的汉字
Write the characters consisting of the following radicals

口：_____   讠：_____

12 写一写 Writing exercise

tā	她
jiě	姐
mèi	妹
nǎi	奶
xìng	姓
yào	要
shǐ	始

13 大声朗读下面的词语，并记住它们的意思
Read aloud the following words and remember their meanings

她们（they; them <for female>）　　姓名（name）
姐姐（elder sister）　　　　　　　要是（if）
妹妹（younger sister）　　　　　　要么（or）
奶奶（mother of father）　　　　　开始（begin; start）

14 根据拼音写汉字，并想想句子的意思

Write the characters according to the *pinyin* and think about the meanings of the sentences

(1) _____（tāmen）是我的同学，是日本人。

(2) 你_____（xìng）什么？叫什么名字？

(3) 我_____（yào）去买东西，你去不去？

(4) 我是从1999年_____（kāishǐ）学习汉语的。

15 写一写　Writing exercise

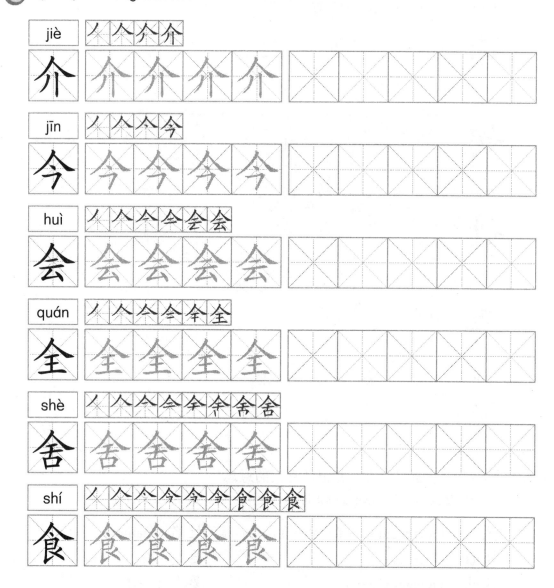

Lesson Eight 第八课 8

16 大声朗读下面的词语，并记住它们的意思
Read aloud the following words and remember their meanings

今天（today） 食堂（canteen） 社会（society）
今年（this year） 开会（have a meeting） *社 shè（community; society）

17 写出带有下列偏旁的汉字
Write the characters consisting of the following radicals

女：_____ 人：_____

18 写一写　Writing exercise

xiè	谢
zuò	做
nǎ	哪
yì	意
lèi	累
cān	参

⑲ 大声朗读下面的词和短语，并记住它们的意思
Read aloud the following words and phrases and remember their meanings

谢谢（thank）　　　哪儿（where）　　　做作业（do homework）
意见（idea; opinion）　哪个（which one）　　非常累（very tired）
注意（pay attention to）　　　　　　　　　参加（take part in）
* 注 zhù（concentrate）　　　　　　　　　* 加 jiā（add）

⑳ 根据拼音写汉字，并想想句子的意思
Write the characters according to the *pinyin* and think about the meanings of the sentences

（1）我_____（cānjiā）了HSK考试，可是考得不好。

（2）我非常_____（lèi），要休息休息。

（3）我要_____（zuò）作业了。

（4）我打听一下，学七楼在_____（nǎr）？

（5）房间里_____（nǎge）桌子是你的？

（6）_____（xièxie）你常常来看我。

㉑ 写一写　Writing exercise

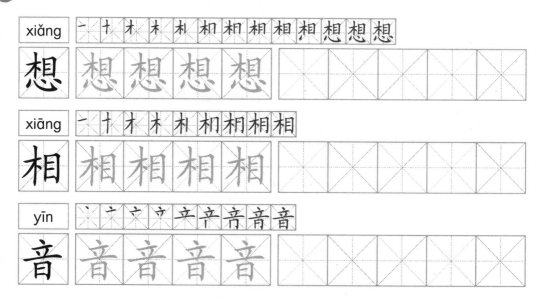

shù	一十十十村权权树树
cūn	一十十十村村村
duì	フヌヌ⁻对对

22 大声朗读下面的词语，并记住它们的意思
Read aloud the following words and remember their meanings

相信（believe）　　村子（village）　　对不起（sorry; excuse me）
互相（each other）　树林（woods）　　音乐（music）
* 互 hù（mutual）　　　　　　　　　　* 乐 yuè（music）

23 根据拼音写汉字，并想想句子的意思
Write the characters according to the *pinyin* and think about the meanings of the sentences

（1）我_____（xiǎng）周日去南京，你_____（xiǎng bu xiǎng）去？

（2）我们一起学习汉语，要_____（hùxiāng）帮助。

（3）我_____（xiāngxìn）你，你也_____（xiāngxìn）我吗？

（4）你家在十七楼，_____（duì bu duì）？

（5）村子前有一片（piàn, *measure word*）小_____（shùlín）。

（6）_____（duìbuqǐ），我没听见你说什么。

Easy Way to Learn Chinese Characters · Workbook

二、本课复习　Review

他	体	位	住	作	信	往	很
得	叫	吃	唱	吧	呢	听	说
语	话	认	识	请	课	试	让
该	她	姐	妹	奶	姓	要	始
介	今	会	全	舍	食	谢	做
哪	意	累	参	想	相	音	树
村	对						
*封	*寄	*社	*注	*加	*互	(*乐)	

① 把上面的汉字写在下面相应的结构后
Group the above characters according to their structures

▭▭ : _____

▯▯▯ : _____

② 写出下列偏旁的笔画数
Give the number of strokes for each of the following radicals

亻（　　）　彳（　　）　口（　　）　讠（　　）　女（　　）

③ 写出带有下列偏旁的汉字
Write the characters consisting of the following radicals

亻：_____　　彳：_____

口：_____　　讠：_____

女：_____

④ 连线组字　Join the components to make up characters

亻	乃		亻	艮
彳	斤		彳	尼
讠	丁		讠	乍
口	木		口	台
女	果		女	舌

5 查字典，写出下列汉字的拼音和意思

Look up the characters in the dictionary, then write down the *pinyin* transcriptions and explanations

使（　　）_____　　记（　　）_____

讲（　　）_____　　让（　　）_____

词（　　）_____　　喝（　　）_____

伴（　　）_____　　嘴（　　）_____

6 根据拼音写汉字，并想想句子的意思

Write the characters according to the *pinyin* and think about the meanings of the sentences

（1）你_____（rènshi）他吗？

（2）你住在_____（nǎr）？

（3）我是从2000年_____（kāishǐ）学汉语的。

（4）A：你的汉语说得很好！

　　　B：_____（xièxie）！

（5）我家一共有七口人：父亲、母亲、_____（jiějie）、弟弟、_____（mèimei）和我。

第九课
Lesson Nine

一、同步练习　Synchronous exercises

1. 写一写　Writing exercise

bīng	丶 冫 冫丨 冰 冰
冰	冰 冰 冰 冰

lěng	丶 冫 冫丿 冷 冷 冷
冷	冷 冷 冷 冷

liáng	丶 冫 冫 冫广 冫亠 冫古 冫古 凉 凉
凉	凉 凉 凉 凉

cì	丶 冫 冫丿 冫丬 次
次	次 次 次 次

jué	丶 冫 冫丨 冫日 冫日 决
决	决 决 决 决

2. 大声朗读下面的词和短语，并记住它们的意思
   Read aloud the following words and phrases and remember their meanings

决心（resolution）　　　凉水（cold water）
冷风（cold wind）　　　冰水（ice water）

一次（once）　　　　　去了一次（have been there once）
两次（twice）　　　　　看了两次（have seen twice）

3 根据拼音写汉字，并想想句子的意思
Write the characters according to the *pinyin* and think about the meanings of the sentences

（1）我去东京（Tokyo）去了＿＿＿＿（liǎng cì），你去了＿＿＿＿（jǐ cì）？

（2）我＿＿＿＿（juéxīn）以后好好学习，天天上课。

（3）夏天我常自己做＿＿＿＿（bīngshuǐ）。

4 写一写　Writing exercise

jiāng 江

shēn 深

jiǔ 酒

xǐ 洗

zǎo 澡

yóu 游

汉字速成课本·练习册 Easy Way to Learn Chinese Characters·Workbook

yǒng 泳 丶 丶 氵 氵 汀 沪 泳 泳
méi 没 丶 丶 氵 氵 沪 沙 没
fǎ 法 丶 丶 氵 氵 汁 泸 法 法

5 大声朗读下面的词和短语，并记住它们的意思
Read aloud the following words and phrases and remember their meanings

长江（the Yangtze River） 白酒（white spirit） 洗澡（shower; bath）
深浅（depth） 啤酒（beer） 游泳（swim）
* 浅 qiǎn（shallow） * 啤 pí（beer）

没有（not have; there be no） 办法（way; means）
有没有（have or not） 方法（method）

6 根据拼音写汉字，并想想句子的意思
Write the characters according to the *pinyin* and think about the meanings of the sentences

（1）吃东西以前该_____（xǐ shǒu）。
（2）夏天，我用冷水_____（xǐzǎo）。
（3）我参加了学校的_____（yóuyǒng）队（duì, team）。
（4）这事儿，你有什么好_____（bànfǎ）吗?
（5）这条_____（jiāng）不太_____（shēn）。

7 写出带有下列偏旁的汉字
Write the characters consisting of the following radicals

冫：_____ 氵：_____

第九课 Lesson Nine

8 写一写 Writing exercise

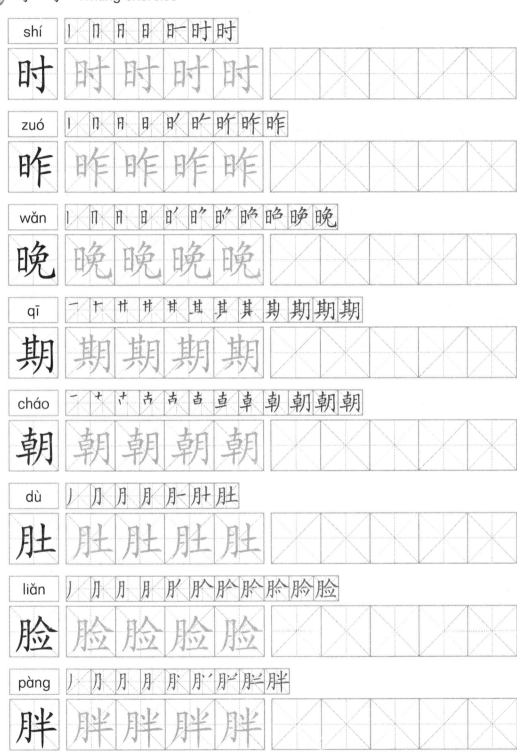

fú 丿 几 月 月 凧 朋 服 服

服 服 服 服 服

9 大声朗读下面的词和短语，并记住它们的意思
Read aloud the following words and phrases and remember their meanings

时间（time）　　昨天（yesterday）　　服务（serve）
小时（hour）　　晚上（evening; night）　　衣服（clothes）
　　　　　　　　　　　　　　　　　＊衣 yī（clothes）

学期（term）　　肚子（belly）　　日期（date）
期中（midterm）　　胖子（fat person）　　两个小时（two hours）

10 根据拼音写汉字，并想想句子的意思
Write the characters according to the *pinyin* and think about the meanings of the sentences

（1）周日_____（wǎnshang）我去朋友家了。

（2）_____（zuótiān），我看书看了两个_____（xiǎoshí）。

（3）他是个_____（pàngzi），_____（dùzi）很大。

（4）这_____（xuéqī）我们九月开始上课。

（5）你来中国多长_____（shíjiān）了？

（6）这儿的_____（fúwù）很好。

11 写出带有下列偏旁的汉字
Write the characters consisting of the following radicals

日：_____　　月：_____

12 写一写　Writing exercise

duì 阝 阝 队 队

队 队 队 队 队

第九课 Lesson Nine

yáng	阳
yīn	阴
yuàn	院
chú	除
fù	附
nà	那
yóu	邮
dōu	都

13 大声朗读下面的词和短语，并记住它们的意思

Read aloud the following words and phrases and remember their meanings

太阳（sun）　　　　医院（hospital）　　　　那儿（there）

Easy Way to Learn Chinese Characters · Workbook

阴天（cloudy） 学院（college） 那么（then; in that way）

附近（nearby; in the vicinity of）

除了……以外（except; besides）

⑭ 根据拼音写汉字，并想想句子的意思
Write the characters according to the *pinyin* and think about the meanings of the sentences

（1）我在外语_____（xuéyuàn）学习日语。

（2）_____（chúle）小王以外，我们_____（dōu）去北京了。

（3）今天是_____（yīntiān），没有_____（tàiyáng）。

（4）我们学院_____（fùjìn）有一家_____（yīyuàn）。

⑮ 写一写 Writing exercise

gòu	够
xiē	此
zuì	最
yuán	圆
néng	能

16 大声朗读下面的词和短语，并记住它们的意思
Read aloud the following words and phrases and remember their meanings

可能（possible; probably）　　　一些（some）
能够（can; be able to）　　　　有些（some）

最近（recently）　　够吃了（enough to eat）　　足够（enough）
最圆（the roundest）　不够吃（not enough to eat）　*足 zú（enough）

17 根据拼音写汉字，并想想句子的意思
Write the characters according to the *pinyin* and think about the meanings of the sentences

(1) 我_____（kěnéng）要马上回国，不能参加考试了。
(2) 我的_____（yìxiē）朋友出国了，_____（yǒuxiē）朋友去了美国。
(3) _____（zuìjìn）我有点儿累，常常晚上十点休息。
(4) 长江是中国_____（zuì）长的江。

18 写出符合下列结构的汉字（1～2个）
Write one or two characters that correspond to the following structures

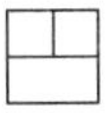

▢: _____　　　▢: _____

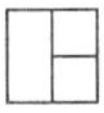

19 写一写　Writing exercise

| zhī | ノ ニ 午 矢 矢 知 知 知 |

知　知 知 知 知

| hào | 丨 口 卩 므 号 |

号　号 号 号 号

| hé | ノ 人 人 仒 合 合 |

合　合 合 合 合

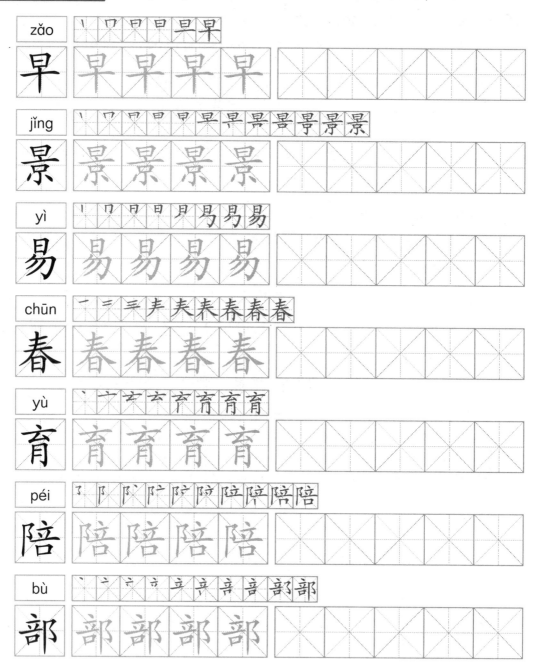

20 大声朗读下面的词语，并记住它们的意思

Read aloud the following words and remember their meanings

早上（morning） 部分（part） 风景（scenery）

春天（spring） 全部（whole; total） 体育（physical training）

早晨（early morning）

＊晨 chén（morning）

第九课 9 Lesson Nine

㉑ 根据拼音写汉字，并想想句子的意思
Write the characters according to the *pinyin* and think about the meanings of the sentences

（1）_____（chūntiān）的天气最好。

（2）我_____（zǎoshang）七点起床，_____（wǎnshang）十一点休息。

（3）我买了很多本子，一_____（bùfen）自己用，一_____（bùfen）给你。

（4）你自己不想去，我_____（péi）你去。

（5）你的生日是几_____（hào）？

（6）今天下午，我们有_____（tǐyù）课。

㉒ 写出含有下列部件的汉字
Write the characters consisting of the following components

日：_____   月：_____

二、本课复习 Review

冰	冷	凉	次	决	江	深	酒
洗	澡	游	泳	没	法	时	昨
晚	期	朝	肚	脸	胖	服	队
阳	阴	院	除	附	那	邮	都
够	些	最	圆	能	知	号	合
早	景	易	春	育	陪	部	
*浅	*啤	(*衣)	*足	*晨			

① 把上面的汉字写在下面相应的结构后
Group the above characters according to their structures

⊞ : _____   ⊟ : _____

⊟ : _____   ⊟ : _____

⊟ : _____

② 写出带有下列形旁的汉字
Write the characters consisting of the following meaning radicals

冫：_____   氵：_____
日：_____   月：_____
阝：_____

③ 给下列汉字注音并组词
Write the pinyin transcriptions for the following characters and make up words with them

次（   ）_____   决（   ）_____
洗（   ）_____   游（   ）_____
期（   ）_____   服（   ）_____
院（   ）_____   附（   ）_____

④ 在下面的空格里填上适当的部件，使它和已有的部件组成一个字
Fill in the blanks with an appropriate component to make a character with the component given below

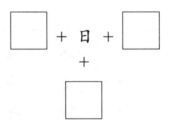

⑤ 根据拼音写汉字，并想想它们的意思
Write the characters according to the pinyin and think about their meanings

chūntiān _____   quánbù _____   xǐzǎo _____
xuéqī _____   nénggòu _____   yóuyǒng _____
bànfǎ _____   fùjìn _____   fúwù _____

⑥ 根据拼音写汉字，并想想句子的意思
Write the characters according to the pinyin and think about the meanings of the sentences

（1）我每天要_____（xǐ liǎng cì zǎo）。
（2）我来北京的_____（shíjiān）不长，才两个多月。

（3）我每天_____（kàn yí ge xiǎoshí de shū），
_____（xiě yí ge xiǎoshí de Hànzì）。

（4）_____（zuìjìn），我父母要来北京看我。

（5）这次考试，汉字_____（bùfen）我考得不好。

（6）这个山的_____（fēngjǐng）比那个山的_____（fēngjǐng）美。

10 第十课
Lesson Ten

一、同步练习　Synchronous exercises

1 写一写　Writing exercise

zhuō	桌
jià	架
xiào	校
bǎn	板
yǐ	椅
lóu	楼

2 大声朗读下面的词和短语，并记住它们的意思
Read aloud the following words and phrases and remember their meanings

桌子（table; desk）　　书架（bookshelf）　　一架飞机（an airplane）

椅子（chair） 　　　　学校（school） 　　　　一张桌子（a table）
* 张 zhāng（measure word for desk, picture, etc.）
大楼（big building） 　　　　上楼（go upstairs）
三楼（the third floor; building 3） 　　　　下楼（go downstairs）

③ 根据拼音写汉字，并想想句子的意思
Write the characters according to the *pinyin* and think about the meanings of the sentences

（1）我家在十九＿＿＿＿（lóu），很高。
（2）我们＿＿＿＿（xuéxiào）不太大，学生也不太多。
（3）这儿有两张＿＿＿＿（zhuōzi）和两把＿＿＿＿（yǐzi），你先用吧。
（4）＿＿＿＿（shūjià）上的书都是我自己买的。

④ 写一写　Writing exercise

| dǎ | 一 十 扌 打 打 |
| 打 | 打 打 打 打 |

| zhǎo | 一 十 扌 找 找 找 |
| 找 | 找 找 找 找 |

| bào | 一 十 扌 扌 扣 扣 报 |
| 报 | 报 报 报 报 |

| sǎo | 一 十 扌 扫 扫 |
| 扫 | 扫 扫 扫 扫 |

| bǎ | 一 十 扌 扌 扣 押 把 |
| 把 | 把 把 把 把 |

guà
挂

jǐ
挤

5 大声朗读下面的词和短语，并记住它们的意思

Read aloud the following words and phrases and remember their meanings

打听（ask about）　　　　　挂号（register at a hospital etc.）
打扫（sweep; clean）　　　　报名（enter one's name）

找东西（look for sth.）　　　一把椅子（a chair）
看报（read newspaper）

6 根据拼音写汉字，并想想句子的意思

Write the characters according to the *pinyin* and think about the meanings of the sentences

（1）我想_____（dǎtīng）一下，学七楼在哪儿？
（2）我要_____（bàomíng）学习画画儿。
（3）这儿太脏（zāng, dirty）了，你应该_____（dǎsǎo）一下。
（4）他_____（bǎ）我的点心都吃了。
（5）我们_____（bǎ）那张画儿_____（guà）上去吧。

7 写出带有下列偏旁的汉字

Write the characters consisting of the following radicals

木：_____　　　扌：_____

8 写一写　Writing exercise

hóng
红

第十课 10 Lesson Ten

lǜ	绿
zhǐ	纸
jīng	经
gěi	给
shào	绍
bié	别
dào	到
guā	刮
gāng	刚

9 大声朗读下面的词和短语，并记住它们的意思
Read aloud the following words and phrases and remember their meanings

已经（already）　　刚才（just now）　　介绍（introduce; introduction）
经常（often）　　　刚刚（just）　　　　报纸（newspaper）

别人（others）　　　到处（everywhere）
别的（other）　　　刮风（blow）

10 根据拼音写汉字，并想想句子的意思
Write the characters according to the *pinyin* and think about the meanings of the sentences

（1）我来北京_____（yǐjīng）一年多了。
（2）晚上，我_____（jīngcháng）去学校看书。
（3）你_____（bié）说话，听他说说。
（4）学校里_____（dàochù）都是_____（lǜ）树。
（5）今天天气不好，_____（guā）大风。
（6）除了我以外，_____（bié de）同学都去上课了。

11 写出带有下列偏旁的汉字
Write the characters consisting of the following radicals

纟：_____　　　　刂：_____

12 写一写　Writing exercise

wàng	忘
nián	念
zěn	怎

第十课 10 Lesson Ten

sī	思	丶 口 曰 田 田 甲 思 思 思
zhì	志	一 十 土 士 志 志 志
jí	急	丿 𠂊 夂 刍 刍 刍 急 急 急
gǎn	感	一 厂 厂 厂 戶 戶 咸 咸 咸 咸 感 感 感
dēng	灯	丶 丶 丷 火 灯 灯
shāo	烧	丶 丶 丷 火 火 灶 烊 烧 烧 烧
yān	烟	丶 丶 丷 火 灯 灯 㶽 烟 烟 烟

13 大声朗读下面的词和短语，并记住它们的意思
Read aloud the following words and phrases and remember their meanings

怎么（how）　　意思（meaning）　　有意思（interesting）
想念（miss）　　思想（thinking）　　没有意思（not interesting）

同志（comrade）　　感谢（thanks）　　电灯（electric light）
杂志（magazine）　　感到（feel）　　香烟（cigarette）
* 杂 zá（miscellaneous）

发烧（have a fever）　感冒（have a cold）　抽烟（smoke a cigarette）

*发 fā（send; feel）　*冒 mào（to risk）　*抽 chōu（take out; draw）

⑭ 根据拼音写汉字，并想想句子的意思
Write the characters according to the *pinyin* and think about the meanings of the sentences

（1）我家的_____（diàndēng）不亮（liàng, bright）了。

（2）今天我_____（gǎnmào）了，有点儿_____（fāshāo）。

（3）这些_____（xiāngyān）都是朋友给我的。

（4）你说的话是什么_____（yìsi）？我_____（zěnme）不明白？

（5）我来中国一年多了，我很_____（xiǎngniàn）我的父母。

（6）我_____（wàng）了他叫什么名字了。

（7）这本书很_____（yǒu yìsi），你看看吧。

（8）_____（gǎnxiè）你来医院看我。

⑮ 写出带有下列偏旁的汉字
Write the characters consisting of the following radicals

心：_____　　　火：_____

⑯ 写一写　Writing exercise

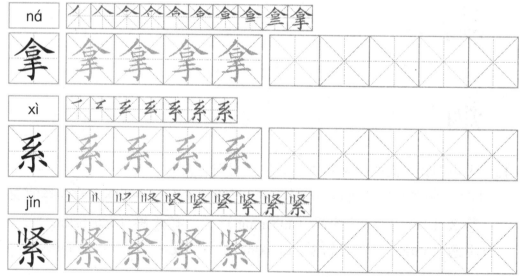

| qiē | 一 七 切 切 |
| 切 | 切 切 切 切 |

| sè | ノ ク ク 名 刍 色 |
| 色 | 色 色 色 色 |

| xiàng | ノ ク ク 个 刍 乌 身 象 象 象 |
| 象 | 象 象 象 象 |

17 大声朗读下面的词和短语，并记住它们的意思
Read aloud the following words and phrases and remember their meanings

拿东西（carry something）　　中文系（Chinese Department）
紧张（nervous）　　　　　　外语系（Foreign Language Department）
* 张 zhāng（stretch）

红色（red）　　　　　　　大象（elephant）
景色（scenery; view）　　　对象（girl or boy friend）

18 根据拼音写汉字，并想想句子的意思
Write the characters according to the *pinyin* and think about the meanings of the sentences

（1）我买了两件（jiàn, *measure word for clothes*）衣服，一件是_____
　　（hóngsè）的，一件是_____（báisè）的。
（2）最近我妹妹找了一个_____（duìxiàng），是个医生。
（3）桂林（Guìlín, name of a city）的_____（jǐngsè）太美了！
（4）我_____（hǎoxiàng）认识他，可是忘了他叫什么了。
（5）我参加 HSK 考试的时候（shíhou, when），有点儿_____
　　（jǐnzhāng）。
（6）我的弟弟和妹妹正在上大学，弟弟在_____（Wàiyǔxì）学
　　日语，妹妹在_____（Zhōngwénxì）学习。

Easy Way to Learn Chinese Characters · Workbook

⑲ 写出带有下列偏旁的汉字

Write the characters consisting of the following radicals

忄：_____　　幺：_____

⑳ 写一写　　Writing exercise

máng	忙
kuài	快
pà	怕
dǒng	懂
guàn	惯
rè	热
zhào	照

94

| hēi | 丨 冂 冃 㓁 㓁 里 里 里 黑 黑 黑 |

黑 黑 黑 黑 黑

21 大声朗读下面的词和短语，并记住它们的意思

Read aloud the following words and phrases and remember their meanings

急忙（in a hurry）　　习惯（be used to; habit）　　黑色（black）
热心（warm-hearted）　照相（take a picture）　　　黑板（blackboard）
　　　　　　　　　　* 相 xiàng（picture; photo）

照个相（take a picture）　　听得懂（can understand what was heard）
照张相（take a picture）　　听不懂（can not understand what was heard）

22 根据拼音写汉字，并想想句子的意思

Write the characters according to the *pinyin* and think about the meanings of the sentences

(1) 王林是个_____（rèxīn）的人。
(2) 你说的是什么意思？我_____（tīng bu dǒng）。
(3) 我已经_____（xíguàn）北京的天气了。
(4) 请您给我们_____（zhào ge xiàng），好吗？
(5) _____（hēibǎn）上写的是什么？我看不见。
(6) 我最近很_____（máng），没有时间看书。
(7) 我没有早上洗澡的_____（xíguàn）。

23 写出带有下列偏旁的汉字

Write the characters consisting of the following radicals

灬：_____　　忄：_____

汉字速成课本·练习册　　Easy Way to Learn Chinese Characters·Workbook

二、本课复习　Review

> 桌　架　校　板　椅　楼　打　找
> 报　扫　把　挂　挤　红　绿　纸
> 经　给　绍　别　到　刮　刚　忘
> 念　怎　思　志　急　感　灯　烧
> 烟　拿　系　紧　切　色　象　忙
> 快　怕　懂　惯　热　照　　　黑
> *张　*杂　(*发)*冒　*抽　(*相)

① 把上面的汉字填在合适的结构后
Group the above characters according to their structures

⊟ : _____　　⊞ : _____

⊟ : _____　　⊞ : _____

② 把下面意义相同的形旁归为一类，并各写出两个例字
Group the meaning radicals below according to the meanings and give two examples for each

刀、手、纟、刂、火、心、扌、灬、忄、幺、灬

_____　　　　_____
_____　　　　_____
_____

③ 写出两个含有下列部件的汉字，并注音、组词
Write two characters for each component, give the *pinyin* transcriptions and make up words with them

纟: _____(　　)_____　　刂: _____(　　)_____
　　_____(　　)_____　　　　_____(　　)_____

灬: _____(　　)_____　　灬: _____(　　)_____
　　_____(　　)_____　　　　_____(　　)_____

96

忄：_____（　）_____　　　　木：_____（　）_____

_____（　）_____　　　　　　　_____（　）_____

4 根据拼音写汉字，然后大声朗读句子，并想一想它们的意思

Write the characters according to the *pinyin* and read the sentences aloud, paying attention to their meanings

（1）我不_____（pà）天气冷，我_____（pà）天气_____（rè）。

（2）小王，你_____（gāngcái）给我打电话了吗？

（3）我只_____（zhǎodào）这一个工作。

（4）我想_____（dǎting）一下，十四楼_____（zěnme）走？

（5）春天到了，_____（dàochù）都是_____（lǜsè）的。

（6）我_____（gǎnmào）了，有点儿_____（fāshāo）。

（7）我给你们全家_____（zhào ge xiàng）吧。

第十一课
Lesson Eleven

一、同步练习 Synchronous exercises

① 写一写 Writing exercise

| biān | 冂 力 边 边 |
| 边 | 边 边 边 边 |

| guò | 一 十 寸 寸 过 过 |
| 过 | 过 过 过 过 |

| jìn | 一 二 牛 井 讲 进 |
| 进 | 进 进 进 进 |

| sòng | 丶 丷 兰 兰 关 关 送 送 |
| 送 | 送 送 送 送 |

| chí | 乛 コ 尸 尺 迟 迟 迟 |
| 迟 | 迟 迟 迟 迟 |

| hái | 一 丆 不 不 还 还 |
| 还 | 还 还 还 还 |

| yíng | 丶 𠂉 卬 卬 迎 迎 |
| 迎 | 迎 迎 迎 迎 |

第十一课 11 Lesson Eleven

shì
适

dào
道

yuǎn
远

2 大声朗读下面的词和短语，并记住它们的意思
Read aloud the following words and phrases and remember their meanings

前边（in front; ahead）　　不过（but）　　永远（forever）
后边（behind; back）　　还是（or）　　* 永 yǒng（forever; always）

过来（come here; come round）　　进来（come in）
过去（go there; formerly）　　进去（go in）

知道（know）　　适合（fit）
迟到（be late）　　合适（proper）
去过上海（have been to Shanghai）

3 从所给词语中选择恰当的填空，然后大声朗读句子
Fill in the blanks with proper words given below and then read the sentences aloud

> 还是　迟到　适合　合适　送　过来　知道

（1）这本书是朋友_____给我的。
（2）他今天上课_____了，8:10才来。
（3）这件衣服不大不小，很_____。
（4）你是韩国（Hánguó, Korea）人_____日本人？
（5）我的脸有点儿黑，白色的衣服不_____我。

（6）请你_____一下，我有话要说。

（7）你_____他的名字吗？

4 写出下列偏旁的笔画数，并写出带有这个偏旁的汉字

Give the number of strokes for the following radical and write the characters with it

辶（　　画）：_____

5 写一写　Writing exercise

| cuò | 丿 𠂉 仁 佐 𠂇 钅 钅 钅 钅 钅 错 错 错 |

错 错 错 错 错

| duàn | 丿 𠂉 仁 佐 𠂇 钅 钅 钅 钅 钅 钅 钅 锻 锻 |

锻 锻 锻 锻 锻

6 大声朗读下面的词和短语，并记住它们的意思
Read aloud the following words and phrases and remember their meanings

不错（good） 围巾（scarf） 错误（error; mistake）
公园（park） 周围（around; surrounding） *误 wù（error; mistake）

分钟（minute） 猜猜（guess）
钱包（wallet） 锻炼（do physical exercise）
*包 bāo（bag） *炼 liàn（refine）

7 从所给词语中选择恰当的填空，然后大声朗读句子
Fill in the blanks with proper words given below and then read the sentences aloud

分钟　周围　锻炼　公园　围巾　错　钱

（1）我家_____的景色很美，前边是个_____，后边是条河（hé, river）。
（2）男朋友送给我一条红色的_____。
（3）他昨天上课迟到了十_____。
（4）我的_____包里没有_____了。
（5）你说_____了，我不是美国人。
（6）我的身体不错，因为我每天早上_____身体。

8 写出下列偏旁的笔画数，并写出带有这个偏旁的汉字
Give the number of strokes for the following radicals and write the characters with them

口（　画）：_____　　钅（　画）：_____

汉字速成课本·练习册　Easy Way to Learn Chinese Characters·Workbook

9 写一写　Writing exercise

fàn	饭
bǎo	饱
è	饿
guǎn	馆
māo	猫
gǒu	狗
zhū	猪
cāi	猜

第十一课 11 Lesson Eleven

⑩ 大声朗读下面的词和短语，并记住它们的意思
Read aloud the following words and phrases and remember their meanings

饭馆（restaurant） 小猫（kitten; kitty） 吃饭（have a meal）
图书馆（library） 小狗（pup; puppy） 早饭（breakfast）

午饭（lunch） 吃饱了（be full） 猜猜（guess）
晚饭（supper） 没吃饱（be not full）

⑪ 从所给词语中选择恰当的填空，然后大声朗读句子
Fill in the blanks with proper words given below and then read the sentences aloud

> 早饭　午饭　晚饭　图书馆　饭馆　小猫　饿　猜

（1）我家没有_____，只有一只小狗。
（2）我每天 7:30 吃_____，12:00 吃_____，17:30 吃_____。
（3）你_____，他今年多大了？
（4）一天没吃东西，我太_____了。
（5）周日我常去_____吃饭。
（6）我们学校的_____里有很多书和杂志。

⑫ 写出带有下列偏旁的汉字
Write the characters consisting of the following radicals

饣：_____　　犭：_____

⑬ 写一写　Writing exercise

yǎn 丨 冂 冃 目 目＾ 目＾ 目＾ 眼 眼
眼　眼 眼 眼 眼

jīng 丨 冂 冃 月 目 目＾ 目＾ 晴 晴 晴 晴 睛
睛　睛 睛 睛 睛

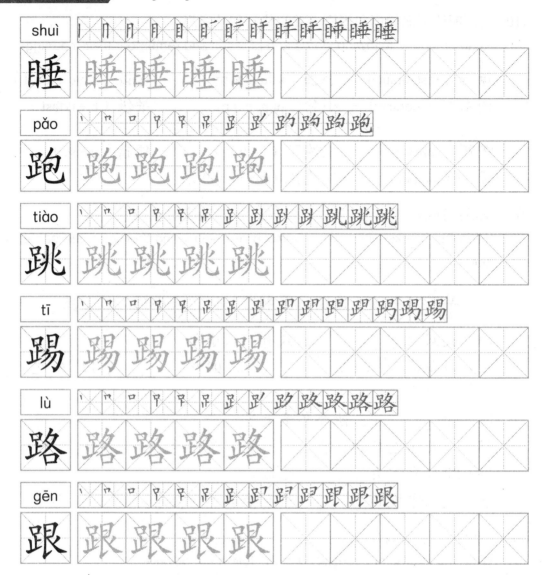

14 大声朗读下面的词和短语，并记住它们的意思
Read aloud the following words and phrases and remember their meanings

眼睛（eye） 公路（highway; road） 路过（pass; go through）
睡觉（sleep） 马路（road） 道路（road; way; path）

跑步（run） 跳舞（dance）
* 步 bù（step; pace） * 舞 wǔ（dance）

睡八个小时的觉（sleep for eight hours）
跑半个小时的步（run for half an hour）

⑮ 从所给词语中选择恰当的填空，然后大声朗读句子

Fill in the blanks with proper words given below and then read the sentences aloud

> 眼睛　马路　跳舞　睡觉　跑步　跟

（1）昨天，我_____朋友一起去香山了。
（2）_____上车多、人多，过_____时要小心。
（3）我每天早上六点_____，晚上十点_____。
（4）小王_____跳得很好。
（5）那个女孩的_____很大、很美。

⑯ 写出带有下列偏旁的汉字

Write the characters consisting of the following radicals

月：_____　　　足：_____

⑰ 写一写　Writing exercise

| huā | 一 十 艹 扩 扩 花 花 |
| 花 | 花 花 花 花 |

| cǎo | 一 十 艹 艹 丱 苎 苎 草 |
| 草 | 草 草 草 草 |

| yīng | 一 十 艹 艹 艹 苎 英 英 |
| 英 | 英 英 英 英 |

| chá | 一 十 艹 艹 艾 苙 苶 苶 茶 |
| 茶 | 茶 茶 茶 茶 |

| cài | 一 十 艹 艹 艹 艹 苎 芯 芯 菜 菜 |
| 菜 | 菜 菜 菜 菜 |

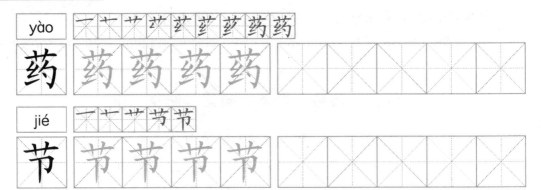

⑱ 大声朗读下面的词和短语，并记住它们的意思
Read aloud the following words and phrases and remember their meanings

花园（garden）　　　英语（English）　　切菜（cut vegetable）
买花（buy flowers）　英国（England）　　喝茶（drink tea）
　　　　　　　　　　　　　　　　　　　*喝 hē（drink）

中药（traditional Chinese medicine）　　节目（program）
西药（Western medicine）　　　　　　　节日（festival）
吃药（take medicine）　　　　　　　　　过节（celebrate a festival）

⑲ 从所给词语中选择恰当的填空，然后大声朗读句子
Fill in the blanks with proper words given below and then read the sentences aloud

> 英国　英语　节目　花　草　药　茶

（1）春天到了，公园里的_____开了，_____绿了。
（2）她是_____人，她的男朋友是美国人。
（3）你感冒了，吃点儿_____吧。
（4）很多中国人都有喝_____的习惯。
（5）我学_____学了三个月了。
（6）你常常看什么电视（diànshì, TV）_____？有意思吗？

⑳ 写一写　Writing exercise

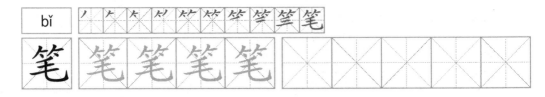

jiǎn	简
dì	第
dá	答
děng	等

㉑ 大声朗读下面的词和短语，并记住它们的意思
Read aloud the following words and phrases and remember their meanings

钢笔（pen）　　　　　　　　回答（answer）
毛笔（writing brush）　　　　答应（promise）
* 毛 máo（hair; feather）

第一（the first）　第一天（the first day）　第一个月（the first month）
第二（the second）　第二天（the second day）　第二个月（the second month）

㉒ 从所给词语中选择恰当的填空，然后大声朗读句子
Fill in the blanks with proper words given below and then read the sentences aloud

钢笔　答应　等　第

（1）我们不用毛笔写字，用_____写字。
（2）你_____一下，我马上来。
（3）他儿子要跟他一起去南京，他没_____。
（4）我来北京已经一个月了，这是_____二个月。

㉓ 写出带有下列偏旁的汉字
Write the characters consisting of the following radicals

艹：_____　　竹：_____

㉔ 写一写　Writing exercise

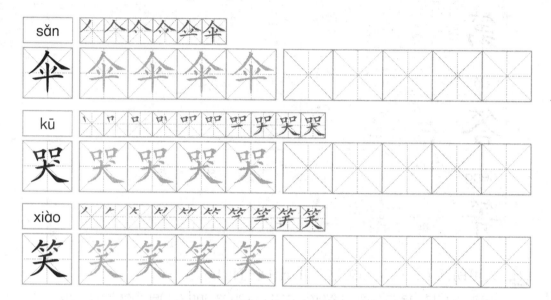

㉕ 大声朗读下面的词和短语，并记住它们的意思
Read aloud the following words and phrases and remember their meanings

雨伞（umbrella）　　　　　哭了（cried）
打伞（hold an umbrella）　　笑了（smiled）

㉖ 从所给词语中选择恰当的填空，然后大声朗读句子
Fill in the blanks with proper words given below and then read the sentences aloud

伞　笑　哭

（1）下雨了，你打把_____吧。
（2）听了我说的话，他们高兴地_____了。
（3）_____比_____好。

二、本课复习　Review

边	过	进	送	迟	还	迎	适
道	远	园	图	围	钱	钟	钢
错	锻	饭	饱	饿	馆	猫	狗
猪	猜	眼	睛	睡	跑	跳	踢
路	跟	花	草	英	茶	菜	药
节	笔	简	第	答	等	伞	哭
笑							

*永　*误　(*包)　(*炼)　*步　*舞　(*喝)
*毛

① 写出两个带有下列形旁的汉字，并注音、组词
　　Write two characters with each of the following radicals. Then transcribe the characters in *pinyin* and make up words with them

辶: _____ ( ) _____　　　口: _____ ( ) _____
　　 _____ ( ) _____　　　　　_____ ( ) _____

钅: _____ ( ) _____　　　饣: _____ ( ) _____
　　 _____ ( ) _____　　　　　_____ ( ) _____

犭: _____ ( ) _____　　　目: _____ ( ) _____
　　 _____ ( ) _____　　　　　_____ ( ) _____

艹: _____ ( ) _____　　　竹: _____ ( ) _____
　　 _____ ( ) _____　　　　　_____ ( ) _____

足: _____ ( ) _____
　　 _____ ( ) _____

② 用汉字写出下列形旁的意思
　　Give in characters the meanings of the following meaning radicals

饣: _____　　目: _____
艹: _____　　竹: _____

Easy Way to Learn Chinese Characters · Workbook

③ 写出含有下列部件的两个汉字，并注音、组词
Write two characters with each of the following radicals. Then transcribe the characters in *pinyin* and make up words with them

舌：_____（　　）_____　　　　勺：_____（　　）_____
　　_____（　　）_____　　　　　　_____（　　）_____

共：_____（　　）_____　　　　艮：_____（　　）_____
　　_____（　　）_____　　　　　　_____（　　）_____

寸：_____（　　）_____
　　_____（　　）_____

④ 按笔画顺序写出下面的汉字，并写出笔画数
Write the following characters in proper stroke order and give the number of strokes

睡（　　画）_____　　　　围（　　画）_____
跳（　　画）_____　　　　等（　　画）_____
迎（　　画）_____

⑤ 从所给词语中选择恰当的填空，然后大声朗读句子
Fill in the blanks with proper words given below and then read the sentences aloud

> 适合　睡觉　不错　分钟　饭馆　眼睛　节目　等　知道

（1）我们下课休息十_____。

（2）这件衣服很_____你。

（3）我的身体_____，因为我每天早上都锻炼身体。

（4）以前我们学校附近有很多小_____。

（5）你每天晚上几点_____？

（6）你的_____红了，怎么了？哭了？

（7）今天晚上电视有什么好_____可以看看？

（8）你_____他为什么今天没来吗？

（9）请你_____我两分钟，我马上来。

12 第十二课
Lesson Twelve

一、同步练习　Synchronous exercises

1. 写一写　Writing exercise

ān	安
kè	客
jiā	家
shì	室
sù	宿
wán	完
róng	容

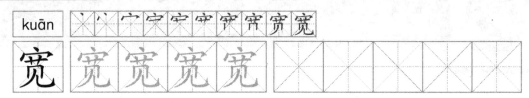

2. 大声朗读下面的词和短语，并记住它们的意思
   Read aloud the following words and phrases and remember their meanings

   客气（polite; courteous）　　安全（safe）
   客厅（parlor）　　　　　　　宿舍（dormitory）
   客人（guest）　　　　　　　 吃完了（finish eating）
   做客（be a guest）　　　　　请客（invite sb. to dinner）

3. 从所给词语中选择恰当的填空，然后大声朗读句子
   Fill in the blanks with proper words given below and then read the sentences aloud

   　　　　安全　客气　做客　宿舍　客人　完

   （1）你来我家_____，你是我们家的_____。
   （2）过马路要小心，注意（zhùyì, pay attention to）_____。
   （3）你的_____在几号楼？
   （4）我已经吃_____晚饭了。
   （5）你有什么事请说吧，别_____！

4. 写一写　Writing exercise

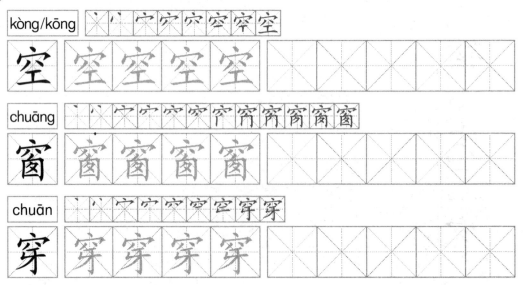

qióng	穷
jiū	究
zhǎi	窄

5 大声朗读下面的词和短语，并记住它们的意思
Read aloud the following words and phrases and remember their meanings

空（kòng）儿（empty space or free time）　　窗户（window）
有空（kòng）儿（have free time）　　空（kōng）气（air）

穿衣服（put on clothes）　　容易（easy）
穷人（poor people）　　内容（content）
研究（study）　　* 内 nèi（inner; inside）
* 研 yán（study）

6 从所给词语中选择恰当的填空，然后大声朗读句子
Fill in the blanks with proper words given below and then read the sentences aloud

> 穷人　窗户　穿　容易　有空儿

（1）我住 17 楼，_____ 请来看看。
（2）我是个_____，没有钱。
（3）学一门外语不_____，要非常努力才能学好。
（4）我宿舍的门上有一个_____。
（5）你_____这件衣服很合适。

7 写出带有下列偏旁的汉字
Write the characters consisting of the following radicals

宀：_____　　穴：_____

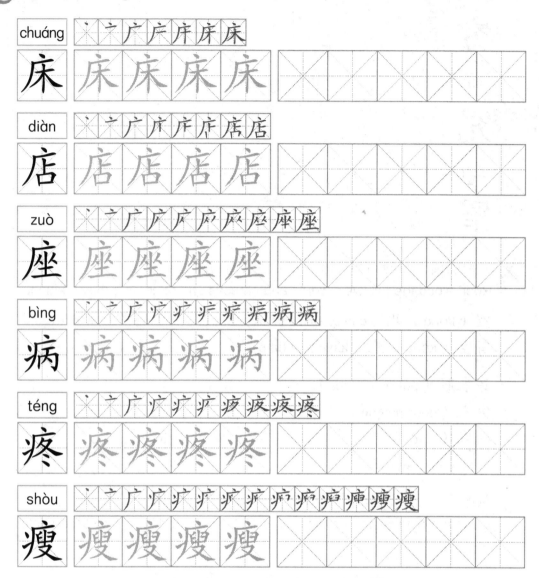

⑧ 写一写 Writing exercise

⑨ 大声朗读下面的词和短语，并记住它们的意思
Read aloud the following words and phrases and remember their meanings

饭店（restaurant）　　　　　座位（seat）
商店（shop）　　　　　　　　病人（patient）
＊商 shāng（trade; business）　起床（get up）

有病（be ill）　　　　　　　　头疼（headache）
生病（be ill）　　　　　　　　肚子疼（stomach ache）

第十二课 12 Lesson Twelve

⑩ 从所给词语中选择恰当的填空，然后大声朗读句子

Fill in the blanks with proper words given below and then read the sentences aloud

> 座位　饭店　商店　起床　病　疼　瘦

(1) 我_____了，头_____。医生让我休息两天。
(2) 我每天早上 6：30_____，7：00 跑步。
(3) 你看那儿有_____，我们去那儿休息休息。
(4) 我常去学校附近的_____买东西。
(5) 这家_____的菜比那家的菜好吃。
(6) 昨天我在马路上看见小王，他比以前_____多了。

⑪ 写出带有下列偏旁的汉字

Write the characters consisting of the following radicals

厂：_____　　　疒：_____

⑫ 写一写　Writing exercise

wū　屋
céng　层
jú　局
zhǎn　展
fáng　房

| shàn | 、 ﹁ ﹂ 户 户 户 户 肩 扇 扇 |

扇 扇 扇 扇 扇

⑬ 大声朗读下面的词和短语，并记住它们的意思
Read aloud the following words and phrases and remember their meanings

屋子（room）　　　　　扇子（fan）
房子（house）　　　　　电扇（electric fan）
房间（room）　　　　　画展（painting exhibition）
邮局（post office）　　　展览馆（exhibition center）

一间屋子（a room）　　　二层（the second floor）
一扇窗户（a window）　　两层（two-storied）

⑭ 从所给词语中选择恰当的填空，然后大声朗读句子
Fill in the blanks with proper words given below and then read the sentences aloud

> 邮局　电扇　屋子　窗户　画展　层

（1）我家有三间_____，最大的一间有三扇_____。
（2）昨天我没在家，我去展览馆看_____了。
（3）夏天，_____很有用。
（4）那个楼很高，一共有三十_____。
（5）我去_____给妈妈寄（jì, to mail）信。

⑮ 写出带有下列偏旁的汉字
Write the characters consisting of the following radicals

尸：_____　　户：_____

⑯ 写一写　Writing exercise

| shì | 、 ﹁ 才 礻 礻 衤 视 视 |

视 视 视 视 视

第十二课 12 Lesson Twelve

lǐ	礼
zhù	祝
yī	衣
chèn	衬
shān	衫
bèi	被
wà	袜
kù	裤
dài	袋

⑰ 大声朗读下面的词和短语，并记住它们的意思
Read aloud the following words and phrases and remember their meanings

口袋（pocket）   被子（quilt）
裤子（trousers）   袜子（socks）
一条裤子（a pair of trousers） 一双袜子（a pair of socks）

衣服（clothes）   电视（TV）
衬衫（shirt）   一台电视（a TV set）
一件衬衫（a shirt） * 台 tái（measure word）
* 件 jiàn（measure word for clothes）

⑱ 从所给词语中选择恰当的填空，然后大声朗读句子
Fill in the blanks with proper words given below and then read the sentences aloud

电视　口袋　裤子　袜子　衬衫

（1）我昨天买了很多东西，有一件_____、一条_____、两双_____。
（2）我很长时间没看_____了，最近有什么好看的节目吗？
（3）这件衣服什么都好，只有一点不好，_____太多，有四个。

⑲ 写出带有下列偏旁的汉字
Write the characters consisting of the following radicals

衤：_____   礻：_____

⑳ 写一写　Writing exercise

huān
欢　⁊ ㄨ ㄨˊ 欢 欢 欢
欢　欢　欢　欢　欢

gē
歌　一 ⼞ ⼞ 哥 哥 哥 哥 哥 哥 歌 歌 歌
歌　歌　歌　歌　歌

第十二课 12 Lesson Twelve

shōu 收
fàng 放
jiāo 教
shǔ 数

21 大声朗读下面的词和短语，并记住它们的意思
Read aloud the following words and phrases and remember their meanings

唱歌（sing a song）　　　　教学生（teach students）
放学（school is over）　　　教唱歌（teach a song）
欢迎（welcome）　　　　　教（jiào）室（classroom）
收到信（receive a letter）

22 从所给词语中选择恰当的填空，然后大声朗读句子
Fill in the blanks with proper words given below and then read the sentences aloud

欢迎　唱歌　放　收　教　第

（1）我是_____二次来北京，以前我来过一次。
（2）_____你有空儿来我的宿舍。
（3）我不常_____，因为我唱得不好。
（4）我不是_____英语的老师，我是_____汉语的老师。
（5）我的书_____在桌子上了。
（6）晚上我要做作业，因为明天老师要_____作业。

㉓ 写出带有下列偏旁的汉字
Write the characters consisting of the following radicals

欠：_____   攵：_____

㉔ 写一写　Writing exercise

㉕ 大声朗读下面的词和短语，并记住它们的意思
Read aloud the following words and phrases and remember their meanings

街上（in the street）　　机器（machine）　　坐下（sit down）
上街（go into street）　　咖啡（coffee）　　班级（class）
　　　　　　　　　　　　*啡 fēi　　　　　　*级 jí（grade）

第十二课 12 Lesson Twelve

26 从所给词语中选择恰当的填空，然后大声朗读句子
Fill in the blanks with proper words given below and then read the sentences aloud

> 机器　班级　咖啡　街上　坐下

（1）我不喝_____，我喝茶。

（2）_____有很多车，你要注意安全。

（3）这是什么_____？我没见过，怎么用？

（4）这个学期，我们一共有十个_____。

（5）_____休息休息，别太累了。

二、本课复习　Review

安	客	家	室	宿	完	容	宽
空	窗	穿	穷	究	窄	床	店
座	病	疼	瘦	屋	层	局	展
房	扇	视	礼	祝	衣	衬	衫
被	袜	裤	袋	欢	歌	收	放
教	数	班	街	咖	器	坐	
*内	(*研)	*商	*台	(*件)	*啡	(*级)	

1 用一个词写出下列形旁的意思，并写出带有下列形旁的汉字
Give in one word the meaning of each of the following meaning radicals, and write the characters with them

例（For example）：宀：__屋顶__（客、完、安、家）

广：_____（　　　　）　　疒：_____（　　　　）

尸：_____（　　　　）　　户：_____（　　　　）

衤：_____（　　　　）　　欠：_____（　　　　）

2 写出带有下列形旁的汉字，并注音、组词

Write the characters with the following radicals and the *pinyin*. Then make up words with them

宀：_____（　　）_____　　　穴：_____（　　）_____
　　 _____（　　）_____　　　　 _____（　　）_____

夂：_____（　　）_____　　　衤：_____（　　）_____
　　 _____（　　）_____　　　　 _____（　　）_____

3 从所给词语中选择恰当的填空，然后大声朗读句子

Fill in the blanks with proper words given below and then read the sentences aloud

> 衬衫　邮局　商店　电视　起床　容易　客气

（1）你别_____了，都是老朋友了，说什么"谢谢"？

（2）这次考试比上次的_____。

（3）你早上_____以后跑步吗？

（4）学校附近有个_____，卖的东西都不错。

（5）我们家前边有个小_____，我常去那儿买报纸、寄信。

（6）我觉得_____里没有好看的节目，都没有意思。

（7）我给男朋友买了一件黑色的_____。

4 朗读　Read aloud

（1）我很喜欢（xǐhuan, like）唱歌，可是我会唱的歌太少了，昨天老师教我们唱歌，第一次我唱得不好，第二次还可以（OK; not bad）。

（2）上周我生病了，头疼，不想吃东西。这两天好了，可是我也瘦了。

（3）我昨天买了很多东西：一件衬衫、一条裤子和两双袜子。

（4）我住在学生宿舍十四楼，六层608号房间，欢迎你有空儿来玩儿。

5 用汉语写出你的住址　Write out your address in Chinese

13 第十三课
Lesson Thirteen

一、同步练习　Synchronous exercises

① 写一写　Writing exercise

dì	地
chǎng	场
chéng	城
qiáng	墙
lā	垃
jī	圾
jī	基

2 大声朗读下面的词和短语，并记住它们的意思
Read aloud the following words and phrases and remember their meanings

地方（place）　　城市（city）　　垃圾（trash）
地图（map）　　城墙（city wall）

广场（square）　　商场（supermarket）　　操场（playground）
体育场（stadium）　　　　　　　　　　*操 cāo（drill; exercise）

3 从所给词语中选择恰当的填空，然后大声朗读句子
Fill in the blanks with proper words given below and then read the sentences aloud

> 地方　地图　广场　城市　喜欢　走路

（1）从_____上看，这个国家不是很大。

（2）昨天晚上，我去天安门_____了。

（3）明天我们十点见面，你说在什么_____好？

（4）上海是中国有名的大_____。

（5）你最_____吃的是什么菜？

（6）图书馆很近，我们_____去吧。

4 写一写　Writing exercise

shí　一ㄏ了石石
石

yán　一ㄏ了石石石'研研
研

chǔ　一ㄏ了石石矿矿砒础
础

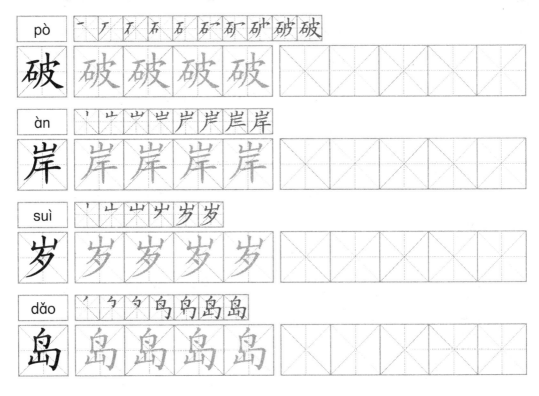

5 大声朗读下面的词和短语，并记住它们的意思

Read aloud the following words and phrases and remember their meanings

石头（stone） 研究（study）
基础（base; foundation） 研究生（graduate student）
岸边（bank） 小岛（small island）

6 从所给词语中选择恰当的填空，然后大声朗读句子

Fill in the blanks with proper words given below and then read the sentences aloud

> 基础　小岛　研究生　岁　破

（1）学习汉语，要打好汉字_____。
（2）这件衣服已经_____了，不能穿了。
（3）日子过得太快了，我已经三十_____了。
（4）他是北京大学的_____。
（5）我去过那个_____，风景不错。

⑦ 写出带有下列偏旁的汉字
Write the characters consisting of the following radicals

石：_____   山：_____

⑧ 写一写　Writing exercise

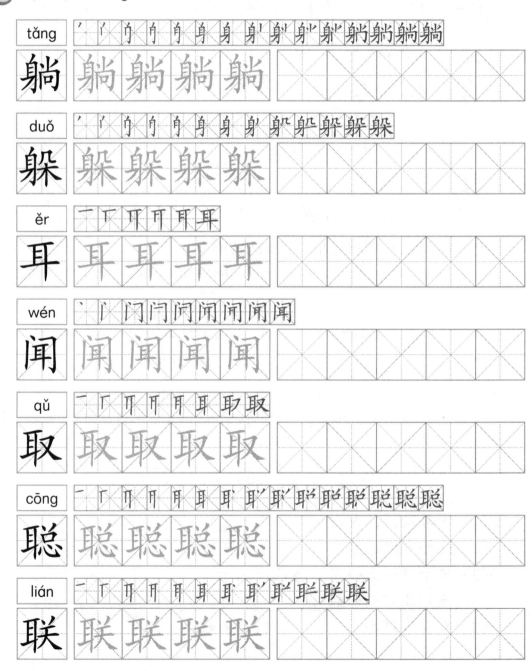

第十三课 13 Lesson Thirteen

zhí 一 丆 丌 爿 爿 耳 耶 耶 职 职

职 职 职 职 职

9 大声朗读下面的词和短语，并记住它们的意思
Read aloud the following words and phrases and remember their meanings

耳朵（duo）(ear)　　取得（get）　　　　　联系（contact; touch）
新闻（news）　　　　聪明（smart; bright）　联欢会（get-together）
* 新 xīn（new; fresh）

职业（occupation）　　　躺在床上（lie in bed）
职员（staff）　　　　　　躲在门后（hide behind the door）

10 从所给词语中选择恰当的填空，然后大声朗读句子
Fill in the blanks with proper words given below and then read the sentences aloud

取得　联系　聪明　职员　职业　新闻　躺

（1）你又_____又努力，一定（yídìng, be sure）能学好汉语。
（2）回国以后，别忘了跟我_____。
（3）我的_____是教师，我男朋友是公司_____。
（4）祝你考试_____好成绩（chéngjì, result）。
（5）我最喜欢_____在床上看书。
（6）我每天都看电视听_____。

11 写一写　Writing exercise

yè 一 丆 丆 页 页 页

页 页 页 页 页

dǐng 一 丁 丅 丅 丆 顶 顶 顶

顶 顶 顶 顶 顶

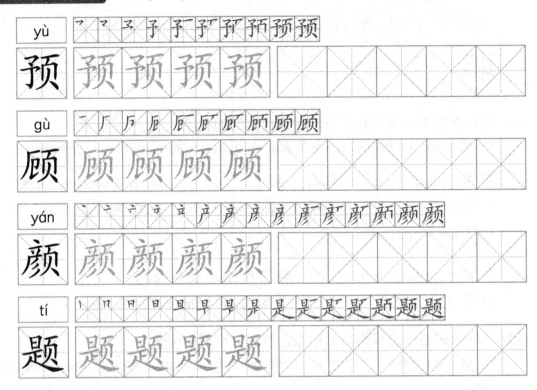

12 大声朗读下面的词语，并记住它们的意思
Read aloud the following words and remember their meanings

山顶（hilltop） 预习（preview）
头顶（the top of the head） 照顾（look after）
颜色（color） 问题（question; problem）

13 从所给词语中选择恰当的填空，然后大声朗读句子
Fill in the blanks with proper words given below and then read the sentences aloud

> 颜色　山顶　问题　预习　照顾　页

（1）我父母老了，我要_____他们。
（2）昨天我没_____新课，今天上课有些我听不懂。
（3）那座山的_____太高，我上不去。
（4）请你回答我几个_____。
（5）你最喜欢什么_____？黑色还是白色？
（6）这本书一共有465_____，你两天能看完吗？

第十三课 13 Lesson Thirteen

14 写出带有下列偏旁的汉字
Write the characters consisting of the following radicals

身：_____   耳：_____   页：_____

15 写一写 Writing exercise

qí	ㄱ 马 马 马' 马* 驴 驴 骑 骑 骑
骑	骑 骑 骑 骑

piàn	ㄱ 马 马 马' 马* 驴 驴 骗 骗 骗 骗
骗	骗 骗 骗 骗

tè	ノ ㄏ 牛 牛 牛' 牛* 牪 特 特 特
特	特 特 特 特

wù	ノ ㄏ 牛 牛 牜 物 物 物
物	物 物 物 物

gào	ノ ㄏ 牛 牛 告 告 告
告	告 告 告 告

yáng	丶 丷 丷 兰 兰 羊
羊	羊 羊 羊 羊

qún	ㄱ ㄱ ㄱ 尹 尹 君 君 君 君' 群 群 群
群	群 群 群 群

zhe	着
着	

chà	差
差	

⑯ 大声朗读下面的词和短语,并记住它们的意思
Read aloud the following words and phrases and remember their meanings

骑车（ride the bicycle） 　特别（special; specially） 　躺着（lying）
骗人（cheat） 　　　　　　礼物（present; gift） 　　　躲着（hiding）

广告（advertisement） 　　羊群（flocks of sheep）
告诉（tell） 　　　　　　　差点儿（almost）
*诉 sù（tell; inform）

⑰ 从所给词语中选择恰当的填空,然后大声朗读句子
Fill in the blanks with proper words given below and then read the sentences aloud

> 广告　礼物　告诉　特别　骑　骗

（1）下雪路滑（huá, slippery），_____车要小心。
（2）你_____人，我不相信你的话。
（3）你相信_____吗？你看了它以后会去买那些东西吗？
（4）你_____小王别等我了，你们先走。
（5）今天对我来说是个_____的日子，因为今天是我三十岁的生日，妻子（qīzi, wife）送了我一个小_____。

⑱ 写出带有下列偏旁的汉字
Write the characters consisting of the following radicals

马：_____　　　牛：_____　　　羊：_____

19 写一写 Writing exercise

chóng	虫
shrimp xiā	虾
shé	蛇
yú	鱼
xiān	鲜
niǎo	鸟
jī	鸡
yā	鸭

Easy Way to Learn Chinese Characters · Workbook

⑳ 大声朗读下面的词语，并记住它们的意思
Read aloud the following words and remember their meanings

虫子（insect; worm）　　　　鲜花（fresh flower）
大虾（big shrimp）　　　　　新鲜（fresh）
小鸡（young bird）　　　　　公鸡（cock）
鸭子（duck）　　　　　　　　母鸡（hen）

㉑ 从所给词语中选择恰当的填空，然后大声朗读句子
Fill in the blanks with proper words given below and then read the sentences aloud

> 新鲜　鲜花　小鸟　大虾　蛇

（1）我喜欢吃_____。
（2）我怕_____，可是不怕吃_____。
（3）妻子送我的生日礼物是一束（shù, a bunch of）_____。
（4）这家饭店的菜很好吃，特别是鸡、鸭、鱼，都是_____的。
（5）教室外面的树上有很多_____。

㉒ 写出带有下列偏旁的汉字
Write the characters consisting of the following radicals

虫：_____　　　鱼：_____　　　鸟：_____

㉓ 写一写　Writing exercise

liǎ　俩

béng　甭

wāi　歪

第十三课 13 Lesson Thirteen

24 大声朗读下面的短语，并记住它们的意思
Read aloud the following phrases and remember their meanings

你们俩（you two）   我们俩（we two）   他们俩（they two）

二、本课复习 Review

地	场	城	墙	垃	圾	基	石
研	础	破	岸	岁	岛	躺	躲
耳	闻	取	聪	联	职	页	顶
预	顾	颜	题	骑	骗	特	物
告	羊	群	着	差	虫	虾	蛇
鱼	鲜	鸟	鸡	鸭	俩	甬	歪
*操	(*新)	*诉					

1 根据下面所给类别写出本课学习的形旁
Group the meaning radicals learned in this lesson according to each category given below

（1）身体部位（part of body）:_____

（2）动物（animal）:_____

（3）自然物（natural thing）:_____

2 写出两个带有下列形旁的汉字，并注音、组词
Give two characters for each meaning radical and the *pinyin* transcriptions. Then make up words with them

土：_____（   ）_____   石：_____（   ）_____
　　_____（   ）_____   　　_____（   ）_____

耳：_____（   ）_____   页：_____（   ）_____
　　_____（   ）_____   　　_____（   ）_____

牛：_____（   ）_____   鸟：_____（   ）_____
　　_____（   ）_____   　　_____（   ）_____

③ 给下列汉字注音并组词

Give the *pinyin* transcriptions for the following characters and make up words with them

鸟（　　）_____　　骑（　　）_____

骗（　　）_____　　差（　　）_____

鲜（　　）_____　　俩（　　）_____

④ 从所给词语中选择恰当的填空，然后大声朗读句子

Fill in the blanks with proper words given below and then read the sentences aloud

> 地方　礼物　研究　喜欢　预习　照顾
> 聪明　新鲜　研究生　联欢会

(1) 你是什么_____人？北方人还是南方人？

(2) 你_____唱中文歌还是英文歌？

(3) 我是南京大学的_____，我_____中国的历史和文化。

(4) 我的弟弟特别_____，他是我们家学习最好的。

(5) 为了欢迎新同学，我们开了一个_____。

(6) 这是我姐姐送给我的生日_____。

(7) 明天的课文我还没_____呢。

(8) 他很忙，可是还要_____孩子。

(9) 这牛奶不_____了，不能喝。

⑤ 填空后朗读　Fill in the blanks and then read aloud

(1) 昨天晚上，我家来了几位_____人。我_____车去市场买菜，市场里东西_____别多。我买了一只鸡、两条鱼和几斤虾。

(2) 一位老人给远方的儿子写了一封（fēng, *measure word for letters*）信，说："儿子，家里要买些_____西，你给我寄点儿钱来。"半个月以_____，他收到了儿子的回信。信上写着："爸爸，您要我寄钱的那封信，我没有收到。"

第十四课
Lesson Fourteen

一、同步练习　Synchronous exercises

① 写一写　Writing exercise

wán	玩
xiàn	现
qiú	球
lǐ	理
wàng	望
guì	贵
huò	货

fèi
费 费 费 费 费

hè
贺 贺 贺 贺 贺

2 大声朗读下面的词语，并记住它们的意思
Read aloud the following words and remember their meanings

现在（now; present） 发现（find） 经理（manager）
网球（tennis） 看望（visit） 货物（goods; commodity）

理由（reason） 学费（tuition） 交费（pay）
理想（ideal） 小费（tip） 收费（collect fees; charge）

祝贺（congratulate）
道理（principle; sense）

3 从所给词语中选择恰当的填空，然后大声朗读句子
Fill in the blanks with proper words given below and then read the sentences aloud

祝贺　发现　理想　现在　学费　交费　网球场

（1）请问_____几点了？
（2）_____你当上了经理。
（3）我的_____是当一名医生。
（4）你们学校的_____贵不贵？
（5）我_____你最近瘦了。
（6）我们学校有个小_____，下了课以后我常去那儿打球，可是那儿是收费的，每次去我要_____。

4 写出带有下列偏旁的汉字
Write the characters cosisting of the following radicals

王：_____　　贝：_____

第十四课 14 Lesson Fourteen

5 写一写 Writing exercise

hé 盒 　丿 人 今 合 合 合 合 슌 슌 盒
盒　盒 盒 盒 盒

pén 盆　丿 八 分 分 分 盆 盆 盆
盆　盆 盆 盆 盆

yì 益　丶 ⺍ 丷 兯 兯 兯 益 益 益 益
益　益 益 益 益

zuì 醉　一 厂 丆 丙 西 酉 酉 酉 酔 酔 酔 酔 酔 醉 醉
醉　醉 醉 醉 醉

xǐng 醒　一 厂 丆 丙 西 酉 酉 酉 酉 酉 酉 酉 酉 醒 醒
醒　醒 醒 醒 醒

pèi 配　一 厂 丆 丙 西 酉 酉 酉 配 配
配　配 配 配 配

6 大声朗读下面的词和短语，并记住它们的意思
Read aloud the following words and phrases and remember their meanings

盒子（box） 　　　　　有益（useful; beneficial）
盆子（basin） 　　　　无益（useless; no good）

分配（distribute） 　　　醉了（drunk）
配合（coordinate; cooperate） 　醒了（waked）

Easy Way to Learn Chinese Characters · Workbook

7 从所给词语中选择恰当的填空，然后大声朗读句子
Fill in the blanks with proper words given below and then read the sentences aloud

> 白酒　啤酒　分配　无益　盆　醉

（1）我的朋友很喜欢花儿，她家里有好几_____花。

（2）我不喝（hē, drink）_____，只喝_____。

（3）你喝酒喝多了，已经_____了。

（4）学校_____给我的工作，我会努力做好。

（5）他一天抽（chōu, smoke）完了一盒烟，我告诉他，抽烟_____于身体。

8 写出带有下列偏旁的汉字
Write the characters consisting of the following radicals

皿：_____　　　　酉：_____

9 写一写　Writing exercise

qīng 轻
liàng 辆
jiào 较
fǔ 辅
shū 输

zhōu	ノ 丿 丹 舟 舟
舟	舟 舟 舟 舟

chuán	ノ 丿 丹 舟 舟 舟 舩 船 船
船	船 船 船 船

bān	ノ 丿 丹 舟 舟 舟 舩 般
般	般 般 般 般

pán	ノ 丿 丹 舟 舟 舟 舟 盘 盘
盘	盘 盘 盘 盘

10 大声朗读下面的词语，并记住它们的意思
Read aloud the following words and remember their meanings

年轻（young）　　比较（compare）　　一般（general; ordinary）

辅导（tutor; train）　　盘子（plate）　　输赢（lose and win）

* 导 dǎo（guide）　　　　　　　　　　* 赢 yíng（win）

11 从所给词语中选择恰当的填空，然后大声朗读句子
Fill in the blanks with proper words given below and then read the sentences aloud

一般　比较　辅导　年轻　船

（1）这本书跟那本书_____，我觉得这本书容易。

（2）教我们汉语的两位老师都很_____。

（3）星期天我_____不工作，只是休息。

（4）这次从日本来中国，我不是坐飞机来的，是坐_____来的。

（5）我_____喜欢红颜色。

（6）为了学好汉语，我请了一位_____老师。

12 写出带有下列偏旁的汉字

Write the characters consisting of the following radicals

车：_____   舟：_____

13 写一写   Writing exercise

jiè	界
界	

liú	留
留	

fù	富
富	

mǐ	米
米	

liáng	粮
粮	

fěn	粉
粉	

cū	粗
粗	

táng 糖 ` ⺊ ⺌ ⺮ ⺮ 米 米' 米⺮ 米⺮ 米⺮ 糖 糖 糖 糖
糖 糖 糖 糖

⑭ 大声朗读下面的词语，并记住它们的意思
Read aloud the following words and remember their meanings

留学（study abroad） 丰富（rich） 米饭（rice）
留学生（student studying abroad） 世界（world） 粮食（food; grain）
＊世 shì（world; generation）

粉笔（chalk）
粉红色（pink） 粗心（careless）

⑮ 从所给词语中选择恰当的填空，然后大声朗读句子
Fill in the blanks with proper words given below and then read the sentences aloud

> 粉笔　米饭　世界　粗心　留学生　糖

（1）你有_____地图吗？我想看看。
（2）我不喜欢吃_____，我喜欢吃面条（miàntiáo, noodles）。
（3）老师上课用_____写字。
（4）他是个_____的人，常常忘了东西放在哪儿。
（5）小孩子都喜欢吃_____。
（6）我们学校的_____比中国学生还多。

⑯ 写出带有下列偏旁的汉字
Write the characters consisting of the following radicals

田：_____　　米：_____

⑰ 写一写　Writing exercise

gǎn 赶 一 十 土 キ 走 走 走 赶 赶
赶 赶 赶 赶

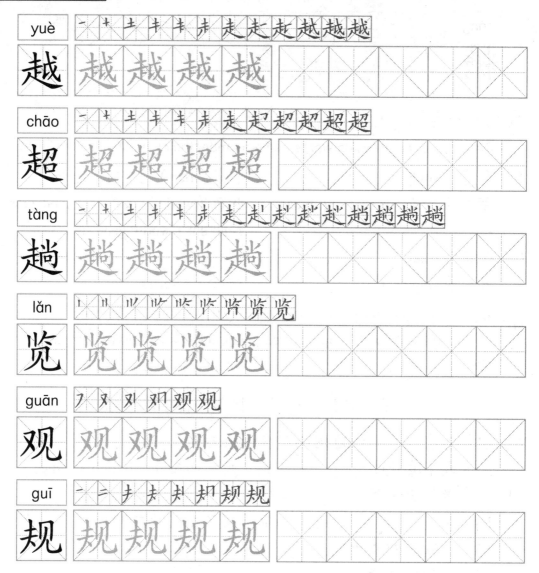

⑱ 大声朗读下面的词和短语，并记住它们的意思
Read aloud the following words and phrases and remember their meanings

赶紧（hurriedly; rush）　　　　超过（exceed）
赶快（at once; quickly）　　　　越来越（more and more）

展览（exhibit; exhibition）　　　观看（look at; watch）
规定（rule; regulation）　　　　参观（visit）

来了一趟（have been here once）
去了一趟（have been there once）

第十四课 Lesson Fourteen

⑲ 从所给词语中选择恰当的填空，然后大声朗读句子
Fill in the blanks with proper words given below and then read the sentences aloud

> 赶紧　规定　展览　参观　越来越

（1）时间快到了，我们_____走吧。
（2）现在我学汉字_____容易了。
（3）周五下午，老师领我们_____了一家工厂。
（4）我们学校有个_____：不来上课的学生不能参加考试。
（5）最近，我看了一个_____，是关于1900～1950年的中国历史的。

⑳ 写出带有下列偏旁的汉字
Write the characters consisting of the following radicals

走：_____　　　　见：_____

㉑ 写一写　Writing exercise

| dòng | 一 二 云 云 动 动 |
| 动 | 动 动 动 动 |

| zhù | 丨 冂 冃 月 且 助 助 |
| 助 | 助 助 助 助 |

| jīn | 丨 冂 巾 |
| 巾 | 巾 巾 巾 巾 |

| dài | 一 十 卄 卅 丗 芇 带 带 |
| 带 | 带 带 带 带 |

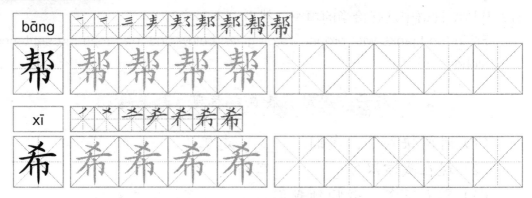

22 大声朗读下面的词语，并记住它们的意思

Read aloud the following words and remember their meanings

帮助（help） 希望（hope） 磁带（tape）
运动（sports; athletics） 毛巾（towel） * 磁 cí（magnetism）
* 运 yùn（motion）

23 从所给词语中选择恰当的填空，然后大声朗读句子

Fill in the blanks with proper words given below and then read the sentences aloud

> 运动　希望　帮助　带

（1）我可以_____我的朋友去你家吗？
（2）谢谢你_____我，非常感谢。
（3）我的身体不错，因为我常常_____。
（4）我_____自己下个学期还在中国学汉语。

24 写一写　Writing exercise

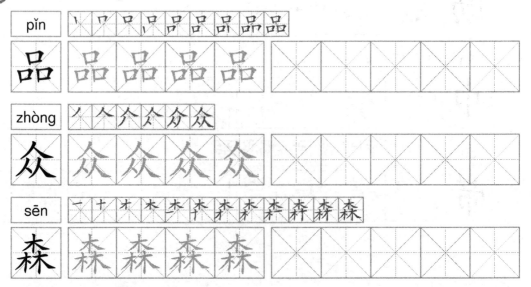

㉕ 大声朗读下面的词语，并记住它们的意思
Read aloud the following words and remember their meanings

食品（food）　　　　　　群众（the masses）
商品（commodity）　　　　森林（forest）

㉖ 从所给词语中选择恰当的填空，然后大声朗读句子
Fill in the blanks with proper words given below and then read the sentences aloud

食品　商品　群众

（1）现在人们的生活好了，_____也丰富多了。
（2）夏天，_____最好放在冰箱（bīngxiāng, refrigerator）里。
（3）上海_____喜欢晚上到外滩（Wàitān, name of a place）走走。

二、本课复习　Review

玩	现	球	理	望	贵	货	费
贺	盒	盆	益	醉	醒	配	轻
辆	较	辅	输	舟	船	般	盘
界	留	富	米	粮	粉	粗	糖
赶	越	超	趟	览	观	规	动
助	巾	带	帮	希	品	众	森
*导	*赢	*世	*磁	*运			

① 写出两个带有下列形旁的汉字，并注音、组词
Give two characters with each meaning radical and the pinyin transcriptions. Then make up words with them

贝：_____（　）_____　　车：_____（　）_____
　　_____（　）_____　　　　_____（　）_____

田：_____（　）_____　　米：_____（　）_____
　　_____（　）_____　　　　_____（　）_____

走：____（　）_____
____（　）_____
　　　　　见：____（　）_____
____（　）_____

力：____（　）_____
____（　）_____
　　　　　巾：____（　）_____
____（　）_____

② 给下列汉字注音并组词
Transcribe the following characters in *pinyin* and make up words with them

理（　）_____　　　球（　）_____
酒（　）_____　　　般（　）_____
品（　）_____　　　森（　）_____

③ 从所给词语中选择恰当的填空，然后大声朗读句子
Fill in the blanks with proper words given below and then read the sentences aloud

> 一般　希望　发现　运动　帮助
> 网球　世界　啤酒　越来越　醉

(1) 我_____很多孩子喜欢看电视广告。
(2) 你喜欢_____吗？你会打_____吗？
(3) 谢谢你对我的_____，我太感谢你了。
(4) 我_____我的孩子以后能当一名医生。
(5) 他喝了很多_____，已经喝_____了。
(6) _____人不喜欢别人说他老了。
(7) 长城是_____上最长的城墙。
(8) 我现在_____喜欢学汉字了。

④ 填空后朗读　Fill in the blanks and then read aloud

　　昨天晚上睡_____时，天气很热，小王_____间里的电扇一直开着。早上起_____时，他的头很疼，他去_____院看病，大夫说他感_____了，给他开了点儿中_____，让他回家休息休息。

⑤ 朗读　Read aloud

(1) 我很累，现在不想起床，想多睡一会儿。
(2) 我弟弟喜欢吃糖，我发现他常常一边看电视一边吃糖，看完电视，一袋糖也吃完了。

第十五课
Lesson Fifteen

一、同步练习　Synchronous exercises

① 写一写　Writing exercise

Easy Way to Learn Chinese Characters · Workbook

fǎng	访
访	访 访 访 访

páng	旁
旁	旁 旁 旁 旁

② 从所给词语中选择恰当的填空，然后大声朗读句子
Fill in the blanks with proper words given below and then read the sentences aloud

号码　经常　年轻　爬山　已经　黄河　何时　爸爸　旁边

（1）这个周日，我要和_____一起去香山_____，妈妈不去。
（2）我不知道他住在哪儿，不过我知道他的电话_____是多少。
（3）我们班的口语老师是个_____的男老师。
（4）以前我_____去电影院看电影；现在总是在家看电视，_____很少去电影院了。
（5）_____是中国的母亲河。
（6）你_____到中国的？你打算_____回国呢？
（7）坐在我_____的是我的同学小何。

③ 写出含有下列声旁的汉字，并注音、组词
Write the characters with the following phonetic radicals and the *pinyin* transcriptions. Then make up words with the characters

马：_____（　　）_____
　　_____（　　）_____
　　_____（　　）_____

巴：_____（　　）_____
　　_____（　　）_____
　　_____（　　）_____
　　_____（　　）_____

至：_____（　　）_____
　　_____（　　）_____

④ 写一写　Writing exercise

qīng	青
青	青 青 青 青

第十五课 15 Lesson Fifteen

qīng	丶 丶 氵 氵 汀 浐 清 清 清 清
清	清 清 清 清

chǔ	一 十 十 木 木 + 林 林 楚 楚 楚 楚
楚	楚 楚 楚 楚

qíng	丨 冂 冃 日 日 日 旷 旷 睛 睛 晴
晴	晴 晴 晴 晴

qíng	丶 丶 忄 忄 忄 忄 忄 情 情 情
情	情 情 情 情

jīng	丶 丶 丷 十 才 米 米 米 米 米 精 精 精
精	精 精 精 精

shén	丶 丶 礻 礻 礻 礻 神 神 神
神	神 神 神 神

jí	丿 乃 及
及	及 及 及 及

jí	乙 乡 纟 幺 级 级
级	级 级 级 级

jí	一 十 才 木 木 极 极
极	极 极 极 极

| gēn | 一十才 木 杧 杧 根 根 根 |

根

5 从所给词语中选择恰当的填空，然后大声朗读句子
Fill in the blanks with proper words given below and then read the sentences aloud

晴天　清楚　事情　精神　请问　来不及　好极了　跟

(1) 那儿出了什么_____? 怎么有那么多人?
(2) _____, 您知道书店怎么走吗?
(3) 你能_____我一起去上海，做我的导游(dǎoyóu, tour guide)，真是_____!
(4) 今天天气不错，是个_____。
(5) 你看，那个男孩真_____!
(6) 你写的字太小，我看不_____!
(7) 已经到时间了，你快点儿，要不(if not)我们_____了。

6 写出含有下列声旁的汉字，并注音、组词
Write the characters with the following phonetic radicals and the *pinyin* transcriptions. Then make up words with the characters

青：_____（　）_____　　及：_____（　）_____
　　_____（　）_____　　　　_____（　）_____
　　_____（　）_____　　艮：_____（　）_____
　　_____（　）_____　　　　_____（　）_____

7 写一写　Writing exercise

| jiāo | 丶 亠 六 亣 交 交 郊 |

郊

| jiǎo | 丿 𠂉 𠂉 饣 饣 饣 饺 饺 |

饺

第十五课 15 Lesson Fifteen

| jì | 记 |
| 记 | |

| jì | 纪 |
| 纪 | |

| lè | 乐 |
| 乐 | |

| kuài | 块 |
| 块 | |

| kuài | 筷 |
| 筷 | |

| huó | 活 |
| 活 | |

8 从所给词语中选择恰当的填空，然后大声朗读句子

Fill in the blanks with proper words given below and then read the sentences aloud

> 生活　说话　郊区　快乐　纪念　记得　饺子　块

（1）我_____，小时候（shíhou, time）我最喜欢吃糖，每次要吃几_____糖。

（2）我们学校在北京的_____，附近都是大学。

（3）中国人春节的时候，习惯吃_____。

（4）我在中国已经_____三年了，我已经习惯这儿了，我觉得住在这儿很_____。

(5) 为了_____白求恩大夫，这个学校叫作白求恩医科（kē, science）大学。

(6) 这学期的听力课老师_____太快，我经常听不懂。

9 写出含有下列声旁的汉字，并注音、组词

Write the characters with the following phonetic radicals and the *pinyin* transcriptions. Then make up words with the characters

交：_____（　　）_____　　　　己：_____（　　）_____
　　　_____（　　）_____　　　　　　_____（　　）_____

夹：_____（　　）_____　　　　舌：_____（　　）_____
　　　_____（　　）_____　　　　　　_____（　　）_____

10 写一写　Writing exercise

cǎi	采
cǎi	彩
xīng	星
xìng	性
shèng	胜
shēng	甥

qí	一十十卄甘甘其其其
其	其 其 其 其

tā	丶丶宀宀它
它	它 它 它 它

qí	一十十木木朾柑柑柑枂棋棋
棋	棋 棋 棋 棋

qí	丶亠方方方方扩扩扩扩挤旗旗
旗	旗 旗 旗 旗

11 从所给词语中选择恰当的填空，然后大声朗读句子

Fill in the blanks with proper words given below and then read the sentences aloud

> 点菜　星期　精彩　其他　胜利　星星　彩旗

（1）天上有多少_____？你数得过来吗？

（2）我和爸爸比游泳，我游得总是比他快，每次都是我取得_____。

（3）我不了解（liǎojiě, know）中国菜，今天你来_____吧。

（4）昨天晚上的电影很_____，看完以后我还想笑。

（5）上个_____五，我们学校开运动会，运动场上很热闹，有很多人，还有各种（zhǒng, kinds）颜色的_____。

（6）我最喜欢的体育运动是下棋，_____我都不太喜欢。

12 写出含有下列声旁的汉字，并注音、组词

Write the characters with the following phonetic radicals and the pinyin transcriptions. Then make up words with the characters

采：_____（　）_____　　生：_____（　）_____

_____（　）_____　　_____（　）_____

其：_____（　　）_____
　　　_____（　　）_____

13 写一写　Writing exercise

gōng 功
dìng 订
fèn 份
pàn 盼
pín 贫

14 从所给词语中选择恰当的填空，然后大声朗读句子
Fill in the blanks with proper words given below and then read the sentences aloud

功课　盼望　预订　空气　份　电灯

（1）昨天刚下过雨，今天_____不错。
（2）我下个月回国，今天去_____飞机票。
（3）我们教室的_____坏了，不亮（liàng, bright）了。
（4）最近我们_____很忙，没有时间出去玩儿。
（5）我_____自己早点儿参加工作。
（6）我现在还不饿，因为今天中午我吃了两_____菜。

第十五课 15 Lesson Fifteen

⑮ 写出含有下列声旁的汉字，并注音、组词

Write the characters with the following phonetic radicals and the *pinyin* transcriptions. Then make up words with the characters

分：_____（　　）_____　　　丁：_____（　　）_____
　　_____（　　）_____　　　　　_____（　　）_____
　　_____（　　）_____　　　　　_____（　　）_____
　　_____（　　）_____　　　　　_____（　　）_____
　　_____（　　）_____　　　　　_____（　　）_____

工：_____（　　）_____
　　_____（　　）_____
　　_____（　　）_____
　　_____（　　）_____

二、本课复习　Review

爸	爬	码	骂	河	黄	何	访
旁	青	清	楚	晴	情	精	神
及	级	极	根	郊	饺	记	纪
乐	块	筷	活	采	彩	星	性
胜	甥	其	它	棋	旗	功	订
份	盼	贫					

① 给下列声旁注音并组词

Transcribe the following phonetic radicals in *pinyin* and make up words with them

可（　　）_____　　　青（　　）_____
及（　　）_____　　　己（　　）_____
采（　　）_____　　　其（　　）_____

② 写出含有下列声旁的汉字并组词

Write the characters with the following phonetic radicals and make up words with the characters

青 （　）_____　　　生 （　）_____
　（　）_____　　　　（　）_____
　（　）_____　　　　（　）_____
　（　）_____　　　　（　）_____
　（　）_____　　　　（　）_____

巴 （　）_____　　　马 （　）_____
　（　）_____　　　　（　）_____
　（　）_____　　　　（　）_____
　（　）_____　　　　（　）_____

交 （　）_____　　　夬 （　）_____
　（　）_____　　　　（　）_____
　（　）_____　　　　（　）_____

③ 给下面的形似字注音并组词

Transcribe in *pinyin* the following characters similar in form and make up words with them

轻 （　）_____　　　级 （　）_____
经 （　）_____　　　极 （　）_____

跟 （　）_____　　　记 （　）_____
根 （　）_____　　　纪 （　）_____

④ 从所给词语中选择恰当的填空，然后大声朗读句子

Fill in the blanks with proper words given below and then read the sentences aloud

> 快乐　何时　清楚　记得　生活　精彩　其他　星期

（1）你说话的声音（shēngyīn, voice; sound）太小了，我听不_____ _____。

第十五课 15 Lesson Fifteen

（2）A：你_____开始学习汉语的？

B：我是从1998年开始学习汉语的。

（3）祝你生日_____！

（4）我三年前来过北京，我_____那时还没有这条马路。

（5）这个_____，我们一共学了五课。

（6）昨晚我看了一个_____的电视节目。

（7）这次考试，听力我考得不好，_____部分还不错。

（8）我在南京_____了三年，对那儿比较了解。

5 填空后朗读　Fill in the blanks and then read aloud

（1）星_____六下午，小何_____自行车回家。他看时_____还早，就（jiù, so; then）去市场看了看，看来看去，最后他_____了一双袜子。

（2）下周六，马力要_____加考试了。这几天，他一_____在复习，他觉_____能来中国学习是件很不容_____的事，他应_____努力学习，以后找一份好工作。

16 第十六课
Lesson Sixteen

一、同步练习 Synchronous exercises

1 写一写 Writing exercise

lìng	令
mìng	命
lǐng	领
dǎo	导
líng	零
líng	铃
lín	邻

第十六课 16 Lesson Sixteen

dī	丿 亻 亻 亻 低 低 低
低	低 低 低 低

dǐ	丶 亠 广 广 庐 底 底 底
底	底 底 底 底

lán	一 十 艹 艹 艹 艹 艹 萨 萨 蓝 蓝 蓝
蓝	蓝 蓝 蓝 蓝

lán	丿 广 广 竹 竹 竹 竺 笠 笠 筥 筥 筥 篮 篮
篮	篮 篮 篮 篮

2 从所给词语中选择恰当的填空，然后大声朗读句子

Fill in the blanks with proper words given below and then read the sentences aloud

领导　邻居　门铃　零钱　蓝色　底下　高低　命令　篮球

（1）下午两点半，我正在宿舍写信。突然，_____响（xiǎng, ring）了，是谁来了？

（2）我给男朋友买了一件_____的衬衫，他很喜欢这个颜色。

（3）张经理是我的_____，所以我得听他的_____，他让我去我就去，他不让我去我就不能去。

（4）我跟_____家的男孩比赛（bǐsài, compete）打_____，这次他赢了，我输了。

（5）我没有_____，给您两个一百的，您找吧。

（6）椅子的_____合适不合适，你要坐上去试试才知道。

（7）你看！桌子_____有一只小猫。

③ 写出含有下列声旁的汉字，并注音、组词
Write the characters with the following phonetic radicals and the *pinyin* transcriptions. Then make up words with the characters

令：_____（　　）_____　　　氏：_____（　　）_____
　　_____（　　）_____　　　　　_____（　　）_____
　　_____（　　）_____　　　监：_____（　　）_____
　　_____（　　）_____　　　　　_____（　　）_____

④ 写一写　Writing exercise

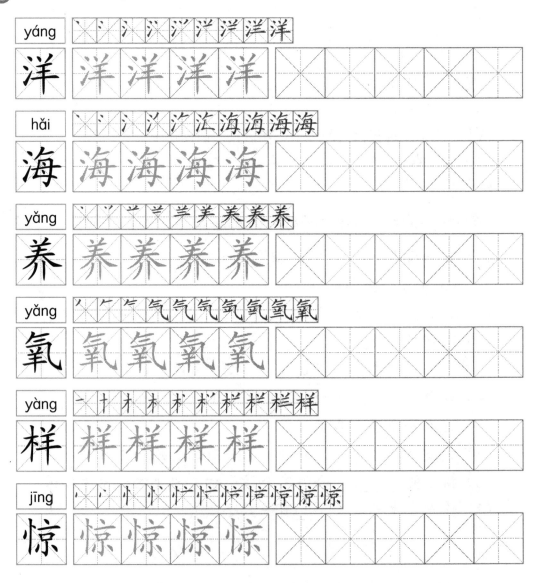

第十六课 16 Lesson Sixteen

yǐng	影
liàn	练
liàn	炼
biàn	遍
piān	篇

5 从所给词语中选择恰当的填空，然后大声朗读句子

Fill in the blanks with proper words given below and then read the sentences aloud

> 锻炼　吃惊　样子　景色　练习　养

（1）我喜欢小动物，我们家_____了一只小猫。

（2）看你的_____，好像病了，是不是感冒了？

（3）到了桂林（Guìlín, name of a city），我真_____，世界上还有这么美的_____。

（4）我每天早上六点起床_____身体，去运动场跑步，六点三刻开始听广播（guǎngbō, broadcast），_____汉语听力。

6 写出含有下列声旁的汉字，并注音、组词

Write the characters with the following phonetic radicals and the *pinyin* transcriptions. Then make up words with the characters

京：_____（　　）_____　　　东：_____（　　）_____
　　　_____（　　）_____　　　　　_____（　　）_____

羊：_____（　　）_____
　　　_____（　　）_____

7 写一写　Writing exercise

第十六课 16 Lesson Sixteen

kē	一 十 木 木 木 杓 杓 朸 桿 楳 楳
棵	棵 棵 棵 棵

kē	丶 冂 冋 曰 旦 甲 果 果 果 果 颗 颗 颗
颗	颗 颗 颗 颗

lún	一 十 车 车 轩 轮 轮
轮	轮 轮 轮 轮

lùn	丶 讠 订 讼 论
论	论 论 论 论

tǎo	丶 讠 计 讨 讨
讨	讨 讨 讨 讨

8 从所给词语中选择恰当的填空，然后大声朗读句子

Fill in the blanks with proper words given below and then read the sentences aloud

> 讨论　水果　回忆　艺术　棵　亿

(1) 我喜欢_____，音乐、画画儿什么的，我都喜欢。

(2) 教室的外面有两_____柿子（shìzi, persimmon）树，秋天树上挂满（mǎn, full）了柿子。

(3) 我们今天下午_____北京的住房问题，欢迎你来听听。

(4) 中国有十多_____人口。

(5) 我常常_____小时候的事情，那时我生活得特别快乐。

(6) 多吃_____对人的身体有益。

汉字速成课本·练习册 Easy Way to Learn Chinese Characters · Workbook

9 写出含有下列声旁的汉字，并注音、组词

Write the characters with the following phonetic radicals and the *pinyin* transcriptions. Then make up words with the characters

果：_____（　）_____　　　乙：_____（　）_____
　　_____（　）_____　　　　_____（　）_____

仓：_____（　）_____
　　_____（　）_____

10 写一写　Writing exercise

zhēng	争
jìng	净
jìng	静
píng	平
píng	评
píng	苹

bāo	丿 ㄅ 勺 勺 包
包	包 包 包 包

bào	一 十 扌 扌 扚 扚 抱 抱
抱	抱 抱 抱 抱

pào	丶 丷 少 火 火 炉 炉 炮 炮
炮	炮 炮 炮 炮

bì	一 ト ヒ 比 比 毕
毕	毕 毕 毕 毕

pī	一 十 扌 扌 扗 批 批
批	批 批 批 批

pì	一 コ 尸 尸 尸 屁 屁
屁	屁 屁 屁 屁

11 从所给词语中选择恰当的填空，然后大声朗读句子

Fill in the blanks with proper words given below and then read the sentences aloud

> 苹果　批评　平时　干净　安静　毕业

（1）我常去教室看书，教室里很_____。
（2）你的宿舍没有我的_____，因为我昨天打扫了一下。
（3）孩子做错了事，父母应该_____他，让他知道这样做是不对的。
（4）我是2010年从南京大学_____的，我已经_____三年了。
（5）我最爱吃的水果是_____。_____吃过晚饭，我都要吃一个。

12. 写出含有下列声旁的汉字，并注音、组词
Write the characters with the following phonetic radicals and the *pinyin* transcriptions. Then make up words with the characters

争：_____（　　）_____　　　平：_____（　　）_____
　　　_____（　　）_____　　　　　_____（　　）_____

比：_____（　　）_____
　　　_____（　　）_____

13. 写一写　Writing exercise

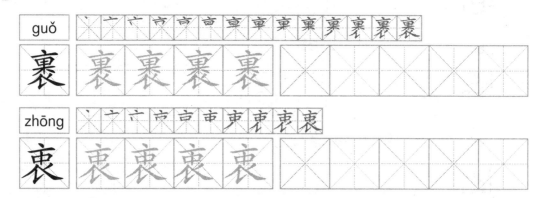

二、本课复习　Review

令	命	领	导	零	铃	邻	低
底	蓝	篮	洋	海	养	氧	样
惊	影	练	炼	遍	篇	乙	艺
术	亿	忆	果	棵	颗	轮	论
讨	争	净	静	平	评	苹	包
抱	炮	毕	批	屁	裹	衷	

1. 给下列声旁注音并组词
Transcribe the phonetic radicals in *pinyin* and make up words with them

令（　　）_____　　　果（　　）_____
平（　　）_____　　　争（　　）_____
乙（　　）_____　　　比（　　）_____

第十六课 16 Lesson Sixteen

2 写出含有下列声旁的汉字，并注音、组词
Write the characters with the following phonetic radicals and the *pinyin* transcriptions. Then make up words with the characters

令：_____（　）_____　　羊：_____（　）_____
　　_____（　）_____　　　　_____（　）_____
　　_____（　）_____　　　　_____（　）_____

京：_____（　）_____　　平：_____（　）_____
　　_____（　）_____　　　　_____（　）_____
　　_____（　）_____　　　　_____（　）_____

乙：_____（　）_____　　争：_____（　）_____
　　_____（　）_____　　　　_____（　）_____
　　_____（　）_____　　　　_____（　）_____

3 给下面的形似字注音并组词
Transcribe in *pinyin* the following characters similar in form and make up words with them

蓝（　）_____　　练（　）_____
篮（　）_____　　炼（　）_____

棵（　）_____　　轮（　）_____
颗（　）_____　　论（　）_____

低（　）_____　　抱（　）_____
底（　）_____　　炮（　）_____

4 从所给词语中选择恰当的填空，然后大声朗读句子
Fill in the blanks with proper words given below and then read the sentences aloud

| 篮球　样子　锻炼　邻居　水果　电影　讨论　安静　干净 |

（1）我的_____是个美国人，我们是好朋友。
（2）我很喜欢打_____，每天下课以后我常去打_____。

（3）看你的_____，我就明白你不会不答应的。

（4）每天_____身体，多吃_____，对身体有益。

（5）_____比电视好看，因为电视太小了。

（6）我们去什么地方郊游，要_____以后决定。

（7）请大家_____，不要说话。

（8）今天我把房间打扫了一下，现在_____多了。

5 填空后朗读 Fill in the blanks and then read aloud

　　不知道_____什么，山本今天没来上课。他平时学习很_____力，上课也很少_____到。艾米给他打电_____，服_____小姐说，山本昨天晚上生_____了，住进了医院。听_____山本住院了，大家都想去看望他。老师告_____了同学们怎么走，让他们过马路要小_____，注意安全。

第十七课
Lesson Seventeen

一、同步练习　Synchronous exercises

① 写一写　Writing exercise

| gǔ | 一 十 十 古 古 |
| 古 | 古 古 古 古 |

| hòu | 丿 亻 亻 亻 伊 伊 伊 伊 候 候 |
| 候 | 候 候 候 候 |

| gù | 一 十 十 古 古 古 古 故 故 |
| 故 | 故 故 故 故 |

| gū | 乚 ㄑ 女 女 女 女 姑 姑 |
| 姑 | 姑 姑 姑 姑 |

| láng | ` ㄱ ㄹ ㄹ 良 良 郎 郎 |
| 郎 | 郎 郎 郎 郎 |

| xīn | ` 一 亠 立 立 辛 辛 亲 亲 新 新 新 |
| 新 | 新 新 新 新 |

| láng | 丿 犭 犭 犭 犷 狉 狼 狼 狼 |
| 狼 | 狼 狼 狼 狼 |

lǎng	朗
dú	读
niáng	娘
jié	结
hūn	婚
jié	洁

2 从所给词语中选择恰当的填空，然后大声朗读句子

Fill in the blanks with proper words given below and then read the sentences aloud

> 新娘 新郎 结婚 故事 姑姑 古时候

昨天_____给我讲了一个_____：_____，一位老人和他的儿子住在草原上，他的儿子就要当_____了，_____是邻居家的女儿。在他们_____的前一天，老人的儿子接到了参军（cān jūn, join the army）的命令。

第十七课 17 Lesson Seventeen

③ 写出含有下列声旁的汉字，并注音、组词

Write the characters with the following phonetic radicals and the *pinyin* transcriptions. Then make up words with the characters

良：_____（   ）_____   古：_____（   ）_____
_____（   ）_____   _____（   ）_____
_____（   ）_____   吉：_____（   ）_____
_____（   ）_____   _____（   ）_____

④ 写一写 Writing exercise

piào	票
piāo	飘
piāo	漂
liàng	亮
qiǎn	浅
xiàn	线

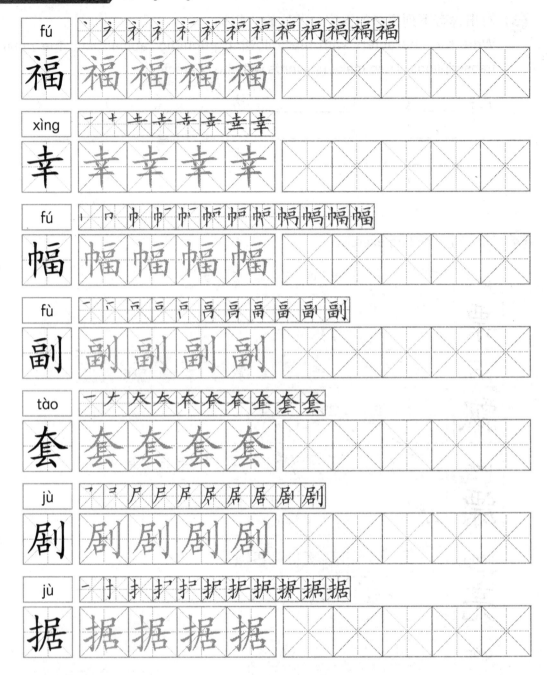

5 从所给词语中选择恰当的填空，然后大声朗读句子

Fill in the blanks with proper words given below and then read the sentences aloud

> 副　幅　线　据说　漂亮　门票　剧场　深浅

（1）邻居家的女儿是一个_____的姑娘。

（2）当你不知道河的_____的时候，最好不要下去游泳。

（3）你知道颐和园（Yíhé Yuán, the Summer Palace）的_____是多少钱一张吗？

（4）丁老师家的客厅里挂着一_____中国山水画。

（5）_____，以后每年一月可以有一次大学入（rù, enter）学考试。

（6）我女朋友送我一_____手套，是用黑_____织（zhī, knit）的。

（7）我好久没去_____看京剧了。

6 写出含有下列声旁的汉字，并注音、组词

Write the characters with the following phonetic radicals and the *pinyin* transcriptions. Then make up words with the characters

票：_____（　　）_____　　戈：_____（　　）_____
　　_____（　　）_____　　　　_____（　　）_____

畐：_____（　　）_____　　居：_____（　　）_____
　　_____（　　）_____　　　　_____（　　）_____

7 写一写　Writing exercise

zhěng　整

qí　齐

zhèng　证

zhèng　政

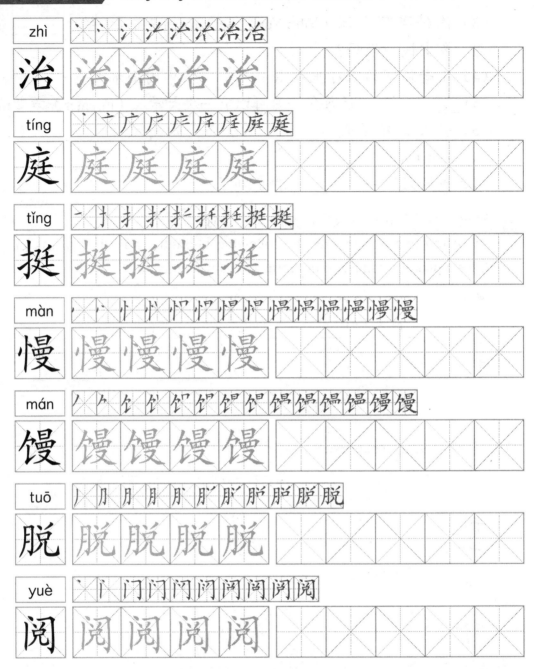

⑧ 从所给词语中选择恰当的填空，然后大声朗读句子
Fill in the blanks with proper words given below and then read the sentences aloud

> 政治　整齐　证书　家庭　阅览室　慢一点儿

（1）你说得太快，我听不懂，请你说_____。

（2）马丁（Martin）的桌子上_____地放着几本汉语书，他的房间很干净。

（3）学习三年以后，我们就可以得到毕业＿＿＿＿了。

（4）我们家是个小＿＿＿＿，只有三口人。

（5）他希望以后成为一名＿＿＿＿家（expert），所以他在大学学习＿＿＿＿学。

（6）我常去图书馆的＿＿＿＿看杂志。

⑨ 写出含有下列声旁的汉字，并注音、组词

Write the characters with the following phonetic radicals and the *pinyin* transcriptions. Then make up words with the characters

廷：＿＿＿（　）＿＿＿＿　　　正：＿＿＿（　）＿＿＿＿
　　＿＿＿（　）＿＿＿＿　　　　　＿＿＿（　）＿＿＿＿
　　　　　　　　　　　　　　　　　＿＿＿（　）＿＿＿＿

曼：＿＿＿（　）＿＿＿＿
　　＿＿＿（　）＿＿＿＿

⑩ 写一写　Writing exercise

| qiě | 丨 冂 冃 月 且 |
| 且 | 且 且 且 且 |

| ér | 一 ア 冂 丙 而 而 |
| 而 | 而 而 而 而 |

| zū | 一 二 千 禾 禾 利 和 租 租 租 |
| 租 | 租 租 租 租 |

| zǔ | ㄑ ㄠ 纟 纠 纫 纫 组 组 |
| 组 | 组 组 组 组 |

175

汉字速成课本·练习册 Easy Way to Learn Chinese Characters·Workbook

zhī 织
zǔ 祖
xiāng 箱
xiāng 厢
gāng 纲
tí 提

⑪ 从所给词语中选择恰当的填空，然后大声朗读句子
Fill in the blanks with proper words given below and then read the sentences aloud

> 而且　祖国　组织　租房　提纲　刚才

（1）上个周日，学校_____我们去参观了故宫。
（2）写论文以前，要先把_____写好。
（3）我们都热爱自己的_____。
（4）_____马丁来了一趟，又走了。
（5）买房子不仅每月的费用便宜，_____房子以后是自己的了，比_____住好。

第十七课 17 Lesson Seventeen

12 写出含有下列声旁的汉字，并注音、组词
Write the characters with the following phonetic radicals and the *pinyin* transcriptions. Then make up words with the characters

且：_____（　　）_____　　冈：_____（　　）_____
　　_____（　　）_____　　　　_____（　　）_____

13 写一写　Writing exercise

| yáng | 一 † 扌 扬 扬 扬 |
| 扬 | 扬 扬 扬 扬 |

| yáng | 一 † 扌 木 朽 杨 杨 |
| 杨 | 杨 杨 杨 杨 |

| qiāng | 一 † 扌 木 朴 枪 枪 |
| 枪 | 枪 枪 枪 枪 |

| qiǎng | 一 † 扌 扌 扩 抢 抢 |
| 抢 | 抢 抢 抢 抢 |

| gòu | 丨 冂 冂 贝 贝 购 购 购 |
| 购 | 购 购 购 购 |

14 从所给词语中选择恰当的填空，然后大声朗读句子
Fill in the blanks with proper words given below and then read the sentences aloud

> 手枪　抢购　杨树　表扬

（1）我家门前有两棵大_____。
（2）因为我上课从来不迟到，所以老师_____了我。

（3）这种新商品卖得很好，刚一出来就被_____完了。

（4）在中国，私（sī, private）人不能有_____。

二、本课复习　　Review

古	候	故	姑	郎	新	狼	朗
读	娘	结	婚	洁	票	飘	漂
亮	浅	线	福	幸	幅	副	套
剧	据	整	齐	证	政	治	庭
挺	慢	馒	脱	阅	且	而	租
组	织	祖	箱	厢	纲	提	扬
杨	枪	抢	购				

① 给下列声旁注音并组词

Transcribe the following phonetic radicals in *pinyin* and make up words with them

古（　　）_____　　　票（　　）_____

且（　　）_____　　　相（　　）_____

② 写出含有下列声旁的汉字，并注音、组词

Write the characters with the following phonetic radicals and the *pinyin* transcriptions. Then make up words with the characters

正：____（　　）_____　　　且：____（　　）_____

　　____（　　）_____　　　　　____（　　）_____

　　____（　　）_____　　　　　____（　　）_____

古：____（　　）_____　　　廷：____（　　）_____

　　____（　　）_____　　　　　____（　　）_____

③ 给下面的形似字注音并组词

Transcribe in *pinyin* the following characters similar in form and make up words with them

浅（　　）_____　　　幅（　　）_____

线（　　）_____　　　副（　　）_____

剧（　　）_____　　　　洁（　　）_____
据（　　）_____　　　　结（　　）_____

慢（　　）_____　　　　杨（　　）_____
馒（　　）_____　　　　扬（　　）_____

4 从所给词语中选择恰当的填空，然后大声朗读句子
Fill in the blanks with proper words given below and then read the sentences aloud

> 京剧　姑姑　结婚　整齐　邮票　提纲　组织　租房

（1）我丈夫（zhàngfu, husband）是我的大学同学，我们_____已经三年多了。

（2）我们把爸爸的姐姐或者（huòzhě, or）妹妹叫_____。

（3）往日本寄一封（fēng, measure word for letters）信要多少钱的_____？

（4）_____是中国的一种传统（chuántǒng, traditional）艺术，很多人都喜欢听。

（5）他的房间打扫得很干净，东西放得也很_____。

（6）我现在没有住在学校的宿舍里，我在外面_____住。

（7）下个星期，学校要_____我们去大同旅行（lǚxíng, travel）。

（8）要是你想说得清楚点儿，可以先写个_____。

5 填空后朗读　Fill in the blanks and then read aloud

　　我来中国已_____一个月了。我们_____校在北京的郊区，这里空气比_____好。我们的校园很_____亮，有红的花、绿的草，我很_____欢我们的校园。

　　平时我们的功_____很多，可是我没忘了锻_____身体。周末我们几个_____轻人经常在一起做饭、包饺子，有_____候出去玩儿。上个星期天，我们去了香山，在那儿我们爬山、种树，玩儿得很_____兴。

6 写一段话，介绍一下你的校园生活

Write a paragraph to introduce your campus life

第十八课
Lesson Eighteen

一、同步练习　Synchronous exercises

1. 写一写　Writing exercise

shéi/shuí	谁
duī	堆
tuī	推
bó	伯
hài	害
pāi	拍
yuán	原

汉字速成课本·练习册　　Easy Way to Learn Chinese Characters·Workbook

| yuán | 丶丶氵氵沪沪沪沪沥源源源 |
| 源 | 源 源 源 源 |

| yuàn | 一厂厂厂原原原原原原愿愿愿 |
| 愿 | 愿 愿 愿 愿 |

| qún | 丶丿衤衤衤衤衤衤裙裙裙 |
| 裙 | 裙 裙 裙 裙 |

2 从所给词语中选择恰当的填空，然后大声朗读句子

Fill in the blanks with proper words given below and then read the sentences aloud

　　　裙子　害怕　愿望　源头　原来　拍手　伯伯

（1）我们把爸爸的哥哥叫_____。

（2）我的_____是以后能环游世界。

（3）我_____这次考试考不好，妈妈就不会让我去旅行了。

（4）_____我认为学汉字很难，现在我觉得比较容易了。

（5）看了他的表演，大家都_____叫好。

（6）你昨天穿的那条_____很好看，在哪儿买的？

（7）民歌（míngē, folk song）是文学的一个_____。

3 写出含有下列声旁的汉字，并注音、组词

Write the characters with the following phonetic radicals and the pinyin transcriptions. Then make up words with the characters

隹：_____（　）_____　　　白：_____（　）_____

　　_____（　）_____　　　　　_____（　）_____

　　_____（　）_____　　　　　_____（　）_____

原：_____（　）_____　　　君：_____（　）_____

　　_____（　）_____　　　　　_____（　）_____

182

第十八课 18 Lesson Eighteen

4 写一写　Writing exercise

pinyin	character
hē	喝
kě	渴
jìng	镜
jìng	境
huán	环
zhuān	专
zhuàn	传
zhuǎn	转

zhí	一 十 才 木 木 朽 朽 桔 柿 植 植 植

植 植 植 植 植

zhí	丿 亻 亻 仁 佔 佔 佔 值 值 值

值 值 值 值 值

zhì	一 冂 罒 罒 罒 罒 罩 罩 罩 置

置 置 置 置 置

⑤ 从所给词语中选择恰当的填空，然后大声朗读句子
Fill in the blanks with proper words given below and then read the sentences aloud

传记　环境　植树　镜子　口渴　布置　值班　喝水　专心

（1）女孩子都喜欢照_____，看看自己漂亮不漂亮。
（2）我们学校的_____不错，有山有水，还有很多树。
（3）快考试了，你要_____学习，不能总想着玩儿了。
（4）跑完步以后，我特别_____，我想_____。
（5）他正在写一个名人的_____，是关于这位名人在中国的生活。
（6）每年的3月12日是中国的_____日，那天很多人都会去郊区种树。
（7）你的房间_____得很特别，有点儿像咖啡馆。
（8）这个周末我要在公司_____，不能休息。

⑥ 写出含有下列声旁的汉字，并注音、组词
Write the characters with the following phonetic radicals and the *pinyin* transcriptions. Then make up words with the characters

曷：_____（　）_____　　竟：_____（　）_____
　　_____（　）_____　　　　_____（　）_____

直：_____（　）_____　　专：_____（　）_____
　　_____（　）_____　　　　_____（　）_____

第十八课 18 Lesson Eighteen

7 写一写 Writing exercise

pinyin	character
zhàn	占
zhàn	站
zhàn	战
zhān	粘
tiē	贴
chéng	成
chéng	诚
shí	实

Easy Way to Learn Chinese Characters · Workbook

chéng	一 厂 厂 成 成 成 成 盛 盛 盛
盛	盛 盛 盛 盛

wěi	ノ 亻 亻 亻 伟 伟
伟	伟 伟 伟 伟

wéi	一 二 ㄢ 韦 韦 沣 违
违	违 违 违 违

⑧ 从所给词语中选择恰当的填空，然后大声朗读句子
Fill in the blanks with proper words given below and then read the sentences aloud

诚实　成功　成为　伟大　车站　战争　盛

（1）我的愿望是_____一名律师（lǜshī, lawyer）。
（2）人们都热爱和平（hépíng, peace），不喜欢_____。
（3）我们下午四点坐车出发，你差一刻四点到_____就行。
（4）他是一个_____的人，不会骗我们的。
（5）他是一个_____的、_____的政治家。
（6）你多吃点儿饭，我再给你_____一点儿吧。

⑨ 写出含有下列声旁的汉字，并注音、组词
Write the characters with the following phonetic radicals and the pinyin transcriptions. Then make up words with the characters

占：_____（　　）_____　　　　成：_____（　　）_____
　　　_____（　　）_____　　　　　　　_____（　　）_____

韦：_____（　　）_____
　　　_____（　　）_____

⑩ 写一写　Writing exercise

zhēn	一 二 ⺜ 王 王 圡 珍 珍 珍
珍	珍 珍 珍 珍

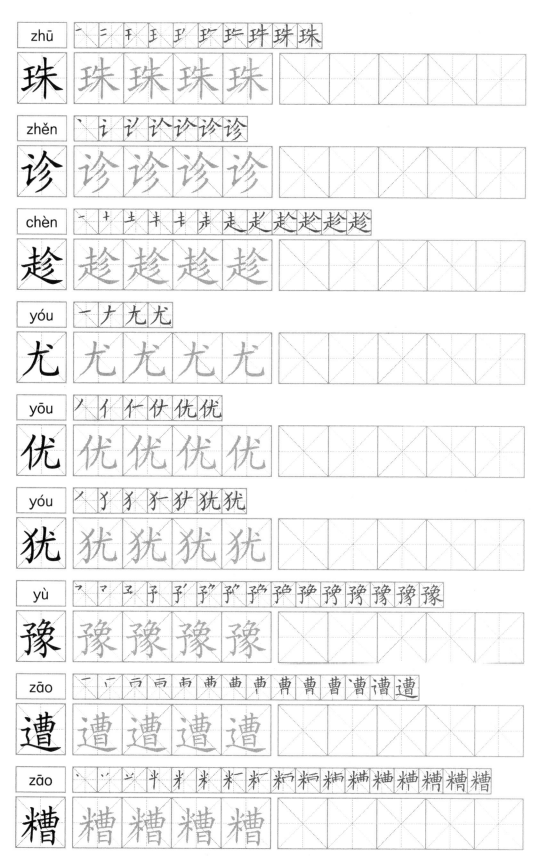

gāo 丶 丶 丷 半 半 米 米 米 米 粐 糕 糕 糕 糕

糕

⑪ 从所给词语中选择恰当的填空，然后大声朗读句子
Fill in the blanks with proper words given below and then read the sentences aloud

犹豫　尤其　优点　珍珠　糟糕

（1）我喜欢吃中国菜，_____是中国的四川（Sìchuān, a province of China）菜。
（2）_____！我忘了戴（dài, put on; wear）眼镜了，我怎么看电影呢？
（3）很多女孩子喜欢戴_____项链（xiàngliàn, necklace）。
（4）去还是不去，我很_____。
（5）我的男朋友有很多_____，所以（suǒyǐ, so）我喜欢他。

⑫ 写出含有下列声旁的汉字，并注音、组词
Write the characters with the following phonetic radicals and the *pinyin* transcriptions. Then make up words with the characters

尤：_____（　）_____　　参：_____（　）_____
　　_____（　）_____　　　　_____（　）_____
　　　　　　　　　　　　　　　　_____（　）_____
曹：_____（　）_____
　　_____（　）_____

⑬ 写一写　Writing exercise

wèi 一 二 キ 才 未

未

mò 一 二 キ 才 末

末

第十八课 18 Lesson Eighteen

wěi 一 コ 尸 尸 屋 尾
尾 尾 尾 尾 尾

Zhū ノ ト ヒ 牛 牛 朱
朱 朱 朱 朱 朱

二、本课复习　Review

谁	堆	推	伯	害	拍	原	源
愿	裙	喝	渴	镜	境	环	专
传	转	植	值	置	占	站	战
粘	贴	成	诚	实	盛	伟	违
珍	珠	诊	趁	尤	优	犹	豫
遭	糟	糕	未	末	尾	朱	

① 给下列声旁注音并组词

Transcribe the following phonetic radicals in *pinyin* and make up words with them

原（　　）_____　　专（　　）_____

成（　　）_____　　尤（　　）_____

② 写出含有下列声旁的汉字，并注音、组词

Write the characters with the following phonetic radicals and the *pinyin* transcriptions. Then make up words with the characters

隹：____（　　）____　　直：____（　　）____

　　____（　　）____　　　　____（　　）____

　　____（　　）____　　　　____（　　）____

原：____（　　）____　　专：____（　　）____

　　____（　　）____　　　　____（　　）____

③ 给下面的形似字注音并组词
Transcribe in *pinyin* the following characters similar in form and make up words with them

喝（　　）_____　　　镜（　　）_____
渴（　　）_____　　　境（　　）_____

怕（　　）_____　　　站（　　）_____
伯（　　）_____　　　粘（　　）_____

④ 从所给词语中选择恰当的填空，然后大声朗读句子
Fill in the blanks with proper words given below and then read the sentences aloud

专门　原来　布置　违反　诚实　愿望　伯伯　环境

（1）我们把爸爸的哥哥叫作_____。
（2）_____我不想出去玩儿，我弟弟一定让我陪他去，我只好去。
（3）我的_____是能到世界各地去旅行。
（4）我们校园里的_____不错，有很多树，树上还有很多小鸟。
（5）我这次来北京是_____学习汉语的。
（6）你的房间_____得很漂亮。
（7）他是一个_____的人，从来不骗人。
（8）你这样做_____了学校的规定，是不对的。

⑤ 填空后朗读　Fill in the blanks and then read aloud

（1）小何经_____往美国寄包裹，今天她又去邮_____寄了两本中文书和几张照_____，她在包裹上贴了好几张邮_____。
（2）我们学_____在市中心，离我家比较远，坐车要二十分_____。我家_____近的环境不错，种了很多树。我有几个星_____没回家了，有点儿想_____我的_____母。

第十九课
Lesson Nineteen

一、同步练习　Synchronous exercises

1. 写一写　Writing exercise

yè	夜
píng	瓶
biǎo	表
shì	示
yǎn	演
tián	填
dài	代

② 从所给词语中选择恰当的填空，然后大声朗读句子
Fill in the blanks with proper words given below and then read the sentences aloud

打电话　打篮球　手表　表演　表扬　日报

（1）我每天都看《北京_____》。
（2）请看一下你的_____，现在几点了？
（3）这次我的工作完成得很好，经理_____了我，我很高兴。
（4）这次联欢会，我们班_____什么节目呢？
（5）我最喜欢的运动是_____。
（6）回国以后，请给我_____。

③ 给下面的多义字注音、组词
Transcrible the following multi-meaning characters in *pinyin* and make up words with them

外（　　）_____　　　现（　　）_____
　　　　_____　　　　　　　_____

习（　　）_____　　　起（　　）_____
　　　　_____　　　　　　　_____

④ 写一写　Writing exercise

jì	绩
huàn	换
liú	流

第十九课 19　Lesson Nineteen

tōng 　一 フ ア 丹 丹 甬 `甬 涌 通
通　通 通 通 通

yuē 　ㄥ 乡 乡 纟 约 约
约　约 约 约 约

5 从所给词语中选择恰当的填空，然后大声朗读句子
Fill in the blanks with proper words given below and then read the sentences aloud

> 节　节目　成绩　成为　交通　交往

（1）我们每天上午有四_____课。
（2）这座城市的_____情况不是很好，路上的车很多。
（3）昨天晚上的电视_____很有意思。
（4）我跟他_____十多年了，我很了解他。
（5）长大以后，我想_____一名医生。
（6）这次考试我的_____不错。

6 填空后朗读　Fill in the blanks and then read aloud

　　上大学的时候，我很喜欢打篮球，日_____练习。那些日子，我很累，可是很快乐，我们最好的成_____是学校第一名。那时候，很多姑娘给我_____电话，有一个姑娘还给我_____了一件毛衣，现在她已经成_____我的妻子了，我也是一个成_____的篮球教师了。

7 写一写　Writing exercise

guā 　一 厂 爪 瓜 瓜
瓜　瓜 瓜 瓜 瓜

ròu 　丨 冂 内 内 肉 肉
肉　肉 肉 肉 肉

Easy Way to Learn Chinese Characters · Workbook

8 从所给词语中选择恰当的填空，然后大声朗读句子

Fill in the blanks with proper words given below and then read the sentences aloud

> 发言　发烧　发展　一生　生病　安心　安全　安排

(1) A：你的脸色不太好，是不是_____了？

　　B：是的，我有点儿_____。

(2) 过马路时要注意_____。

(3) 上海的经济_____得很快，已经成为中国最重要的经济城市了。

(4) 我会帮你把这事办好的，你别着急，就_____养病吧。

第十九课 19 Lesson Nineteen

（5）来北京的这两个星期，你是怎么_____的？你打算去哪些地方？

（6）这次开会我没_____，因为这个问题我还没想好怎么说。

（7）人的_____，最重要的是健康（jiànkāng, health）。

⑨ 给下面的多义字注音、组词

Transcribe the following multi-meaning characters in *pinyin* and make up words with them

参（　　）_____　　　现（　　）_____

_____　　　　　　　_____

⑩ 写一写　Writing exercise

zhuǎ	爪
lì	厉
ài	爱
shòu	受
jiē	接

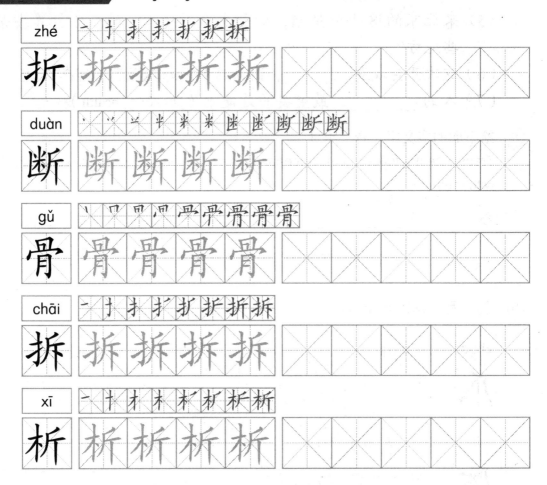

⑪ 从所给词语中选择恰当的填空，然后大声朗读句子

Fill in the blanks with proper words given below and then read the sentences aloud

> 拆开　西瓜　接受　厉害　受不了

（1）他病得很_____，得赶快去医院。

（2）我最喜欢吃的水果是_____。

（3）我的朋友送给我的生日礼物是一件毛衣，我_____了。

（4）他给我寄来的包裹，我还没_____呢，不知道里面是什么。

（5）今年夏天太热了，没有空调我们可_____。

第十九课 19 Lesson Nineteen

二、本课复习 Review

夜	瓶	表	示	演	填	代	绩
换	流	通	约	瓜	肉	词	发
件	言	排	慰	爪	厉	爱	受
接	折	断	骨	拆	析		

① 用下列汉字组词或短语
Make up words or phrases with the following characters

日：_____、_____、_____、_____

表：_____、_____、_____、_____

生：_____、_____、_____

发：_____、_____、_____、_____

② 从括号中选出合适的词语填入空格
Fill in the blanks with proper words given in the brackets

(1) 祝你考试取得好_____。（成功、成绩）

(2) 这支笔_____上跟那支笔一样。（表面、表示）

(3) 老师_____同学们汉语说得不错。（表示、表扬）

(4) 春节是中国最主要的_____。（节日、节目）

(5) 那儿_____了什么事？我们去看看。（发生、发展）

(6) 过马路时要小心，注意_____。（安全、安心）

③ 从所给词语中选择恰当的填空，然后大声朗读句子
Fill in the blanks with proper words given below and then read the sentences aloud

成为　安排　节约　表演　发言　安慰　日报

(1) 今天的_____上有什么新闻？

(2) 我叫杨力，希望我们以后_____好朋友。

(3) 过日子要_____，不该花的钱就不能花。

(4) 这次旅行，我们_____了两天时间住在上海。

（5）新年联欢会上，我们_____了一个小合唱。

（6）今天下午开会我要_____，我得准备（zhǔnbèi, prepare）一下。

（7）她哭了，你去_____她一下吧。

④ 朗读　Read aloud

广州（Guǎngzhōu, name of a city）是中国的文化名城，有很多古老的故事。那里冬天不冷，夏天不热，一年四季都有鲜花，是一座花城。

在它的郊区有一座山，山顶常常有白云，叫白云山。山上有大树、青草、鲜花和清清的小溪（xiǎo xī, stream）。天晴的时候，在山顶可以清楚地看见整个广州城。

20 第二十课 Lesson Twenty

一、同步练习　Synchronous exercises

① 写一写　Writing exercise

jiě
ノ ⺈ ⺈ ⺈ 钅 角 角 角¹ 角² 解 解 解

解

② 从所给词语中选择恰当的填空，然后大声朗读句子
Fill in the blanks with proper words given below and then read the sentences aloud

　　　拿不了　吃不了　睡着了　爱好　干净

（1）服务员每天打扫教室，我们的教室很_____。
（2）这么多糖，我_____。
（3）我的_____是听音乐。
（4）昨天晚上我躺着看书，一会儿就_____。
（5）这箱子太重，我_____。

③ 写一写　Writing exercise

duǎn
ノ ⺈ ⺊ 矢 矢 矢 知 知 知 短 短

短

shī
丨 丿 丿 丿 师 师

师

bēi/bèi
丨 ㇀ ⺈ ⺈ 北 北 背 背 背

背

④ 从所给词语中选择恰当的填空，然后大声朗读句子
Fill in the blanks with proper words given below and then read the sentences aloud

> 教室　教课　后背　长大　背包　有空儿

（1）好久（jiǔ, long time）不见，你的女儿_____了，我都快不认识了。
（2）教师的工作就是_____，工作的地方就是_____。
（3）你今天晚上_____吗？我想请你吃饭。
（4）你的_____重不重？我帮你背吧。
（5）他的 T 恤衫（T xùshān, T-shirt）很特别，前面没有字，_____上画着一只手。

⑤ 写一写　Writing exercise

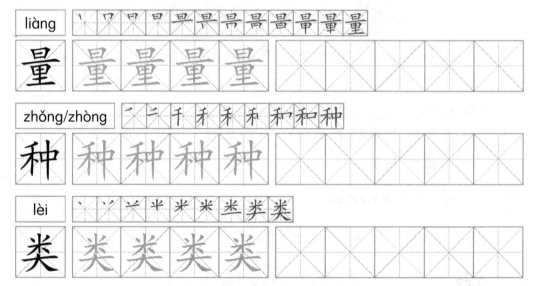

⑥ 从所给词语中选择恰当的填空，然后大声朗读句子
Fill in the blanks with proper words given below and then read the sentences aloud

> 相处　处处　数不清　多少

（1）学校里_____都很干净。
（2）我和我的同屋_____得很好。
（3）A：你有_____根头发？
　　　B：我_____，你数得清吗？

第二十课 20 Lesson Twenty

⑦ 给下面的多音多义字注音并组词
Transcribe the following multi-phonetic and meaning characters in *pinyin* and make up words with them

数（　　）_____　　　　长（　　）_____
　（　　）_____　　　　　（　　）_____

教（　　）_____　　　　种（　　）_____
　（　　）_____　　　　　（　　）_____

⑧ 写一写　Writing exercise

biàn/pián
便

yí
宜

shǒu
首

jiǎ/jià
假

⑨ 从所给词语中选择恰当的填空，然后大声朗读句子
Fill in the blanks with proper words given below and then read the sentences aloud

方便　首都　便宜　放假　假话

（1）北京是中国的_____。
（2）学校附近有商店、市场，买东西很_____，商店里的东西特别_____。

(3) 他总是说_____，我不相信他。

(4) 我们明年一月_____。

⑩ 给下面的多音多义字注音并组词

Transcribe the following multi-phonetic and meaning characters in *pinyin* and make up words with them

觉（　　）_____　　　　还（　　）_____
　（　　）_____　　　　　（　　）_____

大（　　）_____　　　　乐（　　）_____
　（　　）_____　　　　　（　　）_____

⑪ 朗读　Read aloud

天安门广场（Tiān'ān Mén Guǎngchǎng, Tian'anmen Square）在首都北京的中心。每年的十月一日，那里处处都是鲜花，又干净又漂亮。那几天，学校、工厂都放假，人们都喜欢去天安门看看。

⑫ 写一写　Writing exercise

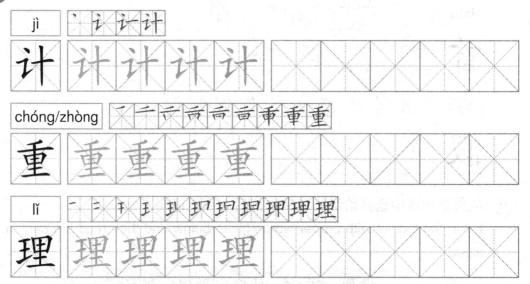

第二十课 20 Lesson Twenty

⑬ 从所给词语中选择恰当的填空，然后大声朗读句子
Fill in the blanks with proper words given below and then read the sentences aloud

> 重量 重复 会计 还书 发现

（1）我要去图书馆_____，这本书快到期了。
（2）我_____现在很多年轻人都喜欢穿黑色的衣服。
（3）对不起，我没听清你说什么，请你_____一遍。
（4）我觉得女孩子做_____工作比较好，因为女孩子比较细心（xìxīn, careful）。
（5）你的包裹的_____只是我的包裹的一半。

⑭ 写一写 Writing exercise

què 确 一 丆 丆 石 石 矿 矿 矿 确 确 确
确 确 确 确 确

⑮ 从所给词语中选择恰当的填空，然后大声朗读句子
Fill in the blanks with proper words given below and then read the sentences aloud

> 出差 中文系 差不多 的确

（1）我是北京大学_____的学生。
（2）这本书一共二十课，现在我们学到了十九课，我们_____快学完这本书了。
（3）我_____喜欢这儿的生活，这不是说假话。
（4）我爸爸_____去广东了，下个星期回来。

⑯ 给下面的多音多义字注音并组词
Transcribe the following multi-phonetic and meaning characters in *pinyin* and make up words with them

差（　　）_____　　　发（　　）_____
　（　　）_____　　　　（　　）_____

汉字速成课本·练习册　Easy Way to Learn Chinese Characters·Workbook

会（　　）_____　　　重（　　）_____
　（　　）_____　　　　（　　）_____

17 写一写　Writing exercise

xiě/xuè	血
yè	液
báo/bó	薄
bǐng	饼
ruò	弱
xià/hè	吓
kǒng	恐

18 从所给词语中选择恰当的填空，然后大声朗读句子
Fill in the blanks with proper words given below and then read the sentences aloud

> 吓（xià）　血液　流血　薄弱

（1）他切菜时，不小心切了手，他的手_____了。
（2）_____是人体中重要的一部分。
（3）我的汉字学得不错，听力方面有点儿_____。
（4）我正在看书，他突然（tūrán, suddenly）大叫了一声，我_____了一跳。

二、本课复习　Review

解	着（zháo）	干（gān）	好（hào）	长（zhǎng）
短	教（jiào）	师	背（bēi）	少（shào）
数（shù）	量	种	类	处（chǔ）
便（pián）	宜	都（dū）	首	乐（yuè）
假	还（huán）	会（kuài）	计	重（chóng）
发（fà）	理	系（jì）	差（chāi）	的（dí、dī）
确	得（dé、děi）	血	液	薄
饼	弱	吓	恐	

1 给下面的多音多义字注音并组词
Transcribe the following multi-phonetic and meaning characters in *pinyin* and make up words with them

长（　　）_____　　少（　　）_____
　（　　）_____　　　（　　）_____

种（　　）_____　　重（　　）_____
　（　　）_____　　　（　　）_____

处（　　　）_____　　　乐（　　　）_____
　（　　　）_____　　　　（　　　）_____

便（　　　）_____　　　觉（　　　）_____
　（　　　）_____　　　　（　　　）_____

2 给下列句中加点的字注音

Transcribe the underdotted characters in *pinyin*

（1）这么多东西，我们拿不了（　　　）。
（2）安静点儿，别说话！孩子已经睡着（　　　）了。
（3）我的姐姐是个会（　　　）计。
（4）你的头发长（　　　）了，该理发（　　　）了，
（5）上个星期我出差（　　　）去了西安。
（6）明天参加考试，今天我得（　　　）好好复习复习。

3 从所给词语中选择恰当的填空，然后大声朗读句子

Fill in the blanks with proper words given below and then read the sentences aloud

> 便宜　音乐　的确　假话　首都　放假　方便

（1）他是个诚实的人，从不说_____。
（2）我喜欢听_____，你喜欢吗？
（3）北京是中国的_____。
（4）学校附近有很多小饭馆，吃饭比较_____。
（5）春天到了，商店里冬天的衣服都_____了。
（6）我们7月18号开始_____，9月1号开学。
（7）学汉字_____很有意思。

4 朗读　Read aloud

　　一天，我正在家里写钢笔字，门铃响了。我去开门，门口是我的邻居——一个卖花的姑娘。她告诉我，刚才她在路边发现了一个钱包，里边有我的名片（míngpiàn, name card）。我看了一下，真是我的钱包，我非常感谢她。